CRITICAL INSIGHTS

Contemporary Immigrant Short Fiction

CRITICAL INSIGHTS

Contemporary Immigrant Short Fiction

Editor
Robert C. Evans
Auburn University at Montgomery

SALEM PRESS
A Division of EBSCO Information Services, Inc.
Ipswich, Massachusetts

GREY HOUSE PUBLISHING

∞ The paper used in these volumes conforms to the American National Standard for Permanence of Paper for Printed Library Materials, Z39.48-1992 (R1997).

Publisher's Cataloging-In-Publication Data
(Prepared by The Donohue Group, Inc.)

Contemporary immigrant short fiction / editor, Robert C. Evans. -- [First edition].

    pages ; cm. -- (Critical insights)

    Edition statement supplied by publisher.
    Includes bibliographical references and index.
    ISBN: 978-1-61925-832-7 (hardcover)

    1. Immigrants' writings, American--History and criticism. 2. Short stories, American--History and criticism. I. Evans, Robert C., 1955- II. Series: Critical insights.

PS508.I45 C66 2015
813.9/086912

First Printing

PRINTED IN THE UNITED STATES OF AMERICA

Contents _____

Resources

About This Volume

Robert C. Evans

The United States has long prided itself on being a nation of immigrants, and certainly immigrants or their immediate descendants have long made valuable contributions to the nation's literature. Wave after wave of immigrants from many nations—at first mainly from Europe, but then (more recently), mostly from other continents or regions—have added both to the population and to the culture of the country. Immigrant writers and their children have brought with them both memories and dreams, both experiences and aspirations. Sometimes they have found their status as immigrants exciting; sometimes they have found it exasperating; usually their attitudes have been mixed. In the process of sharing their thoughts and experiences with readers of fiction, they have often enriched both American literature and the English language.

In her introductory essay to this volume, Natalie Friedman offers helpful reminders of the history of the often close relations between immigrants and short fiction. She suggests that short stories—because of their simultaneous brevity and possibilities for complexity—have frequently been ideal forms for immigrant writers. Stories can often be written more quickly and read more widely than novels, and many have appeared first in periodicals especially designed for immigrant readers. Friedman discusses the early twentieth-century Jewish writer Abraham Cahan as a good example of larger trends. In so doing, she also provides valuable background information about the roots of American immigrant short fiction in the writings of immigrants who often came from Europe.

A similar emphasis on an earlier writer from Europe appears in Solveig Zempel's illuminating essay on the short fiction of the Norwegian American writer O. E. Rølvaag. As Zempel notes, writers and their works "do not exist in isolation; instead, they are embedded in a wide variety of historical situations. Discussing those situations in broadly general terms can be useful, but even more useful, in some respects, is an examination of a particular author in light of contexts both specific and broad." Many of the aspects of Rølvaag's life and career that she explores will seem quite similar to the experiences of numerous other immigrant writers, both of the distant and the very recent past. Moreover, Zempel's essay nicely exemplifies *how* a writer's life and works can be related to their historical contexts. The kinds of topics Zempel discusses, and the kinds of methods she uses, are relevant to every other writer discussed in this book.

In two additional "contextual" essays, Robert C. Evans first offers an overview of sources relevant to the critical reception of recent immigrant short fiction, and then he shows how one kind of critical approach (formalism) can be used to explicate such fiction. In the first of the two essays, Evans surveys some of the numerous works (especially reference works and scholarly essays and monographs) that can help readers make sense of the ever-expanding number of short stories by recent immigrant writers. In the second essay, he suggests that formalist approaches, which involve the very careful "close reading" of literary texts *as* literary texts, can be among the most fruitful ways of treating immigrant writing as complex literature rather than simply as evidence for historical or sociological generalizations. In this essay, Evans focuses on the relatively neglected genre of "flash fiction," in which individual word choices matter even more obviously than they do in longer forms of short fiction.

Finally, in the last of the four opening "contextual" essays, Anupama Arora compares and contrasts the works of two of the most important of contemporary immigrant writers of short fiction—Chimamanda Ngozi Adichie (originally from Nigeria) and Jhumpa Lahiri (born to parents from India). Both, she notes, have won "major awards—the Pulitzer and the Guggenheim for Lahiri and the Orange Broadband and the MacArthur for Adichie—and have published novels and short fiction that have been on best-seller lists." Both writers also illustrate a trend that will be obvious in the rest of the book: the fact that many of the best recent immigrant authors of short stories come from regions outside Europe, which for centuries had been the source of most freely chosen immigration to America. Many slaves, of course, were brought forcibly from Africa, but Adichie is one of a growing number of Africans who have recently resettled voluntarily on this continent. Arora shows how much the writings of an African and a "South Asian" writer have in common, especially in terms of the themes about which they write.

The next major section of the book consists of a variety of "Critical Readings" of numerous works by a real cross-section of recent immigrant authors. John Paul Russo, for instance, offers insightful readings of two short stories ("The Angel Esmeralda" and "Baader-Meinhof") by Don DeLillo, an author of Italian American heritage who is better known for his novels than his short fiction. Although born in the US himself, DeLillo grew up in a neighborhood full of immigrants and remembers speaking a mixture of Italian and English at home. He symbolizes, in a sense, the receding influence of immigrants from Europe on recent American short fiction.

More typical of the rest of the present volume is the essay that follows Russo's. In that ensuing piece, King-Kok Cheung argues that "Yiyun Li's 'The Princess of Nebraska' and 'Gold Boy, Emerald Girl' bring out the pressure on Chinese gays and lesbians to lead compromised lives so as to create the semblance of heterosexual families and to avoid the homophobic gaze of their larger societies. The suspense in reading these two stories lies in ferreting out the secrets and pains the characters try to hide from one another and even from themselves." As is common in much recent literary scholarship, Cheung explores alienation that is often both sexual and ethnic. Fifty years ago, Asian American writers dealing with "gay" themes would have been highly unusual, both ethnically and in their willingness to tackle sexual issues that were once taboo. Today, both Asian American and gay writers are far more prominent than was once the case.

In another essay on a Chinese American writer, Te-hsing Shan discusses two short story collections by Ha Jin, an immigrant author whose rise to prominence has been nothing short of astonishing.

As Shan notes, Ha Jin has won a number of prestigious awards, including the Flannery O'Connor Award for Short Fiction (for *Under the Red Flag*, 1996), the PEN/Hemingway Award (for *Ocean of Words*, 1997), the National Book Award (for *Waiting*, 1999), the PEN/Faulkner Award (for *Waiting*, 2000, and *War Trash*, 2005), and the Asian American Literary Award (for *The Bridegroom*, 2001). His 2014 novel, *A Map of Betrayal*, was a *Christian Science Monitor* Best Book of the Year. In recognition of his literary achievements, he was elected a fellow of the American Academy of Arts and Sciences (2006) and a fellow of the American Academy of Arts and Letters (2014).

This list of achievement suggests that the US still welcomes and celebrates talented writers from abroad in ways and to degrees that might seem extremely unusual in other countries. Asian American writers have been among the most successful of all immigrant authors and perhaps none more so than Ha Jin.

Several subsequent essays focus, however, on another group of writers who have also made a huge impact on recent American fiction in general (and short fiction in particular). These are writers who are either from (or closely associated with) Spanish-speaking countries. Bridget Kevane, for instance, explores the themes of silence and language in stories by Ernesto Quiñonez. Quiñonez, she notes, was "born in 1969, of an Ecuadorian father and a Puerto Rican mother" and "is best known for his dynamic portraits of New York City's Spanish Harlem, *el barrio*, in his two novels *Bodega Dreams* (2000) and *Chango's Fire* (2004), as well as in his short stories. Quiñonez's own childhood," Kevane reports, "was spent in *el barrio* and all of his fiction is firmly rooted in this neighborhood's gritty and yet vibrant streets."

In another essay on another writer highly familiar with the Spanish language and Caribbean culture, David A. Colón discusses "Heroic Insecurity in Junot Díaz's *Drown* and *This Is How You Lose Her*," two collections of short fiction. Díaz, an immensely gifted writer who was born in the Dominican Republic, rose to prominence with his 2007 novel *The Brief Wondrous Life of Oscar Wao*, for which he was awarded the 2008 Pulitzer Prize. Many critics regard him as one of the most lively, inventive American authors writing today, and his rapid and sustained success suggests, once more, that the US remains a country open to, and invigorated by, influences from other cultures. The same argument might be made about the career of Edwidge Danticat, who was born in Haiti (a nation right next door to the Dominican Republic) and who has regularly been winning awards and receiving honorary degrees since at least 1994. Danticat's short fiction is discussed in Rebecca Fuchs's essay "Resignifying Wounds Through Silences in Edwidge Danticat's *The Dew Breaker.*" Once again, the US has done itself great credit by being so ready to honor a writer who reflects the nation's ongoing multinational, multicultural heritage. Finally, in another essay on another talented writer with close links to a Caribbean nation, Alli Carlisle explores "Experimentation and Reference in Ana Menéndez's *Adios, Happy Homeland!*" Menéndez, although born in the United States, is the daughter of Cuban immigrants and remains centrally concerned with her Cuban heritage.

The next several essays in the "critical readings" section of this book focus on writers associated with areas far to the east of the Caribbean. Randa Jarrar, for instance, is identified in various ways with such places as Palestine (where her father was born), Egypt and Greece (through her mother), and Kuwait and Egypt (where Jarrar herself has lived). Jarrar is an enormously talented writer, and an essay by Robert Evans tries to do justice to Jarrar's literary skills rather than being mainly concerned with the cultural or sociological implications of her work. In another essay dealing with writers from outside the Western Hemisphere, Maryse Jayasuriya explores two short stories similar in themes and methods: "the Indian-American writer Chitra Banerjee Divakaruni's 'Mrs. Dutta Writes a Letter' (1998) and the Nigerian writer Chimamanda Ngozi Adichie's 'The Thing Around Your Neck' (2009)." Both stories deal with epistolary topics and techniques, so that discussion of one work helps illuminate discussion of the other.

Finally, Brian Yothers discusses four different works by one of the most successful of all recent immigrant writers of short fiction, Jhumpa Lahiri, who was born in London to parents from India before she immigrated to the United States. Lahiri's work is the subject of much recent writing about immigrant authors and their works. And, since the book that first brought her to prominence was a collection of short stories, she seems an appropriate figure with whom to end this wide-ranging collection of essays. One finishes the collection with a real sense of the strength of immigrants' contribution to American literature and culture and also with genuine pride in the nation's welcoming reception of these new and distinct voices.

On Contemporary Immigrant Short Fiction␣␣␣␣␣␣

Natalie Friedman

The short story has the economy of language and the emotional
punch of a lyric poem, with the development of a narrative arc and
the fully-drawn characters found in most novels. It was through
the short story that some of America's earliest immigrant writers
first shone a light on the experience of moving to a strange new
land and writing in a strange new language; it is in this form that
contemporary immigrant writers—and their children—explore the
same rich literary terrain today. Contemporary immigrant writers,
whether in short stories or full-length novels, hark back to a long
tradition of encapsulating an experience of global proportions in a
brief, exquisite package.

   The short story has a lengthy history, originating in oral
storytelling and crystallizing as a literary genre in the nineteenth
century, with the rise of periodical publication (Boyd). Anton
Chekhov and Nikolai Gogol are considered the European fathers
of the genre (one of the contemporary writers featured in this
collection, Jhumpa Lahiri, quotes, in her 2004 novel *The Namesake*,
Dostoyevsky's famous one-liner, "We all came out of Gogol's
overcoat"), but the form was embraced by all nationalities, each
leaving an impression on its execution. One could find evidence
in Gogol's tales, from "The Nose" to "The Overcoat," which are
fundamentally, and perhaps one could say, inherently, Russian. One
might say, then, that there are certain shared "American" qualities
in the American short story and that contemporary writers, like the
ones featured in this collection, owe an equal literary debt to the
likes of Henry James, Nathaniel Hawthorne, Edgar Allen Poe, and
Herman Melville. The immigrant to America might call upon the use
of exaggerated satire—a typical Gogolian story trait—to highlight
the absurdity that often plagues the immigrant's daily affairs; but one
can see, also, formal elements of the supernatural, or of journalistic

reportage, which emerge from "The Turn of the Screw," "The Tell-Tale Heart," and "Bartleby, the Scrivener."

If, then, we follow this line of reasoning and say that American contemporary writers like Jhumpa Lahiri, Junot Diaz, Ha Jin, and others in this collection came not only out of Gogol's overcoat, but also out of James's haunted nursery or Melville's bizarre Wall Street office, then it is safe to say that an ethnic American chronicler of the immigrant experience also came out of the ethnic American writers who preceded them. The short stories of ethnic writers, like the ones represented in this volume, are not just celebrating the form of the novella à *la* Henry James. They are also representing the unique relationship that immigrants and their children have to this complex nation and to the English language in which they all write. Their stories are not only about the absurdities of Fate, but also about the hardships of labor, the struggle to learn a new language, the subtle or outrageous shifts in a family when parents are uprooted and their children adapt more easily—in short, their stories are about the personal narrative arcs of people who are part of a national narrative of migration to this particular country.

We can, therefore, say that these writers came out of the overcoats of those like Mary Antin, Anzia Yezierska, and Abraham Cahan—or rather, out of their Lower East Side. If we trace a line of influence backwards from today's ethnic American writers to those who first established a subgenre of immigrant literature in America, we would find a tradition stretching back to the first Jewish Americans who described the crossings, losses, and triumphs of the immigrant experience.

Mary Antin is best known for her memoir of 1915, *The Promised Land*, one of the first English-language immigrant memoirs. In it, Antin describes her life in Russia, one that she remembered as filled with sun-dappled forests and fear of the Czar. The poverty and violence suffered by Jews in Eastern Europe at that time drove hundreds of thousands of immigrants away from their homes, and Antin's family, fearing conscription into the Czar's army for their sons, fled to America. Antin then goes on to describe the new urban poverty her family encounters in a Jewish and Irish enclave in

Boston at the turn of the twentieth century. The only way to rise out this poverty was, for Antin and her compatriots, education.

Antin's memoir is nonfiction, but it gives us the contours of much immigrant fiction that follows. Stories of immigration usually begin in the homeland, then describe the difficult crossing of the ocean to America; that story is followed by the encounter of hardships in America, followed by a period of change, transformation, and eventually, a rise in both economic and social status. The critic William Boelhower, in his examination of Italian American immigrant autobiography, calls the initial scene in the homeland a moment of "dream anticipation." This phrase is useful in understanding what drives the immigrant character, in any story, be it one of forced exile or one of voluntary migration: the anticipation of finding something better in America (Boelhower 20). This dream, in fiction, is often dashed—or revised—upon encountering the various challenges of a new life in a new country where one's race, traditions, and language potentially mark a barrier; but it is often the memory of this "dream anticipation" that keeps immigrant here. Even if they visit their homelands, characters in immigrant stories often choose to remain in America, which offers a different, but durable, kind of dream.

Antin's escape from hatred and poverty eventually ends in a realized dream of American blending: Antin receives an excellent education, learns standard English, and earns a modicum of fame; her memoir, therefore, is filled with patriotism for her new land. Antin, however, was writing what amounts to long-form journalism; the short story form belonged to other writers, her contemporaries. One of these is often considered the father of the American immigrant short story, the person with the most durable reputation: Abraham Cahan. Cahan, best known as the long-time editor of the *The Jewish Daily Forward* or *Der Forverts*, one of America's oldest and most venerated dual-language publications (still published today in both English and Yiddish), was also a short story writer and a novelist. In a 2009 interview with the *Pittsburgh Post-Gazette*, the Dominican American author Junot Díaz cited Cahan as one of the three greatest influences on him as an ethnic writer. He calls Cahan's 1917 novel,

The Rise of David Levinsky, "a beast of a book...one of the earliest, great immigrant novels" (Pitz). Díaz's statement is confirmation of an unspoken homage most contemporary immigrant writers pay to Cahan's novels and stories—for it was Cahan who paved the way, as early as 1898, for the heartbreaking tales of interpersonal and individual struggle that newcomers to America faced and continue to face even today.

Cahan's short stories, in particular, were heavily influenced by his journalism—and some of the characters and ideas seem drawn from the very tales of the lives of Cahan's readers. But Cahan was also influenced by the realism of his literary mentor, William Dean Howells, as well as by the humorous and tragic tales of the Yiddish short story writer Sholom Aleichem (most famous for his "Tevye the Dairyman" tales, which form the basis of the musical, "Fiddler on the Roof"). The stories in Cahan's collections are recognizably realist, but the tone—one of sadness, but also one of a kind of satirical self-deprecation—owes a debt to both Aleichem and Russian writers, like Chekhov and Gogol. His stories are decidedly not Antin's long-form journalism; they are, like the writings of his predecessors, fictional explorations of psychology and setting, and portraits of characters that remain indelible. They also seem heir to Henry James's stories of New York and Boston's society families, even though their focus is on impoverished immigrants who live in crowded tenements, just a few city blocks south of Washington Square (the title of one of James's novels). Cahan's stories are filled with interpersonal drama, not descriptions of the political or economic battles fought by immigrants. One can say, then, that immigrant fiction became, in Cahan's skilled hands, what it is today: the development of a particular set of characters against the backdrop of immigration. Immigration defines their experience, but the stories are about the subjectivities of each person. These are people who could have existed—this is realist fiction, which represents the possible and the probable. But it is about imaginary characters and their imagined thoughts and responses to the peculiar and particular aftereffects of immigration, not the actual ones. The actual feelings and facts and events are in some ways irretrievably lost to history—but Cahan's stories, and his literary heirs, keep the spirit of these alive.

Cahan's most famous contribution to his own newspaper is an advice column he started in 1906 called "*A Bintl Brief*" (roughly translated as "A Bundle of Letters"). Cahan would edit and present letters from his readers—many of them women—who struggled mightily against forces much greater than themselves. They wrote to the wise, anonymous columnist asking for help in rebuffing the advances of a lecherous factory boss, making peace between a squabbling Jewish husband and his Gentile wife, or locating a missing husband. Cahan's responses were sensitive and optimistic and somehow also managed to convey his incessantly pro-assimilationist perspective: he encouraged people to learn English, stand up to bad bosses, agitate for better wages, and learn to live with their wives and husbands, warts and all.

Cahan's stories, however, show him to be more of a psychologist and student of the immigrant personality than his peppy advice columns do. For, while his stories are also tales of unrelenting upward mobility, of people breaking with Jewish tradition in order to integrate more fully into American society, they are also stories of loss and grief—of what it means to cut one's self off from family, from one's country of origin, from one's language. He asks questions of his characters, just as those characters ask of themselves: what does it mean to choose work over love? To choose assimilation over tradition? To be brave or to be homesick? Again and again, in his stories as in his great novel, his characters grapple with the hardship of leaving loved ones "back home," pursuing new loves in America, and of working towards economic success at all costs. Cahan was himself a socialist, but he understood that immigrants often chose personal economic fulfillment over the cause of a better society for all. He wanted his characters, like his column-readers, to succeed in America—but his characters, like Jake in the short story "Yekl"—are fully aware of what they must give up in order to find that fulfillment.

And that is perhaps the greatest gift Cahan bequeathed to the contemporary generation of writers: the awareness and, therefore, the agency of self that so many people in this nation fail to see in migrant, ethnic, or otherwise marginalized groups. Read any political science journal or media news outlet, and you will see stories of immigrants as victims, trapped by political, economic, or criminal circumstances, immigrants denied asylum, taken advantage of by those who promise to help them, migrants abandoned and left for dead under the most heinous of circumstances. Cahan knew that immigrants of his own time faced similar harsh realities daily, but he also knew them as fighters, survivors—American bootstrappers with European accents, making sacrifices in order to redeem themselves from hardship. Often, these characters fail—the personal sacrifice is too much, too costly, and it can break their hearts. In *The Rise of David Levinsky*, for example, David becomes richer than he ever dreamed, but laments the lack of lasting love in his life: "I am lonely. Amid the pandemonium of my six hundred sewing-machines and the jingle of gold which they pour into my lap I feel the deadly silence of solitude" (Cahan, *Rise* 526). Similarly, in the short story *Yekl*, the Americanized Jake divorces his "greenhorn" wife and abandons his son to marry the stylish Mamie, only to feel, as their cable car nears City Hall, that he wishes for the halting ride to "be prolonged indefinitely" (Cahan, *Yekl* 89).

Interestingly, it is often Cahan's women characters whose inner lives prove even more complex than those of his male characters. In the short story *Yekl,* Cahan gives his readers a glimpse not only into Yekl's dreams and ambitions, but also into Yekl's wife's consciousness. Gitl, the "greenhorn," is at first bewildered by her husband's rejection of her, but quickly rallies and remarries, consolidating her family as well as her economic power. Her loss becomes a gain, and she translates her homesickness into financial stability for herself and her son in America. Her heart is only a little bit broken, Cahan tells us—even as she weeps for her lost marriage, she is already making plans for the next one: "…[A]t the bottom of her heart, she felt herself far from desolate, being conscious of the existence of a man who was to take care of her and her child, and even relishing the prospect of the new life in store for her…there had fluttered through her imagination a picture of the grocery business which she and Bernstein were to start..." (Cahan, *Yekl* 88–89). Gitl's disappointment in Yekl gives way to a new American dream, proving that Cahan's optimism for even the aggrieved immigrant types he encountered through his advice column never flagged and took shape in the self-motivated and ambitious female characters he created.

If Cahan is the father of the modern immigrant short story, then the mother, the person who took female immigrant characters and made them central to the story, is Anzia Yezierska. Although Yezierska died penniless and unknown in 1970, she had enjoyed, at the height of her writing powers, literary fame that drew even the attention of Hollywood. She is most well-known for her novel, *Bread Givers*, which historian Alice Kessler-Harris discovered in a library archive. Working with the publishers at Persea Books, Kessler-Harris had the book reprinted and put back into circulation. The novel has since become a staple of immigrant literary curricula, and for good reasons—it tells the story of one immigrant's struggle out of poverty from a distinctly female perspective, while charting her economic rise through the power of education.

But Yezierska's short stories deserve equal praise, as they first garnered the attention of publishers and journalists. Her first collection of stories, *Hungry Hearts*, was published in 1920, and each one builds upon the foundation laid by Abraham Cahan, while also adding Yezierska's signature. Each story in the collection is about an immigrant woman; some stories describe the crossing and leaving of Russia, Yezierska's country of origin; others begin *in medias res* on the Lower East Side, the adopted homeland of so many Jewish Eastern European immigrants. No matter the setting, each story delves into the psychology of the laboring immigrant woman as she chafes not only against the yoke of employers and unfair landlords, but also of family. Every woman in Yezierska's stories seeks relief and liberation from the soul-crushing work of the factory, the constant domestic toil of housework, and the demands of both fathers and husbands—sometimes, even children. In one iconic story, "The Lost Beautifulness," a Jewish mother awaits her son's arrival home from the army. He, having fought in World War I, has proven his inarguable Americanness and patriotism. She decides to paint her apartment a dazzling white. Her neighbors are awed by its cleanliness, but her landlord, a fellow Jewish immigrant, raises her rent. Unable to pay the fee and so angry that she becomes embroiled in a battle with the landlord, the mother is evicted, and is left crying on the street amid all of her possessions when her son arrives home.

In another story, "How I Found America," a young woman describes the wrenching separation from Russia, the difficult boat crossing, and the grinding poverty and toil she finds on the Lower East Side; she sees all around her young girls wasting their energies under the watchful eye of their male bosses, while the girls wish for good marriages to change their lives. But then the narrator discovers a night school teacher who gives her hope of escaping her circumstances, not through marriage, but through education.

Yezierska's characters, like Cahan's, paint a realist portrait of the conditions of the early twentieth-century immigrant, but they also engage the reader through the inner emotional life of the immigrant worker, a life rich and multi-faceted, born of a clash of cultures and the drive to succeed. These are not characters who sit and bemoan their state; it is their ability to change, adapt, and reflect upon the emotional cost of their economic choices that makes them more complex than the limited representation of immigrants that the nation's media outlets would have us believe. We see echoes of these self-motivated characters in Cahan's literary inheritors: in the scrappy character Yunior of Díaz's collection *Drown*; in Lahiri's intrepid research scientist in *The Interpreter of Maladies*; or in the brave, religious, questioning women of Ernesto Quiñonez's novel *Bodega Dreams*.

These are also characters who remain, for better or worse, attached to their countries of origin, even by the most tenuous threads. The conventional wisdom surrounding most immigrant stories, and the stereotype that helps to underscore the perceived helplessness of the migrant, is that immigrants effectively cut themselves off from their homelands once they reach America; this idea becomes increasingly believable of those migrants who leave behind dictatorships or totalitarian states. In Cahan's stories, characters voice their homesickness, and indulge in acts of letter-writing; they write letters to their families back home in Russia or Poland, creating a transnational connection that becomes a literary trope. Similarly, it is a letter in Yezierska's story "How I Found America" that inspires the narrator and her family to uproot their lives and try to find employment in America (there, clearly, is the scene of "dream anticipation," initiated by a letter, which can probably be seen as a work of fiction itself). Again and again, we see letters exchanged between families and nations, in the works of Díaz, Lahiri, Edwidge Danticat, Ha Jin, and others. In some cases, these letters become the pivot point upon which a story plot turns; in others, they become examples, metaphors, for the other forms of transnational discourse in which migrants engage.

Transnationalism is a term much in vogue in the early twenty-first century among critics of ethnic literature, but as a concept, it predates the newer arrivals to this nation, and can be seen as stretching back to Cahan and his contemporaries. Being transnational does not require return trips to the homeland, but can, instead, be a form of discourse, a literary element, a quality of feeling—one can, and does, feel connected to one's country of origin by speaking in, writing in, loving in, or grieving in one's language, while moving about the confines of Brooklyn, the Bronx, Harlem, or the Lower East Side. We find that the connection Cahan's and Yezierska's characters felt so deeply for their lost Eastern European homelands remained with them throughout the narrative arcs of the stories, and we find that such connections—sorely tested as they might be—form the basis of many of the works by writers in this collection. One need only read a small bit of Ha Jin's work, or an excerpt from Díaz or Cofer, to recognize that these writers feel as rooted in their countries of origin as they do in America and that this rootedness is reinforced by the contact they have—either through visits or through media communication—in the contemporary, global marketplace. Cahan's characters could not seek return to their physical homelands, but they did return there, often, in their letters, hearts, and sorrows. Such is the case for the illegal exiles in Ha Jin's stories in *A Good Fall*, and for the Haitian exiles living in Brooklyn in Edwidge Danticat's connected stories in *The Dew Breaker*.

Abraham Cahan was a Yiddish-speaker, and he wrote mostly in Yiddish; his short stories and his novel were excursions into an adopted language. There is something of the unfamiliar in his English, and he peppers the dialogue between characters in his stories with foreign words or mispronounced sentences. Similar features appear in Anzia Yezierska's language—particularly in her Yiddish-inflected syntax, where the subject comes at the end of sentences, and characters say things like "Long years on you!," a common Yiddish saying. Both writers seem not only to be translating their characters' dialogue from one language to another, but doing something even more interesting: changing the English language, molding it so that it becomes nearly hybrid. Later literary heirs also explore the permeable border between home language and adopted language, and the melding of discursive practices and code-switching that naturally occur in immigrant enclaves, or wherever groups of migrants come together. *Call It Sleep*, Henry Roth's renowned immigrant novel, plays with this technique of reinventing English, as does Pietro Di Donato in his gorgeously written 1939 novel *Christ in Concrete*, which focuses on Italian American immigrants. Late twentieth-century authors push this idea of a hybrid language even further, mixing sentences and words in one language with English, creating nearly bilingual works, such as Gloria Anzaldúa's collection of essay-stories, *Borderlands/La Frontera: The New Mestiza*. Junot Díaz adopts a similar technique in his short stories, which contain not only Spanish phrases, but English phrases that echo with both the Spanish of the Dominican Republic, as well as the hip-hop and African American inflected Spanglish of the New Jersey suburb where he sets his tales.

The reader is encouraged by this kind of writing to enter, again and again, a new space, one created by these writers out of their hardships, but also out of their joys, especially the pleasures of language. For to be a chronicler of an experience so jarring, so destabilizing, and so transformative, one must be ready with new words, a new grammar, an entirely new system of communicating—

and one must love the means of communication. There is love on every page of every book examined in this collection, a reveling in language that is a hallmark of contemporary ethnic writing. It is the immigrants we have to thank for the revitalization and reinvention of English and of the short story in its contemporary form. As they reinvent themselves, they reinvent America.

Works Cited

Boelhower, William. *Immigrant Autobiography in the United States: Four Versions of the Italian-American Self.* Verona: Essedue Edizioni, 1982.

Boyd, William. "A short history of the short story." *Prospect Magazine.* Prospect Magazine Limited, 10 Jul. 2006. Web. 8 Oct. 2015. <http://www.prospectmagazine.co.uk/arts-and-books/william-boyd-short-history-of-the-short-story>.

Cahan, Abraham. *Yekl, and The Imported Bridegroom.* 1898. Ed. Bernard G. Richards. New York: Dover, 1970.

_____. *The Rise of David Levinsky.* 1917. Ed. Jules Chametzsky. New York: Penguin, 1993.

_____. *A Bintel Brief.* Ed. Isaac Metzker. New York: Schocken Books, 1971.

Pitz, Marylynne. "Feeling Like an Outsider Inspires Work of Junot Díaz." *Pittsburgh Post-Gazette.* PG Publishing Co., Inc., 16 Nov. 2009. Web. 8 Oct. 2015. <http://www.post-gazette.com/ae/books/2009/11/16/Feeling-like-an-outsider-inspires-work-of-Junot-Diaz/stories/200911160201>.

CRITICAL
CONTEXTS

O. E. Rølvaag in His Various Historical Contexts_____

Solveig Zempel

Understanding writers and their works in their various historical contexts is one of the most important approaches one can take when studying any kind of literature. Writers and works, after all, do not exist in isolation; instead, they are embedded in a wide variety of historical situations. Discussing those situations in broadly general terms can be useful, but even more useful, in some respects, is an examination of a particular author in light of contexts both specific and broad. This is especially true when dealing with immigrant writers, since the experiences of immigrants, no matter where they individually come from, are often similar in many ways.

To illustrate this argument, I will focus on the Norwegian American writer O. E. Rølvaag. Rølvaag is one of the preeminent immigrant authors of the first half of the twentieth century. Best known for his classic American novel, *Giants in the Earth*, Rølvaag also wrote a number of short pieces, which also belong in the category Werner Sollors calls "American literature written in languages other than English." A selection of Rølvaag's short stories has, in fact, been translated into English and thus made available to a wider American reading public.

Rølvaag's Background

Ole Edvart Rølvaag was born on the island of Dønna off the northern coast of Norway in 1876. His father was, like almost everyone on the island, a fisherman. Though schooling was meager—a mere nine weeks a year for seven years—the island boasted a well-used library, and the family subscribed to a national newspaper. In addition to reading, storytelling was a favorite entertainment during the long dark nights of winter. After his brief schooling, Rølvaag began his career as a fisherman at the age of fourteen, sailing to the Lofoten Islands in the winter and spring. Fishing was then, as it is now, a dangerous occupation. In 1893, Rølvaag barely survived a fierce storm, and that seems to have been an impetus for him to consider emigration. He wrote about this storm years later, describing how the sea was boiling with fish and the men did not want to go ashore, even though they knew a storm was coming. When the storm hit, they rowed for their lives. Many did not survive, and for some who did, their health was ruined. After this harrowing experience, Rølvaag wrote to his uncle in America to ask for a pre-paid ticket, a common story for immigrants. Two years later, the precious ticket arrived, and then he had to make a difficult choice: leave his family forever and relinquish the chance to skipper his own boat or set out into the unknown. Feeling that something better was waiting for him drove him on, and in 1896, he became one of nearly seven thousand Norwegians who traveled from Norway to the United States in that year.

He entered the United States through Castle Garden in New York not knowing a word of English, and after three days on the train, he arrived in Elk Point, South Dakota. Unfortunately, his uncle thought he was coming the next day and wasn't there to meet him. Rølvaag began work as a farmhand, but as a fisherman, he was unaccustomed to farm work, and besides, in Norway, the women took care of livestock and much of the agricultural chores. This was not the life he had left home for. Encouraged by a local pastor, Rølvaag enrolled in Augustana Academy, a Norwegian American preparatory school where many of his classes were taught in Norwegian, but where he also was able to study English. He went on to attend St. Olaf College in Northfield, Minnesota. After Rølvaag graduated from St. Olaf with honors in 1905, the college president lent him enough money for a year of graduate study at the University in Oslo, provided Rølvaag return to teach at St. Olaf afterward. His year in Oslo was wonderful, both because he got the first opportunity to visit his beloved home on Dønna and because he was engaged in learning from renowned scholars the subjects dear to his heart: literature, language, psychology, and history. In Norway at that time, for a poor northern fisherman's son to attend university was impossible; it was only by emigrating to America that such an opportunity was opened to him.

After returning from Norway in 1906, Rølvaag began his teaching career at St. Olaf College and Academy. At first, in addition to Norwegian, he taught geometry, physiology, geography, Bible history, and Greek and, for a time, was resident head in the boys' dormitory. Later, he was able to focus on teaching Norwegian language and literature and to develop his favorite courses (taught in English), on the plays of Henrik Ibsen and on Norwegian immigration history. Rølvaag was enthusiastic about his subject matter and wanted to impart to his students an appreciation for the heritage their families had brought with them and for what they had accomplished in the new world. Though Rølvaag loved teaching and working with youth, and was intensely loyal to St. Olaf College, his position there was burdensome at times, especially when he felt that his real calling was to be a writer.

Rølvaag the Writer

Rølvaag started practicing writing while at Augustana Academy, and his academy notebooks contain several of his earliest short compositions. He started writing fiction and essays in earnest as a student at St. Olaf College. His first published work was in the St. Olaf student paper, the *Manitou Messenger*, which accepted several of his short pieces in the years 1903–1906. He wrote to his fiancée, Jennie Berdahl from Garretson South Dakota, in 1904 (while still a student at St. Olaf) that he could get one dollar per page for writing short stories for the literature section of the Norwegian-American newspaper *Decorah Posten*. But, he added, "one dollar per page does not amount to much for one that composes so slowly as I do, and I am very much afraid I should starve by it." Instead, he took a job as a handyman and carpenter and spent the summer painting and repairing college buildings.

Already at this time, however, his ambition was to be a writer, and he completed a novel during his undergraduate days. He submitted the manuscript to a major Norwegian publisher when he was in Norway doing graduate work, but it was turned down. During this year in Norway, he wrote a rather sentimental short story, which he sent in a letter to his fiancée as he had no other Christmas present for her.

Several early short pieces were published in Norwegian-American periodicals in 1907, 1912, 1913, 1914, and 1917. He frequently submitted poems and sketches to the journal of the association of people from north Norway, and the newspaper *Decorah-Posten* also took a few of his pieces. When the time came for him to collect and edit selections for the declamation book that he edited in 1918, he filled out the gaps with some of his own previously published short pieces. In 1919 and 1920, Volumes 1 and 2 of a reader for use in Norwegian-American schools and homes, which he compiled and edited, contain even more of his pieces, including several children's stories and descriptive pieces, which he wrote especially for these readers.

Much of Rølvaag's early experiences, as well as reflections on his life in the old country, are told in fictional form in his first novel, published in 1912 by Augsburg Press in Minneapolis under the pseudonym Paal Mörck. The Norwegian title *Amerika-Breve* (Letters from America) indicates the form of the novel, and the title of the 1971 English translation, *The Third Life of Per Smevik,* hints at its content. The English title comes from a statement made by the protagonist in one of his first letters home. His first life, he explains, was lived in his old home in Smeviken, Norway. His second life, which seemed like an eternity to him, was lived on the three week journey by sea, railroad, and foot to his new home in South Dakota. He is now about to embark on his third life as an immigrant in a new land. The letters to his father and brother that make up the remainder of the book describe this new life and his reactions to it, showing the protagonist's gradual process of assimilation and acculturation. Though this is, of course, fiction, there is also no doubt that many of the incidents and certainly the feelings expressed in the book are based on Rølvaag's own experiences and emotional reactions. He even inserted portions of one of his own speeches into the novel by having his protagonist copy it out for his father and brother to help them decide whether or not to emigrate. The message of the speech on the gains and losses of the immigrant seems to warn against emigration, but the message of the novel as a whole, in showing the success of the protagonist, emphasizes the gains. Throughout his writing career, Rølvaag continued, with ever increasing skill and sensitivity, to focus his work on the intertwined themes of this first, apprentice novel, the dangers to the immigrant of rootlessness and the importance of preserving immigrants' heritage and cultural traditions.

Rølvaag's third published novel, *To Tullinger* ("Two Fools" translated as *Pure Gold*) came out in 1920, this time under his own name. Here Rølvaag focuses on the bitterness and disillusionment of the World War I period, a very ugly period in American history characterized by anti-immigrant hysteria and inflammatory nativist rhetoric. The fates of protagonists Louis and Lizzie in this bleak book illustrate Rølvaag's theme of the emptiness of those who lose their traditions and cultural background. Nothing is left for them but a barren and fruitless materialism, leading to a cold and lonely death.

Rølvaag interrupted his writing of fiction in 1922 to gather his thoughts on issues of immigration, culture, and heritage. The resulting book, *Omkring Fædrearven* (*Concerning Our Heritage*) is a volume of polemical essays aimed at Norwegian Americans. In it, Rølvaag exhorts them to preserve their ancestral heritage and Norwegian language and culture as a means of strengthening their spiritual life as well as adding dimension to their contribution to their new home in America. Rølvaag had a two-fold purpose with his preaching about the importance of maintaining the Norwegian cultural heritage. First, he was trying to foster a sense of self-knowledge and self-worth among Norwegian Americans in the face of the negative attitudes of American society towards immigrants. In addition, he firmly believed that preserving the best elements in the heritage of each immigrant group would lead to a stronger and finer America. Rølvaag's vision of America was of a mosaic of ethnic communities, each preserving and promoting its own language, culture, and traditions, but united around American political ideals (Zempel, *Concerning* 3–37).

Giants in the Earth

In 1923–24, Rølvaag finally got a sabbatical and spent part of that fall at his cabin in the northern Minnesota woods, working on his story of pioneer immigrants. Though he himself had not experienced the pioneer period, his wife's family had, and her father and uncle provided much important detail about their experience on a wagon train and homesteading in Dakota Territory. Rølvaag finished the manuscript on a visit to Norway, where it was published in two volumes by the major Norwegian publisher Aschehoug. This was a tremendous coup for an unknown Norwegian American. These novels were received enthusiastically by the Norwegian public and critics and made Rølvaag famous in Europe. When the English translation came in 1927, the two parts were published by Harper's in one volume under the title *Giants in the Earth*. The novel became a Book-of-the-Month Club selection, and overnight Rølvaag went from being an obscure professor to a famous writer. *Giants in the Earth* has been in print continuously to this day, has been widely anthologized, and has been translated into many languages. Two plays and two operas have been based on the novel, and several screenplays have been written, though no film has resulted so far.

This epic novel uses Norwegian immigrant pioneers to provide a psychologically realistic portrait of the immigrant's struggle, a portrait that, in its artistic greatness, allows immigrants from other cultures and other time periods to see themselves and their situations reflected. Rølvaag himself said that he saw two movements looming above all others: the westward migration and the movement of immigration. *Giants in the Earth* depicts both the cost and the promise of the great westward movement, the plus and the minus of immigration. It does this by presenting the reader with a husband and wife, Per Hansa and Beret, pitting them and their immigrant compatriots against the prairie, depicted both as a dangerous enemy and one filled with beauty and richness. Per Hansa is the model pioneer, constantly looking for new things and building his kingdom on the prairie. His overabundance of pride and self-confidence become his downfall. Beret clings to old traditions and old ways of thinking, sensitive and fearful of the unknown. Rølvaag understood very well these immigrant pioneers: they indeed needed to be giants if they were to defeat the forces confronting them—forces of nature (storm, drought, plague, fire, hunger); psychological forces (loneliness, fear, madness); and spiritual forces (greed, materialism, and rootlessness). While Per Hansa and the rest of the pioneers are concerned with physical survival and establishing their new homes, his wife Beret feels most keenly the spiritual loss that results from being cut off from homeland and ties of family and tradition. Per Hansa, however, can be seen as using his heritage, rather than losing it, when he applies his knowledge of sailing and fishing to new situations in the new culture. We may see this as a form of healthy adaptation in contrast to Beret's longing for a perhaps idealized former life and home.

Later Works

Rølvaag continued the story of the Holm family in two more novels. *Peder Victorious* opens with an image reminiscent of *The Third Life of Per Smevik*. As a child, the American-born Peder feels that he lives in three different rooms. One room is in English; here, he is happiest and most himself. In another room, he is with his mother and family—there, everything is in Norwegian—and in a third room, which is also in Norwegian, he is unhappily alone with God. Unfortunately, Peder is never able to fully integrate these various strands of his personality. The novel gives an insightful portrait of the psychology of an adolescent and also continues Beret's story, relating how she carries on the work of Per Hansa and becomes the best farmer in the settlement.

The final novel from Rølvaag's pen, *Their Fathers' God*, continues with the story of Peder's young adulthood, his marriage to the Irish American Susie Doheny, and his growing political ambitions. Peder Victorious is a young man in revolt against his mother and her insistence on the importance of maintaining the Norwegian language, church, and culture. If Peder could only have understood and accepted his own heritage, then he might also have understood and accepted that of his Irish American wife Susie. Instead, the novel ends with his marriage and his life in shambles.

We aren't surprised to find in these two novels Rølvaag's familiar themes of the importance of maintaining ancestral heritage, faith, and language. The two final novels also show what happens to the second generation and to the communities of immigrants as they adapt to American lives and conditions.

There is no doubt in anyone's mind that Norwegian American immigrant author O.E. Rølvaag is best known as a novelist and that his best-known novel is the American classic, *Giants in the Earth*. However, before writing this famous novel, Rølvaag served a long apprenticeship. Unknown in America outside of the Norwegian American community, within that community, Rølvaag was a leading figure. He wrote constantly in newspapers and journals, he gave speeches throughout the Midwest, he was active in many Norwegian American organizations, and his novels, poems, and short stories (all written in Norwegian) were familiar to the Norwegian American reading public. Rølvaag, himself a teacher of Norwegian, worked tirelessly to promote Norwegian instruction in schools and colleges through his textbook writing and through his work with language and heritage preservation groups.

Other Writings

In addition to his novels, Rølvaag published a book-length collection of articles; wrote numerous editorials, articles, and reviews in newspapers and journals; prepared glossaries, textbooks, and anthologies for use in the school and the home; and wrote numerous poems, both published and unpublished. He also wrote and published a number of short stories. Untangling the writing and publication history of Rolvaag's short stories is an interesting saga in itself. All of his writing was done in Norwegian, most of it published by Norwegian American presses and aimed at an audience of Norwegian immigrants. A few of his short stories, however, were published first in Norway, mostly in Christmas annuals. Rølvaag did not hesitate to work and rework the same material and to publish the same or similar pieces in more than one place. In a letter to a friend, he explains that the editor at Augsburg Publishing House had begged him for another story for the Christmas annual, *Jul i Vesterheimen*.

The title of this popular journal translates as "Christmas in the Western Home." "Vesterheim," or "Western Home" was how Norwegians as well as Norwegian Americans referred to the United States and, even today, is the name of the Norwegian immigration museum in Decorah, Iowa. Rølvaag wrote in this letter that he was busy proofreading a novel, so he was going to submit a story that had already been published in Norway. He would just give it a new title, and no one would know the difference.

Rølvaag's Short Fiction

Many of the places Rølvaag's short stories appeared are, at least today, rather obscure. They consist mostly of short-lived journals and papers with a restricted audience of Norwegian Americans. His short stories probably reached their widest audience when they appeared in the popular Norwegian and Norwegian American Christmas annuals. A selection of Rølvaag's short stories was collected and published after his death by his friend Waldemar Ager, a Norwegian-American newspaper editor from Eau Claire, Wisconsin. However, this long out-of-print collection was also not very widely distributed nor well known. Rølvaag wrote most of his stories in Norwegian, though a few were written in English, mostly for college publications.

Rølvaag himself prepared translations of several of his own stories and tried to sell them to the American magazine market. Considering his fame as an author after *Giants in the Earth*, it is somewhat surprising that they were never accepted for publication. Rølvaag placed two of these stories with a literary agency, which submitted them to an impressive list of major American magazines ranging from *McCall's* to *Farm and Fireside*, but he got only rejections. Unfortunately, few of the actual rejection letters are available in the Rølvaag papers in the archives of the Norwegian-American Historical Association (NAHA), so we can't see if the editors commented on the stories or merely sent form letters. Perhaps the editors feared the short stories were aimed too specifically at a Norwegian American audience and would not appeal to a broader American public. Rølvaag paid a former student to translate at least one of his stories, but from the typescript found in the Rølvaag papers, it is clear that he did substantial revision on it himself. Rølvaag tended to rewrite as he translated, and his translations of the short stories are no exception. In the English texts that he prepared, descriptive passages have been expanded, dialog added (including profanity), and, in one case, an expression has been turned from negative to positive. In spite of these re-workings, the American magazine market of his day was not interested in Rølvaag's stories. None of Rølvaag's Norwegian-language stories were published in English translation during his lifetime. Since his death, however, one story, "When Snow Drifts Down at Christmastide," was published in *American Prefaces* in 1936, and the short story collection *When the Wind is in the South* was published in 1984 by the Center for Western Studies in Sioux Falls, SD.

Even though Rølvaag used some of the same material over several times, he did not lack for new story ideas. In his pocket-calendars and on other handy pieces of paper, he jotted down many ideas for stories and novels, as well as scraps of poetry. In his calendar for 1921, he made a list of seven ideas for short stories, and he outlined a story that ends with a father hanging himself in the corncrib, the mother taken to the poor farm, and the children rejecting their heritage. He also made a note to himself to write a poem about "the source of love" and to write a legend on the same theme. In his calendar for 1925, he outlined a plot for a story in which a Norwegian American man marries a cold American woman. He finally awakens her passion, but then is burned by the fire. These many jottings show some of the directions Rølvaag was interested in pursuing with his writing, though not all of them were fully developed into complete stories.

In many of Rølvaag's short stories, Nature personified becomes a secondary character or functions symbolically. Stylistic influence from the Old Norse sagas can be seen in his use of a mixture of direct and indirect speech. What one critic calls Rølvaag's "crisp, wry style" might also reflect the influence of the sagas (Jordahl 26). His love of Norwegian folk literature and oral narrative have also clearly left their mark on Rølvaag's writing, both in turn of phrase and in theme and characterization. Just to give some examples of his use of stylistic elements of the folktale, some of his stories start with the Norwegian equivalent of "Once upon a time." In folk literature, characters are most often types, and we see this when Rølvaag has a protagonist who is simply "the boy" and the other characters are "the aunt" and "the mother." The place is, of course, also unnamed, just as in folk tales. In many of his short stories, Rølvaag makes effective use of dialect to indicate character as well as regional origin. We see this clearly in "Molla's Heart Attack," where the father uses the dialect from the Trøndelag region of Norway and sprinkles his speech with nautical expressions, and the speech patterns of the smooth salesman Erlie Ingolf show clearly that he is from Bergen. Rølvaag also never hesitates to put English words and Norwegian American expressions into the mouths of his characters, which makes them seem all the more real. In his short stories, as in his novels, Rølvaag demonstrates great psychological insight and presents characters that are complex in their motivations and actions.

Rølvaag's short works can be placed in several categories. He wrote a number of pieces that could be called prose poems, lyrical descriptions of nature. In contrast to many immigrant writers who tended to focus on nostalgic views of the mountains, valleys, and the shores of the homeland, Rølvaag waxed poetic about the prairie, woods, and lakes of what he called "the Northwest," the home of "his people," the Norwegian Americans, in what we would now call the Upper Midwest. Nature personified can be both a positive and a negative force. Perhaps the best of these pieces is "Prairie Moods," which appeared in a number of different publications, but has never been published in English. Here Rølvaag portrays the beauty and power of nature on the prairie in all the seasons. Humans and their reactions to nature and the changing weather are included, and Rølvaag's description of the farmer testing the quality of the spring rain is both true to life and moving.

Another group of stories are those written for and about children. These include a charming tale about the rabbit Long-Ears and his friend Hop-Hop and their brief lives on the farm. Told from the point of view of the rabbit, the tale does not avoid the harshness of reality in describing the death of the protagonist in the jaws of its enemy, the farm dog. The abrupt shift at the end to a scene with the two rabbits in rabbit heaven seems a bit contrived, but perhaps the ending would otherwise have been too harsh for the child audience. The story "The New Hired Hand" is a delightful description of an eight year-old boy whose father takes him on as a helper on the farm. In its realistic description of farm and family life and its psychological insight, this story shows Rølvaag as a master of portraying the child's mind and reality. "The Boy Who Had No Jackknife" suffers from the sentimentality that was so common in Norwegian American literature. However, it, too, shows Rølvaag's keen insight into the psychology of childhood.

The stories Rølvaag himself tried to have published in English belong to a category we might call tragic-comic sketches of immigrant life. In these humorous and yet somewhat tragic stories, Rølvaag pokes fun at the foibles of humanity and particularly at the weaknesses of Norwegian Americans. The characters, in some cases, become almost cartoon figures, caricatures that exaggerate and emphasize certain aspects of personality or experience.

"Molla's Heart Attack" and "The Christmas Offering" show Rølvaag's ability to create strong female characters. We cannot help but laugh at the sight Rølvaag presents of the two-hundred-fifty-pound Molla stripping her erstwhile suitor, Erlie Ingolf, then driving off with his clothes, leaving him naked in the cornfield. Her revenge for his betrayal was indeed sweet, and her life seems to go on afterward on a more-or-less even keel. The fate of Anna Katrina in "The Christmas Offering" (which Rølvaag titled in the version published in Norway "Vengeance is Mine, Saith—") is bleaker. Though it is true she has won the battle for power over her husband, the picture of their lives together both past and future is grim. In "The Butter War in Greenfield," no single character dominates the story; instead, using just a few skillful words, Rølvaag sketches for the reader an entire gallery of distinct personalities. The rural Norwegian Americans depicted in this story demonstrate the weakness of humans who compete with neighbors in false generosity. Presented as an amusing anecdote showing the dangers of rubber-necking on

---

the new-fangled party-line telephone, this story also contains an underlying tragedy, as in the end, the rivalries tear a community apart, and it is clear that an innocent person's career is about to be destroyed.

Though humor is evident in many of Rølvaag's stories, one in particular shows the playful side of his personality most clearly. Only a truly dedicated fisherman would find even a hint of tragedy in the story, which in English has been titled "When the Wind is in the South." The English title of this story, also the title of the anthology of short stories, comes from the saying "when the wind is in the south, it blows the bait in the fish's mouth." Here Rølvaag pokes fun at himself and his friends in a description of his favorite activity of fishing, and he invests the most trivial incident with hilarity.

Rølvaag cast one of his more serious stories in the form of an Indian legend, at the same time incorporating many characteristics of Norwegian folk literature. "Whitebear and Greybear" presents one of Rølvaag's constant themes, the necessity of cultural preservation. In this allegory, Rølvaag shows what happens to "hyphenated" Americans when they try to deny their own culture and identity. He makes no claim for the superiority of one culture over another; rather, he shows the foolishness of trying to imitate without understanding the lifestyle of another group, and he takes a poke at American materialism (see Zempel, *When the Wind*).

Rølvaag's biographer, Einar Haugen, comments rather poetically on Rølvaag's short stories that here "we see Rølvaag the author at work, gathering the bricks for the literary mansions he dreamt of creating" (18). Some critics have labeled Rølvaag as a writer who depicted the "tragedy of immigration." However, he was no "Johnny One-Note" and the short stories, with their variety of theme, style, and tone amply demonstrate the breadth of his vision and his artistic virtuosity.

Rølvaag's short stories (like his longer works) were not always well received in the Norwegian American community. His satire apparently sometimes hit a sore nerve, and some readers did not appreciate having their perceived weaknesses revealed. In 1929, he wrote to a friend, "just the other day I got a letter from one of our pastors who scolds me sharply for the story that appeared in the Christmas annual. The letter is a classic when it comes to stupidity." However, in spite of some negative criticism, the editors of the Christmas annual were constantly asking him for new pieces.

In briefly examining his work as a writer of short stories, we see that though *Giants in the Earth* undoubtedly was Rølvaag's greatest artistic success, this novel alone does not demonstrate the full extent of his vision and his artistic abilities. To see that, we must look at the full range of his authorship and seek out of their obscure hiding places his shorter works as well.

Sources of more detailed information in English on Rølvaag's life and art can be found in the two biographies by Einar Haugen (1983) and Jorgenson and Solum (1939), as well as in Reigstad (1972). There are also numerous book chapters and journal articles treating various aspects of his life and writing. A selection of his short stories has been translated and published in *When the Wind is in the South and Other Stories by O. E. Rølvaag* (1984). All of Rølvaag's letters, manuscripts, and other papers are found in the archives of the Norwegian-American Historical Association.

Works Cited

Haugen, Einar. *Ole Edvart Rølvaag*. Boston: Twayne, 1983.

Jordahl, Owen. *Three Essays on O. E. Rølvaag*. MA Diss. University of Utah, 1972.

Jorgenson, Theodore & Nora O. Solum. *Ole Edvart Rølvaag: A Biography*. New York: Harper's, 1939.

Reigstad, Paul. *Rølvaag: His Life and Art*. Lincoln: U of Nebraska P, 1972.

Rølvaag, O. E. *When the Wind Is in the South and Other Stories by O. E. Rolvaag*. Trans. & Ed. Solveig Zempel. Sioux Falls, SD: Center for Western Studies, 1984.

Rølvaag, Ole Edvart. "Papers." Norwegian-American Historical Association Archives. Northfield, MN.

Sollors, Werner, ed. *Multilingual America*. New York: New York UP, 1998.

Zempel, Solveig. "Introduction." *Concerning Our Heritage.* By O.E. Rolvaag. Trans. & Ed. Solveig Zempel. Northfield, MN: NAHA, 1998. 3–37.

_____. "Introduction." *When the Wind Is in the South.* By O. E. Rølvaag. Trans. & Ed. Solveig Zempel. Sioux Falls, SD: Center for Western Studies, 1984. 7–16.

American Immigrant Short Fiction: An Overview of Recent Critical Resources_____

Robert C. Evans

Once upon a time it would have been relatively easy to prepare an overview of critical commentary dealing with short fiction by recent American immigrants. Those days, however, are long past. Now the problem is *not* finding enough to say; instead, the problem is trying to impose some order on the enormous body of material presently available. Another problem is how to do justice to so much material in a limited amount of space. Inevitably, various valuable resources will be left out, either deliberately or inadvertently. (I have intentionally omitted, for instance, the many books available on children's literature.) And no resource will receive the kind of in-depth description it deserves. One can only hope that indulgent readers will appreciate the difficulties of the task.

In discussing the resources described below, I have imposed the following structure on the materials:

- Overview of General Critical Works on American Immigrant Literature
- Overview of Critical Works on American Short Story Writers from Africa
- Overview of Critical Works on American Short Story Writers from East Asia
- Overview of Critical Works on American Short Story Writers from South Asia
- Overview of Critical Works on American Short Story Writers from the Middle East
- Overview of Critical Works on American Short Story Writers from Latin America

Merely to compile this list is to feel intimidated, and I have elected to eliminate altogether writers from Europe, who would require an article all their own. The present project *is* made a bit easier (but also, in some ways, more difficult) because many discussions of recent immigrant writers treat them as novelists, poets, dramatists, and/or essayists rather than as writers of short fiction. Thus, some winnowing of the materials has already occurred. But finding the references to short stories amidst discussions of works in other genres presents its own challenge.

One is reminded of Ben Jonson's famous poem on Shakespeare. After spending sixteen lines describing what he would and would not do when attempting to praise Shakespeare, Jonson finally simply threw up his hands and said "I, therefore, will begin."

Overview of General Critical Works on American Immigrant Literature

One good way to achieve a general overview of any topic is to begin with the available annotated bibliographies. Fortunately, such bibliographies dealing with immigrant writers abound. In 1992, instance, David Peck compiled an early, but still valuable, survey of criticism dealing with Native American, African American, Chicano/Latino, and Asian American writers. Obviously, not all the commentaries surveyed by Peck deal with immigrant writers in the strictest sense; after all, Native Americans and African Americans have lived in the United States for centuries. Peck's book is especially useful, then, when it deals with Hispanic and Asian writers. Two years later, Laurie King produced another annotated guide to multicultural American literature, and by the end of the twentieth century Peck himself had compiled three other helpful works, all containing bibliographical information (and much else; see the Works Cited segment at the conclusion if this chapter). Also helpful, and even more specifically focused than Peck's books on immigrant literature, was another annotated bibliography issued in 1994 by Roberta Simone. Brief annotated bibliographies also appear in the work edited by Maria Lauret, et al., and James K. Bracken's overviews of reference works are also helpful (although they tend to focus on the standard pre-immigrant canon). And, of course, the best place to begin research on any literary-critical topic remains the *Modern Language Association International Bibliography*, which is now available online. For earlier materials, see also Harner (esp. 428–57) and Marcuse (esp. 399–406).

Encyclopedias, dictionaries, and other such works dealing with ethnic and/or immigrant writers are plentiful. These include such works as the massive, five-volume *Greenwood Encyclopedia of Multiethnic American Literature*, edited by the incredibly productive Emmanuel S. Nelson. It covers an enormous range of authors and topics and has recently been abridged as *Ethnic American Literature: An Encyclopedia for Students* (also edited by Nelson). Intended for a similar audience is *Beginning Ethnic American Literatures* by Helena Grice et al. Helpful, too, is the volume edited by Alpana Knippling, which covers literature produced by members of twenty-two different groups and which offers chapters generally organized by "Literary-Cultural History, Dominant Concerns, Major Authors, Early and Recent Efforts, [and] Prevailing Genres" (xii). A search of this book turns up many references to short stories, making this volume especially relevant to the present essay. Even more relevant are the various editions of the huge and ever-expanding *Critical Survey of Short Fiction*, edited by Charles May. It contains numerous essays on individual immigrant writers as well as essays on immigrant traditions in general (such as the discussion of Asian American short fiction).

The volumes edited respectively by Bendixen and Nagel, Fallon et al., and also by the Werlocks are helpful, as is Blanche H. Gelfant's *Columbia Companion*, which, in addition to offering essays on scores of individual authors, also provides overviews of such topics as "The Asian American Short Story" and "Non-English American Short Stories." The encyclopedia edited by Hamilton and Jones touches on a variety of immigrant authors. A more broadly useful reference set is the two-volume encyclopedia on diaspora cultures edited by Ember, Ember, and Skoggard. But the various volumes prepared by Patrick Meanor and his colleagues are especially valuable for anyone interested in American short fiction of the past fifty years.

Essay collections dealing with literature written by immigrant writers and authors representing diverse ethnic groups include the very valuable volumes edited by Baker, Brown, Nanda, Payant and Rose, and Sollors. Brown's book is particularly helpful because it is totally devoted to essays on short fiction. Also useful are the collections assembled jointly by Anzaldúa and Moraga, Brannon and Greene, Dale and Paine, Di Pietro and Ifkovic, Perez and Sandin, and Shell and Sollors.

General critical studies by single authors are also numerous. Gilbert Muller's *New Strangers in Paradise* covers writings by a handful of significant ethnic groups and touches often on short stories, while A. Robert Lee's volume, although not exclusively focused on immigrant writers, does frequently mention them and has been much praised. The books or articles by Birkle, Boddy, Cowart, Cutter, Fitz, Franco, Jin, Kandiyoti, Nyman, and Skardal are also all worth consulting.

Overview of Critical Works on American Short Story Writers from Africa

Surprisingly few guides seem to have been published dealing with African writers who have immigrated to the United States and written here. (Of course, guides abound to literature produced by "native" African Americans.) The few overviews that do exist about American writers with relatively recent connections to Africa tend to deal with Hispano-African writers and will be discussed in a later section of this essay. In the meantime, however, the survey prepared by Parekh and Jagne is a helpful starting point, but its focus is on writers who were born in Africa and who mostly stayed there. Their book does, though, deal with such African creative writers (of short stories and other works) as Kofi Nyidevu Awoonor, Emmanuel Dongala, Femi Euba, Molara Ogundipe-Leslie, and others who have lived and written in the United States. Another reference work that deals with a number of American writers either from Africa or with strong (such as parental) connections to that continent is the encyclopedia edited by Hamilton and Jones. It includes, for instance, articles on such writers as Chimamanda Ngozi Adichie and Uzodinma Iweala. John Arthur's book, meanwhile, does not focus on writers per se, and the same is true of the collection edited by Okpewho and Nzegwu. That volume does, however, contain a useful essay by Sandra Jackson-Opoku titled "Out beyond Our Borders: Literary Travelers of the TransDiaspora," and Jackson-Opoku is herself a writer of fiction.

The encyclopedia edited by Ember, Ember, and Skoggard contains an essay on African diaspora culture in the United States, and the books by Branche, Goyal, and Pinto, along with Kandji's collection, are also worth consulting in this regard, especially since their focus is primarily literary. Books most specifically concerned with short stories include the ones by Balogun and Emenyonu, although the former (unlike the latter) almost exclusively emphasizes writers who chose to stay in Africa. Clearly, then, there is a real need for additional annotated bibliographies, anthologies, essays, and monographs featuring short stories by African immigrants to the United States. The fact that many English-speaking Africans have emigrated to Britain rather than the US may help explain why there seem to be relatively few American scholarly works of the kinds just called for.

Overview of Critical Works on American Short Story Writers from East Asia

If finding information about African immigrant writers is difficult, just the opposite is true about immigrant writers from East Asia. Resources are so plentiful that covering even the best of them is a difficult task. One might begin, for instance, with the (now dated) annotated bibliography by Cheung and Yogi, then move to the guide prepared by Wong and Sumida, and then proceed to 2003 and 2006 volumes by Huang (especially the 2003 book, which focuses exclusively on short fiction), as well as the book prepared by Nelson (2000). Most helpful of all, however, is probably Huang's three-volume *Greenwood Encyclopedia of Asian American Literature*, which covers practically every topic imaginable. Meanwhile, Oh's one-volume encyclopedia is also worth examining, as is the *Cambridge Companion* edited by Parikh and Kim and the *Interethnic Companion* edited by Cheung. Finally, one might consult such works as those by Adams, Bow, Davis, Ghymn, Lee (1999 and 2014), Leonard, Li, Ling, Kim, Ma, Ninh, Rody, Trudeau,

Wong, Yin, and so on. A search for "Asian American literature" in the Library of Congress electronic catalogue turns up 523 items, and the list, of course, is ever-growing. Finding material on short story writers connected with East Asia is by no means difficult, and so it seems best to deal here more extensively with immigrant writers affiliated with other parts of the world.

Overview of Critical Works on American Short Story Writers from South Asia

By "South Asia," I mean, specifically, writers from such nations as India, Pakistan, Afghanistan, Sri Lanka, and other places on or near the Indian subcontinent (and, therefore, sometimes also called "Indic" writers). People from this area tend to be ethnically distinct from the peoples of East or Southeast Asia.

Although not specifically concerned with short fiction, Nelson's *Reworlding: The Literature of the Indian Diaspora* is an essay collection that is a good place to begin to appreciate the sheer range of South Asian literature. Its bibliography, though helpful, chiefly lists primary works of literature, but the notes to individual chapters offer leads to secondary scholarship. This is also true of Nelson's edited collection on *Asian American Novelists*, which contains brief essays on a number of South Asian writers. Equally useful, especially for its annotated bibliographical leads, is the book by Brains. The individual essays on South Asian writing and writers in Nelson's *Greenwood Encyclopedia* should definitely be consulted, as should the guide edited by Sanga, which has especially good bibliographies that include listings of individual short stories.

Useful collections of essays, sometimes containing discussions of short fiction in particular, include those edited by Dhawan, Dominic, Fludernik, and Singh, and also by Kuortti and Rajeshwar, Pal and Chakrabarti, Ramanan and Sailaja, and also Singh and Singh. Authors of helpful monographs include Afzal-Khan, Brians, Kumar, Kuortti, Mani, Maxey, Ponzanesi, Singh, and Srikanth.

Overview of Critical Works on American Short Story Writers from the Middle East

American writers from the Middle East, especially from Arabic-speaking countries, have only recently begun to receive much critical attention. Partly, this is because the Arab population in the United States was not especially large until the last several decades. But Arab American fiction is now being produced much more abundantly than in the past, as evidenced in the two editions (2004 and 2009) of an anthology edited by Kaldas and Mattawa, titled *Dinarzad's Children: An Anthology of Arab American Fiction*. This book is specifically focused on short stories.

One of the most useful guides to Arab American writing is the 2011 overview by Steven Salaita, which surveys fiction in general and also contains a chapter on short fiction in particular. Also helpful is the 2006 special issue of the journal *MELUS*, guest-edited by Hassan and Newman, which contains a good introductory chapter as well as many solid bibliographical leads. The various works by Orfalea, especially his 1984 monograph, are very much worth consulting, as are the books by Abdelrazek, Fadda-Conrey, Hassan, and especially Salaita. Helpful edited collections include those by Al Maleh and by Majaj and Amireh, and the essay by Majaj should also be consulted. Discussions of Arab American writing, like discussion of works by other immigrant writers, often tend to focus on novels and poetry rather than short fiction, but as more short fiction is produced, more scholarship will undoubtedly be generated as well.

Overview of Critical Works on American Short Story Writers from Latin America

If the number of American immigrant writers from the Middle East is still relatively small, the same cannot be said of writers from countries in the Western Hemisphere where Spanish and Portuguese are the dominant languages. The US has long had a large Hispanic American population, and that population continues to grow. Short stories by American writers originally from (or closely associated with) Mexico, Puerto Rico, Cuba, the Caribbean, and other parts of Central and South America abound. The critical literature on

Hispanic American literature is also quite abundant. The guides prepared by Augenbraum and also by Augenbraum and Olmos are especially valuable. Also helpful are the works by Aldama, Bost and Aparicio, Caminero-Santangelo, Caulfield and Davis, and also Dalleo and Sáez. Useful, too, are the works by Kevane, Leonard, Magill, Poey, Quintana, and Stavans. Special mention should be made of the four books by Kanellos, one of them dealing specifically with short fiction.

More specialized volumes, among many others that could easily be mentioned, include the works by Acosta-Belen, Cudjoe, Fabre, Hernández, Horno-Delgado, Kafka, McKenna, Rahming, Rivera, Sandin, Socolovsky, and the volumes by Antonio López and Marissa López. As the sheer number of primary and secondary works suggests, immigrant fiction by Hispanic-speaking writers and critics is thriving and will surely continue to do so.

Conclusion

As the preceding survey suggests, there is still a great deal of work to be done on recent American immigrant writing, especially on short fiction. Of all the genres, short fiction often receives relatively little attention, despite the fact that so many writers often compose short stories and so many readers read them. Short fiction in general—and short fiction by recent American immigrant writers—deserves far more study than it has heretofore received. Opportunities for original scholarship are plentiful, especially concerning immigrant writers.

Works Cited & Consulted

Abdelrazek, Amal Talaat. *Contemporary Arab American Women Writers: Hyphenated Identities and Border Crossings*. Youngstown, NY: Cambria Press, 2007.

Acosta-Belen, Edna. "Beyond Island Boundaries: Ethnicity, Gender, and Cultural Revitalization in Nuyorican Literature." *Callaloo* 15.4 (1992): 979–998.

Adams, Bella, et al. *Asian American Literature*. Edinburgh, UK: Edinburgh UP, 2008.

Afzal-Khan, Fawzia. *Cultural Imperialism and the Indo-English Novel: Genre and Ideology in R.K. Narayan, Anita Desai, Kamala Markandaya, and Salman Rushdie.* University Park: Pennsylvania State UP, 1993.

Al Maleh, Layla, ed. *Arab Voices in Diaspora: Critical Perspectives on Anglophone Arab Literature.* New York: Rodopi, 2009.

Aldama, Frederick Luis. *Latino/a Literature in the Classroom: 21st Century Approaches to Teaching.* New York: Routledge, 2015.

_____. *The Routledge Concise History of Latino/a Literature.* New York: Routledge, 2013.

Anzaldúa, Gloria & Cherrie Moraga, eds. *This Bridge Called My Back, Fourth Edition: Writings by Radical Women of Color.* Albany State U of New York P, 2015.

Arthur, John A. *Invisible Sojourners: African Immigrant Diaspora in the United States.* Westport, CT: Praeger, 2000.

Augenbraum, Harold, et al. *Latinos in English: A Selected Bibliography of Latino Fiction Writers of the United States.* New York, NY: Mercantile Library of New York, 1992.

Augenbraum, Harold & Margarite Fernández Olmos, eds. *U.S. Latino Literature: A Critical Guide for Students and Teachers.* Westport, CT: Greenwood Press, 2000.

Baker, Houston A., Jr., ed. *Three American Literatures: Essays on Chicano, Native Americans and Asian American Literature for Teachers of American Literature.* New York: MLA, 1982.

Balogun, F. Odun. *Tradition and Modernity in the African Short Story: An Introduction to a Literature in Search of Critics.* New York: Greenwood, 1991.

Bendixen, Alfred & James Nagel, eds. *A Companion to the American Short Story.* Malden, MA: Wiley-Blackwell, 2010.

Birkle, Carmen. *Migration, Miscegenation, Transculturation: Writing Multicultural America into the Twentieth Century.* Heidelberg, Germany: Universitätsverlag Winter, 2004. American Studies: A Monograph Ser.

Boddy, Kasia. *The American Short Story since 1950.* Edinburgh, UK: Edinburgh UP, 2010.

Bost, Suzanne & Frances R. Aparicio, eds. *The Routledge Companion to Latino/a Literature.* New York: Routledge, 2013.

Bow, Leslie. *Betrayal and Other Acts of Subversion: Feminism, Sexual Politics, Asian American Women's Literature*. Princeton, NJ: Princeton UP, 2001.

Bracken, James K. *Reference Works in British and American Literature*. 2nd ed. Englewood, CO: Libraries Unlimited, 1998.

_____ & Larry G. Hinman. *The Undergraduate's Companion to American Writers and Their Web Sites*. Englewood, CO: Libraries Unlimited, 2001.

Brians, Paul. *Modern South Asian Literature in English*. Westport, CT: Greenwood Press, 2003.

Branche, Jerome. *The Poetics and Politics of Diaspora: Transatlantic Musings*. New York: Routledge, 2015.

Brannon, Lil & Brenda M. Greene, eds. *Rethinking American Literature*. Urbana, IL: National Council of Teachers of English. 1997.

Brown, Julie, ed. *Ethnicity and the American Short Story*. New York: Garland, 1997.

Caminero-Santangelo, Marta. *On Latinidad: U.S. Latino Literature and the Construction of Ethnicity*. Gainesville: UP of Florida, 2007.

Caulfield, Carlota & Darién J. Davis, eds. *A Companion to U.S. Latino Literatures*. Rochester, NY: Tamesis/Boydell & Brewer, 2007.

Cheung, King-Kok, ed. *An Interethnic Companion to Asian American Literature*. New York: Cambridge UP, 1997.

_____ & Stan Yogi. *Asian American Literature: An Annotated Bibliography*. New York: Modern Language Association of America, 1988.

Cowart, David. *Trailing Clouds: Immigrant Fiction in Contemporary America*. Ithaca, NY: Cornell UP, 2006.

Cudjoe, Selwyn R., ed. *Caribbean Women Writers: Essays from the First International Conference*. Wellesley, MA: Caloux, 1990.

Cutter, Martha J. *Lost and Found in Translation: Contemporary Ethnic American Writing and the Politics of Language Diversity*. Chapel Hill: U of North Carolina P, 2005.

Dale, Corrine H. & J. H. E. Paine, eds. *Women on the Edge: Ethnicity and Gender in Short Stories by American Women*. New York: Garland, 1999.

Dalleo, Raphael & Elena Machado Sáez. *The Latino/a Canon and the Emergence of Post-Sixties Literature*. New York: Palgrave Macmillan, 2007.

Davis, Rocío G. *Transcultural Reinventions: Asian American and Asian Canadian Short-Story Cycles*. Toronto, Ontario: TSAR, 2001.

Dhawan, R. K., ed. *Indian-American Diasporic Literature*. New Delhi, India: Prestige Books International, 2013.

Di Robert, Pietro & Edward Ifkovic, eds. *Ethnic Perspectives in American Literature: Selected Essays on the European Contribution, A Sourcebook*. New York: MLA, 1983.

Dominic, K. V., ed. *Concepts and Contexts of Diasporic Literature of India*. New Delhi, India: Gnosis, 2011.

Ember, Melvin, Carol R. Ember, & Ian Skoggard, eds. *Encyclopedia of Diasporas: Immigrant and Refugee Cultures Around the World*. London: New York: Springer, 2005.

Emenyonu, Ernest, ed. *Writing Africa in the Short Story*. Rochester, NY: Boydell & Brewer, 2013.

Fabre, Geniève, ed. *European Perspectives on Hispanic Literature of the United States*. Houston: Arte Publico P, 1988.

Fadda-Conrey, Carol. *Contemporary Arab-American Literature: Transnational Reconfigurations of Citizenship and Belonging*. New York: New York UP, 2014.

Fallon, Erin, et al., eds. *A Reader's Companion to the Short Story in English*. Westport, CT: Greenwood, 2001.

Fitz, Earl E. *Rediscovering the New World: Inter-American Literature in a Comparative Context*. Iowa City: U of Iowa P, 1991.

Fludernik, Monika, ed. *Hybridity and Postcolonialism: Twentieth Century Indian Literature*. Tübingen, Germany: Stauffenburg Verlag, 1998.

Franco, Dean J. *Ethnic American Literature: Comparing Chicano, Jewish, and African American Writing*. Charlottesville: U of Virginia P, 2006.

Ghymn, Esther Mikyung. *The Shapes and Styles of Asian American Prose Fiction*. New York: P. Lang, 1992.

Goyal, Yogita. *Romance, Diaspora, and Black Atlantic Literature*. New York: Cambridge UP, 2010.

Hamilton, Geoff & Brian Jones, eds. *Encyclopedia of Contemporary Writers and Their Works*. New York: Facts On File, 2010.

Harner, James. *Literary Research Guide: An Annotated Listing of Reference Sources in English Literary Studies*. 4th ed. New York: Modern Language Association, 2002.

Hassan, Salah &Marcy-Jane-Knopf Newman, eds. *MELUS: The Journal of the Society for the Study of Multi-Ethnic Literature of the United States*. Special Issue: Arab American Literature 31.4 (Winter 2006).

Hassan, Waïl S. *Immigrant Narratives: Orientalism and Cultural Translation in Arab American and Arab British Literature*. Oxford: Oxford UP, 2011.

Hernández, Carmen Dolores. *Puerto Rican Voices in English: Interviews with Writers*. Westport, CT: Praeger, 1997.

Horno-Delgado, Asunción, et al., eds. *Breaking Boundaries: Latina Writing and Critical Readings*. Amherst: U of Massachusetts P, 1989.

Huang, Guiyou, ed. *Asian American Short Story Writers: An A-to-Z Guide*. Westport, CT: Greenwood, 2003.

_____. *The Columbia Guide to Asian American Literature Since 1945*. New York: Columbia UP, 2006.

_____. *The Greenwood Encyclopedia of Asian American Literature*. 3 vols. Westport, CT: Greenwood, 2009.

Jin, Ha. *The Writer as Migrant*. Chicago: U of Chicago P, 2008.

Kafka, Phillipa. *"Saddling la Gringa": Gatekeeping in Literature by Contemporary Latina Writers*. Westport, CT: Greenwood Press, 2000.

Kaldas, Pauline & Khaled Mattawa, eds. *Dinarzad's Children: An Anthology of Contemporary Arab American Fiction*. Fayetteville, AR: U of Arkansas P, 2004. Rev. ed. 2009.

Kandiyoti, Dalia. *Migrant Sites: America, Place, and Diaspora Literatures*. Lebanon, NH: UP of New England, 2009.

Kandji, Mamadou, ed. *Women's Studies, Diasporas and Cultural Diversity: Essays in Literary Criticism and Culture*. Dakar, Senegal: Dakar UP, 2008.

Kanellos, Nicolás. *Biographical Dictionary of Hispanic Literature in the United States: The Literature of Puerto Ricans, Cuban Americans, and Other Hispanic Writers*. New York: Greenwood Press, 1989.

_____. *Hispanic Immigrant Literature: El Sueño del Retorno*. Austin: U of Texas P, 2011.

_____. *Hispanic Literature of the United States: A Comprehensive Reference*. Westport, CT: Greenwood Press, 2003.

Kevane, Bridget A. *Latino Literature in America*. Westport, CT: Greenwood Press, 2003.

Kim, Elaine H. *Asian American Literature: An Introduction to the Writings and Their Social Context*. Philadelphia: Temple UP, 1982.

King, Laurie. *Hear My Voice: Bibliography: An Annotated Guide to Multicultural Literature from the United States*. Menlo Park, CA: Addison-Wesley, 1994.

Knippling, Alpana Sharma, ed. *New Immigrant Literatures in the United States: A Sourcebook to Our Multicultural Literary Heritage*. Westport, CT: Greenwood, 1996.

Kumar, Nagendra. *The Fiction of Bharati Mukherjee: A Cultural Perspective*. New Delhi: Atlantic Publishers, 2001.

Kuortti, Joel. *Writing Imagined Diasporas: South Asian Women Reshaping North American Identity*. Newcastle, UK: Cambridge Scholars, 2007.

_____ & Mittapalli Rajeshwar, eds. *Indian Women's Short Fiction*. New Delhi: Atlantic, 2007.

Lauret, Maria, Helena Grice, Candida Hepworth, & Martin Padget, eds. *Beginning Ethnic American Literatures*. Manchester: Manchester UP, 2001.

Lee, Rachel C. *The Americas of Asian American Literature: Gendered Fictions of Nation and Transnation*. Princeton, NJ: Princeton UP, 1999.

_____, ed. *The Routledge Companion to Asian American and Pacific Islander Literature*. New York: Routledge/Taylor & Francis Group, 2014.

Leonard, George J., ed. *The Asian Pacific American Heritage: A Companion to Literature and Arts*. New York: Garland Press, 1999.

Leonard, Kathy S. *Index to Translated Short Fiction by Latin American Women in English Language Anthologies*. Westport, CT: Greenwood, 1997.

_____. *Latin American Women Writers: A Resource Guide to Titles in English*. Lanham, MD: Scarecrow P, 2007.

Li, David Leiwei. *Imagining the Nation: Asian American Literature and Cultural Consent*. Stanford, CA: Stanford UP, 1998.

Ling, Amy. *Between Worlds: Women Writers of Chinese Ancestry*. New York: Pergamon Press, 1990.

López, Antonio M. *Unbecoming Blackness: The Diaspora Cultures of Afro-Cuban America*. New York: New York UP, 2012.

López, Marissa K. *Chicano Nations: The Hemispheric Origins of Mexican American Literature*. New York: New York UP, 2011.

Ma, Sheng-Mei. *Immigrant Subjectivities in Asian American and Asian Diaspora Literatures*. Albany: State U of New York P, 1998.

Magill, Frank N., ed. *Masterpieces of Latino Literature*. New York: HarperCollins, 1994.

Maitino, John R. & David R. Peck, eds. *Teaching American Ethnic Literatures: Nineteen Essays*. Albuquerque: U of New Mexico P, 1996.

Majaj, Lisa Suhair. "Arab American Literature and the Politics of Memory." *Memory and Cultural Politics: New Approaches to American Ethnic Literatures*. Ed. Amritjit Singh, Joseph T. Skerrett, & Robert E. Hogan. Boston: Northeastern UP, 1996. 266-90.

_____ & Amal Amireh, eds. *Etel Adnan: Critical Essays on the Arab-American Writer and Artist*. Jefferson, NC: McFarland, 2002.

Mani, Bakirathi. *Aspiring to Home: South Asians in America*. Stanford, CA: Stanford UP, 2012.

Marcuse, Michael J. *A Reference Guide for English Studies*. Berkeley: U of California P, 1990.

Maxey, Ruth. *South Asian Atlantic Literature, 1970–2010*. Edinburgh, UK: Edinburgh UP, 2012.

May, Charles E., ed. *Critical Survey of Short Fiction*. 4th ed. 10 vols. Ipswich, MA: Salem, 2012.

McKenna Teresa. *Migrant Song: Politics and Process in Contemporary Chicano Literature*. Austin: U of Texas P, 1997.

Meanor, Patrick. *American Short-Story Writers Since World War II*. Detroit: Gale Research, 1993.

_____ & Gwen Crane. *American Short-Story Writers Since World War II*. Detroit: Gale, 2000. Second Ser.

_____ & Richard E. Lee. *American Short-Story Writers Since World War II*. Detroit: Gale Group, 2001. Third Ser.

_____ & Joseph McNicholas. *American Short-Story Writers Since World War II*. Detroit: Gale, 2001. Fourth Ser.

_____ & Richard E. Lee. *American Short-Story Writers Since World War II*. Detroit: Thomson Gale, 2007. Fifth Ser.

Muller, Gilbert. *New Strangers in Paradise: The Immigrant Experience and Contemporary American Fiction*. Lexington: U of Kentucky P, 2008.

Nanda, Aparajita, ed. *Ethnic Literatures and Transnationalism: Critical Imaginaries for a Global Age*. New York: Routledge, 2014.

Nelson, Emmanuel S., ed. *Asian American Novelists: A Bio-Bibliographical Critical Sourcebook*. Westport, CT: Greenwood Press, 2000.

_____. *Ethnic American Literature: An Encyclopedia for Students*. Westport, CT: Greenwood, 2015.

_____, ed. *The Greenwood Encyclopedia of Multiethnic American Literature*. 5 vols. Westport, CT: Greenwood, 2005.

_____, ed. *Reworlding: The Literature of the Indian Diaspora*. New York: Greenwood Press, 1992.

Ninh, Erin Khuê. *Ingratitude: The Debt-Bound Daughter in Asian American Literature*. New York: New York UP, 2011.

Nyman, Jopi. *Home, Identity, and Mobility in Contemporary Diasporic Fiction*. Amsterdam: Rodopi, 2009.

Oh, Seiwoong, ed. *Encyclopedia of Asian-American Literature*. New York: Facts on File, 2007.

Okpewho, Isidore & Nkiru Nzegwu, eds. *The New African Diaspora*. Bloomington: Indiana UP, 2009.

Orfalea Gregory. *Before the Flames: A Quest for the History of Arab Americans*. Austin: U of Texas P, 1988.

_____. "Doomed by Our Blood to Care: The Poetry of Naomi Shihab Nye." *Paintbrush* 18.35 (Spring 1991): 56–66.

_____. "On Arab Americans: A Bibliographic Essay." *American Studies International* 27.2 (October 1989): 26–41.

_____. *U.S.-Arab Relations: The Literary Dimension*. Washington, DC: National Council on U.S.-Arab Relations, 1984.

Pal, Adesh & Tapas Chakrabarti, eds. *Interpreting Indian Diasporic Experience*. New Delhi: Creative Books, 2004.

Parekh, Pushpa Naidu & Siga Fatima Jagne, eds. *Postcolonial African Writers: A Bio-Bibliographical Critical Sourcebook*. Westport, CT: Greenwood P, 1998.

Parikh, Crystal & Daniel Kim, eds. *Cambridge Companion to Asian American Literature*. New York: Cambridge UP, 2015.

Payant, Katherine B. & Toby Rose, eds. *The Immigrant Experience in North American Literature: Carving out a Niche*. Westport, CT: Greenwood Press, 1999.

Peck, David R. *American Ethnic Literatures: Native American, African American, Chicano/Latino, and Asian American Writers and Their Backgrounds—An Annotated Bibliography*. Pasadena, CA: Salem Press, 1991.

_____, ed. *American Ethnic Writers*. Pasadena, CA: Salem Press, 2000.

_____ & Eric Howard, eds. *Identities and Issues in Literature*. 3 vols. Pasadena, CA: Salem Press, 1997.

Perez, Richard & Lyn Di Iorio Sandin, eds. *Moments of Magical Realism in U.S. Ethnic Literatures*. New York: Palgrave Macmillan, 2012.

Pinto, Samantha. *Difficult Diasporas: The Transnational Feminist Aesthetic of the Black Atlantic*. New York: New York UP, 2013.

Poey, Delia. *Latino American Literature in the Classroom: The Politics of Transformation*. Gainesville: UP of Florida, 2002.

Ponzanesi, Sandra. *Paradoxes of Postcolonial Culture: Contemporary Women Writers of the Indian and Afro-Italian Diaspora*. Albany: State U of New York P, 2004.

Quintana, Alvina E., ed. *Reading U.S. Latina Writers: Remapping American Literature*. New York: Palgrave Macmillan, 2003.

Rahming Melvin R. *The Evolution of the West Indian's Image in the Afro-American Novel*. Millwood, NY: Associated Faculty, 1986.

Ramanan, Mohan & P. Sailaja, eds. *English and the Indian Short Story: Essays in Criticism*. New Delhi, India: Orient Longman, 2000.

Rivera, Carmen S. *Kissing the Mango Tree: Puerto Rican Women Rewriting American Literature*. Houston, TX: Arte Público Press, 2002.

Rody, Caroline. *The Interethnic Imagination: Roots and Passages in Contemporary Asian American Fiction*. New York: Oxford UP, 2009.

Salaita, Steven. *Modern Arab American Fiction: A Reader's Guide.* Syracuse, NY: Syracuse UP, 2011.

Sandín, Lyn Di Iorio & Richard Perez, eds. *Contemporary U.S. Latino/a Literary Criticism.* New York: Palgrave Macmillan, 2007.

Sanga, Jaina C. *South Asian Novelists in English: An A-Z Guide.* Westport, CT: Greenwood Press, 2003.

Shell, Marc & Werner Sollors, eds. *Multilingual America: Transnationalism, Ethnicity and the Languages of American Literature.* New York: New York UP, 1998.

Simone, Roberta. *The Immigrant Experience in American Fiction: An Annotated Bibliography.* Metuchen, NJ: Scarecrow, 1994.

Singh, Manjit Inder, ed. *Contemporary Diasporic Literature: Writing History, Culture, Self.* Delhi: Pencraft International, 2007.

_____ & Joga Singh, eds. *Multiple Perspectives on Indian/Punjabi Diaspora: Identities, Locations and Intersections.* Patiala: Publication Bureau, Punjabi University, 2014.

Skardal, Dorothy Burton. "Revising the American Literary Canon: The Case of Immigrant Literature." *American Studies in Transition.* Ed. D. Nye & C. Thomsen. Odense: Odense UP, 1985. 97–119.

Socolovsky, Maya. *Troubling Nationhood in U.S. Latina Literature: Explorations of Place and Belonging.* New Brunswick, NJ: Rutgers UP, 2013.

Sollors, Werner, ed. *The Invention of Ethnicity.* New York: Oxford UP, 1991.

Srikanth, Rajni. *The World Next Door: South Asian American Literature and the Idea of America.* Philadelphia: Temple UP, 2004.

Stavans, Ilan, ed. *Latina Writers.* Westport, CT: Greenwood Press, 2008.

Trudeau, Lawrence J. ed. *Asian American Literature: Reviews and Criticism of Works by American Writers of Asian Descent.* Detroit: Gale, 1999.

Werlock, Abby H. P. & James P. Werlock, eds. *The Facts On File Companion to the American Short Story.* 2nd. ed. New York NY: Facts On File, 2010.

Wong, Sau-ling Cynthia. *Reading Asian American Literature: From Necessity to Extravagance.* Princeton, NJ: Princeton UP, 1993.

_____ & Stephen H. Sumida. *A Resource Guide to Asian American Literature*. New York: Modern Language Association of America, 2001.

Yin, Xiao-huang. *Chinese American Literature since the 1850s*. Urbana: U of Illinois P, 2000.

Formalism and Latino "Flash Fiction"_____

Robert C. Evans

"Old" New Criticism and Newer Forms of Formalism

From the 1940s to the mid-1970s, commentary on American literature was often dominated by the so-called "New Criticism." Advocated by such prominent figures as Cleanth Brooks, Robert Penn Warren, Rene Wellek, and many others, New Criticism arose as a reaction against various earlier ways of reading literature. Those earlier approaches were largely historical in emphasis, dealing with such matters as the author's life, the author's ideas, and the author's social circumstances. The New Critics, in contrast, wanted to focus on what they often called "the work itself." In other words, they wanted to explore literature *as* literature—that is, as *language*, interesting, powerful, and effective phrasing. They therefore favored "close readings" of individual texts. They argued that in great works of literature, every single word or even sound mattered. Sentence structures were as important as larger forms. Literature was less interesting simply for the ideas it expressed or the topics it explored than for the literary skill with which such expression and exploration were accomplished. To many scholars and teachers in the 1940s and beyond, the New Criticism seemed a breath of fresh air. It seemed to make visible the skill, craftsmanship, and subtleties of language that made literature worth reading and worth studying in the first place. For the New Critics—or "formalists," as they were also called—"form" could not be separated from "content." What mattered most were not the ideas a work dealt with, but the precise, individual word-choices a writer used in order to impose meaning and significance on whatever ideas the work explored.

The rise of the New Criticism was strongly resisted by traditional scholars, but the new approach quickly won the day. By the 1960s, New Criticism had, in fact, become the new orthodoxy, and to increasing numbers of critics it no longer seemed very new at all. In fact, it had come to seem (at least to many) formulaic and old-fashioned. Increasing numbers of critics reacted against it, attracted instead by newer theories and fresher analytical approaches. These included such theories as structuralism, deconstruction, feminism, multiculturalism, dialogical criticism, postmodernism, and, especially, the so-called New Historicism. Many of these newer theories were less interested in the precise phrasing and structures of individual works than in the philosophical, historical, social, political, and cultural significance of texts. In other words, the pendulum had swung back, in many ways, to an earlier emphasis on the content or meaning of works. It had swung away from the formalists' emphasis on precise word choices. Works were now often studied in terms of their "themes" and their relevance to various cultural contexts. The reign of formalism was over.

Or so it seemed. By the beginning of the twenty-first century, increasing numbers of critics had begun to feel that the pendulum (as always) had swung too far—that literature was increasingly "reduced" to its paraphraseable meanings and that literary criticism had often become mere political propaganda. Essays on literature were now often essays on the various ideologies in which literature seem entangled. Studies of works were now often studies of the ways works were relevant to "larger" issues of class, gender, race, and other constructions of human identity. Critics now often saw their job as studying literature in order to expose and oppose various forms of discrimination and oppression. Criticism now often had an overt political agenda. It was now used less often than in the past to study the subtleties of a work's phrasing. That sort of "literary" approach, after all, might actually cloak an intentional or inadvertent reactionary political agenda, and it did nothing to promote economic, political, and social justice. At least (the "Newer" Critics argued) they themselves were absolutely "up-front" about their various nonliterary beliefs and passions. In contrast, the old New Critics (they alleged) had often been closet reactionaries.

This is not the place to debate these broader issues. (For sample discussions, see the "Works Cited or Consulted" section at the conclusion of this chapter.) It *does* seem worth remarking, however, that a critic can easily embrace a definite program for social change and *still* be interested in the precise details of an author's literary craftsmanship. In other words, there seems no *necessary* contrast between a close attention to the literary effectiveness of the words on the page and a concern with social justice. Arguably, in fact, the literary works that will most effectively and lastingly promote various social agendas are precisely the ones that are best-written. Hundreds of religious essays were written in defense of Christianity during John Milton's day, but few of them are as fascinating, memorable, and re-readable as *Paradise Lost*. Many essays have been written over the centuries about the need for powerful people to care for the weak and poor, but few of them pack the lasting literary punch of Shakespeare's *King Lear*. Ethical, social, and political concerns need not conflict with close readings.

Often, however, by the early twenty-first century, actual works of literature had begun to seem less important to some critics than the messages those works contained. Criticism often began to consist of plot summaries embedded in social, cultural, or political commentary. Even worse, the commentary had begun to seem excruciatingly predictable. Anyone picking up an essay using a particular ideological approach could almost guarantee the kinds of conclusions the essay would reach. This charge of predictability, ironically, had also often been leveled at the old New Critics themselves. And sometimes the allegations were true. But at least the old New Critics had been so focused on individual phrasing that they often produced genuine insights into the *literary* details of *literary* works. A reader picking up a New Critical essay might indeed be able to predict that the essay would end by arguing for the complex unity of a work. But rarely could a reader predict precisely *how* and *why* the critic would come to that conclusion. Because New Critics distrusted and even disdained what they called "the heresy of paraphrase," one could at least expect a formalist to focus on a text's unique, precise phrasing. A reader might actually learn something unexpected in the process.

By the early 2000s, therefore, "formalism" had begun to make a comeback. "What goes around comes around," and by this point, formalism had begun to come around again. (Surely it will recede once more, but it is unlikely ever to disappear entirely, at least as long as people love interesting, effective combinations of words.) Many leading figures no longer dismissed formalism, but now in fact embraced it. Perhaps they embraced it in new forms, arguing that older formalist approaches were insufficiently complex. But the important thing is that suddenly it had once again become respectable to pay attention to the precise words on the page.

Formalism and American Immigrant Fiction

Why and how is any of this relevant to fiction (including short fiction) written by "American immigrant" authors? The answer is simple. During the original heyday of the old New Criticism, very little attention was paid to work by American immigrant writers. This was especially true of works by "recent" immigrants, such as Africans, East Asians, Southwest Asians, Latinos, and other groups who were not as prominent in American culture as they are today. Prior to the 1960s, restrictive laws had discouraged immigration from most countries besides European nations. After the mid-1960s, a change in the law had made it possible for more and more non-Europeans to come to the United States. In short, during the decades when the New Criticism dominated the literary-theoretical scene, little "immigrant" literature was being written. By the time such literature had begun to be abundantly produced, most critics were not only uninterested in formalism, but were actually hostile to it. To many of them, it seemed old-fashioned, if not retrograde or reactionary.

This is all a shame because it means that much literature produced during the period from the 1960s to the present has often not received the kind of close, careful, "literary" attention it might have received if formalism had not been, for many years, *verboten*. Instead, immigrant literature (like, in fact, much literature by African Americans and gays) has often been read in terms of its messages and meanings rather than in terms of the ways those messages and meanings are expressed in individual words, sentences, sounds, rhythms, and so on. Matters of characterization, tone, setting, point-of-view, and structure have received far less attention than they merit. Literature by immigrants has often been treated mainly as propaganda rather than primarily as literature. Words *as words* have often been off the radar screens of many commentators, teachers, and students.

The recent renewal of formalism, however, now offers abundant opportunities for commentators on recent literature by immigrants to make up for lost time. Close readings of such literature can now help establish these works as significant parts of the American *literary* canon, not just as political essays dressed up as poems, novels, or short stories. Eventually, as the United States becomes an increasingly cosmopolitan and "welcoming" country, and as immigrants become more and more powerful parts of the national constituency, and as the injustices suffered by many immigrants recede, immigrant literature will more and more need to be studied *as literature* lest it seem to have only historical significance ("that's how they treated us back in the day"). Ultimately, immigrant literature, to survive as literature rather than as sociology, will need to be studied and appreciated in terms of the skill with which it is written.

"Flash" Fiction

"Flash fiction"—sometimes called "sudden fiction," "micro fiction," "very, very short fiction," "short-short fiction," and so on— offers rich opportunities for the kinds of close reading I have just advocated. Of course, defining such fiction is as difficult as defining most literary genres with any precision. But as the various terms suggest, "flash fiction" tends to be unusually brief. "Very, very short stories" are often less than a thousand words in length, sometimes less than three hundred. This means that in these works, even more than in most literary works, every word counts. Novels and "regular" short stories are usually long enough that they can be read mostly in thematic terms—in terms of their apparent messages. In "flash fiction," however, there is usually less time for a writer to expatiate on ideological themes. There is also less incentive for a critic to treat such literature reductively. After all, the writing has already been reduced by the original author to bare (or barer) essentials. Flash fiction, therefore, offers critics and regular readers real chances to examine writing by immigrant authors *as writing*.

In this respect, one of the most helpful anthologies of "flash fiction" by immigrant writers is an anthology titled *Sudden Fiction Latino: Short-Short Stories from The United States and Latin America*, edited by Robert Shapard, James Thomas, and Ray Gonzalez. This collection contains scores of works, many of them by "immigrant" authors. This term, too, is hard to define. But, for the purposes of this essay, I will define it as referring to authors born outside the United States but resident here either now or for long periods of their lives. If we use the term in this sense, a dozen "immigrant" authors of short fiction are included in *Sudden Latino Fiction*. Those authors include Daniel Alarcón, Luna Calderón, Norma Elia Cantú, Omar Castañeda, Judith Ortíz Cofer, Junot Díaz, Dagberto Gilb, Julio Ortega, Tomás Rivera, Luis Alberto Urrea, Luisa Valenzuela, and Marisella Veiga. All twelve of these writers are distinguished, prize–winning authors. In the space remaining, I hope to do several things: (1) quickly survey the anthology's stories written by these twelve authors; (2) briefly indicate which stories seem most effectively written; and (3) finally concentrate on the work of Judith Ortíz Cofer, who has written a number of powerful pieces of "flash fiction." Her pieces are included not only in *Sudden Latino Fiction*, but elsewhere. She is, I believe, an immigrant writer of short fiction who merits even more attention than she has already received.

Latino Flash Fiction: A Quick Survey

Julio Ortega's story, which concludes the volume, is titled "Epilogue: Migrations." It begins with an effective opening sentence: "Monday morning walking down the hill toward the bus stop, I was expecting to see Charlie but he was not there" (Ortega 289). The phrasing is simple and clear; it thrusts us immediately into the midst of things (*in medias res*); it creates interest in the narrator and in Charlie; and in its final words, it makes us experience, along with the narrator, the sudden sense of Charlie's absence. (Imagine how different the effect would be if the sentence had been structured this way: "Charlie was not there on Monday morning when I walked . . .”). Soon, however, the story devolves into what sounds like intellectual name-dropping by a self-involved academic:

> I was reading *The Frog*, John Hawkes's recent novel . . . . Borges has written . . . . Perhaps Heraclitus's river flows in the reverberance of speech. . . .Marx and Fournier start their visions . . . . I sent the first version of my poem to Guy Davenport . . . . I helped my dear friend the Brazilian poet Haroldo de Campos . . . . No less telling is the case of Gregory Rabassa. Greg becomes another person when he translates a book. . . . Once in a conference at the Crystal Room, John Hawkes felt short of words and turned to me . . . . (Ortega 290–96)

Perhaps this is not a short story at all (although it is mentioned as one in the book's Introduction [Valenzuala 21]). Perhaps it is instead a personal essay. If it is indeed a work of creative fiction, it might perhaps be read as a satire of the narrator. In any case, little about the style catches or holds one's attention. As literature—as writing interesting *as* writing—this text never quite matches the interest generated by its opening sentence.

Similar problems arguably arise in some of the other texts by "immigrant" writers included in *Sudden Latino Fiction*, but many of the stories are genuinely striking, almost from the very first words. Thus the story titled "The Visitor," by Daniel Alarcón, is intriguing right from the start. It opens with these words: "It had been three months and I thought things would have gotten easier. The children still cried at night. They still asked about their mother" (Alarcón 213). Instantly, Alarcón creates sympathy and suspense. As his tale unfolds, we discover that the narrator and his young children have survived a massive mudslide that has wiped out their remote village, killing the wife and mother and an even younger sibling of the three remaining children. This story is subtly understated in phrasing and rich in moral implications, and its conclusion is particularly thought-provoking. Asked by a visitor, near the very end of the tale, how many loved ones he has lost in the slide, the narrator replies "Only one" (218), even though the story has made it abundantly clear that a fourth child was also killed. Why does the narrator not include this fourth child when he responds to the visitor's question? The story, like many good stories, leaves us uncertain and therefore leaves us thinking and wondering. It closes with a fascinating ambiguity that makes it even more memorable than it had been already.

Powerful in other ways is a story titled "Alma," by Junot Díaz, which grabs readers' attentions from the very first paragraph and never lets go:

> You have a girlfriend named Alma, who has a long tender horse neck and a big Dominican ass that seems to exist in a fourth dimension beyond jeans. An ass that could drag the moon out of orbit. An ass that she never liked until she met you. Ain't a day that passes that you don't want to press your face against that ass or bite the delicate sliding tendons of her neck. You love how she shivers when you bite, how she fights you with those arms that are so skinny they belong on an after-school special. (Díaz 39)

The word "You" instantly involves readers: the speaker talks about himself as if he were talking both *about* us and *to* us. The tone of the story is immediately dialogic and colloquial. Sentences flow with the rhythm, syntax, and diction of actual speech, as in the double fragments, the idiomatic "Ain't," and the crude but credible specificity of "ass . . . ass . . . ass . . . ass"—repetition that underscores in the phrasing the speaker's focus on one part of Alma's body. The speaker is obviously at home in the lingo of the streets, but his language is also precise, inventive, and often surprising, as in the paradoxical description of the girlfriend's "long tender horse neck" or in the claim that her ass is big enough that it "could drag the moon out of orbit." As he describes Alma, the speaker even more thoroughly, if implicitly, describes himself. He seems young, energetic, cocky, smart, observant, potent, aggressive, raunchy, sex-driven, and humorous, and he may also strike some readers as sexist and arrogant. We find ourselves immediately interested in him, in Alma, and in what if anything will happen between them. Ironically, by the very end of the story, the speaker himself will seem a sort of ass and will be perceived as such by Alma, the reader, and even himself. Whether Díaz himself intended this sort of comic structural

---

Formalism and Latino "Flash Fiction"   43

echo between the opening of the story and its end is less important than the irony itself. The speaker, who in the opening paragraph seems in control of everything, has, by the story's final sentence, become a loser in more ways than one.

In the meantime, and in-between the first and last paragraphs, Díaz's story is consistently lively and evocative. Practically every sentence invites close reading and real appreciation for its diction, syntax, tone, rhythms, and sounds. Almost every sentence is a virtuoso performance in one way (or to one degree) or another. Readers never lose interest because they can never predict what Díaz—or, rather, his narrator—will say or do next. The story deals with topical social issues (gender relations, eroticism and the nature of desire, relations between ethnic groups, the ways men abuse women), but it never seems merely sociological or propagandistic. Superficial as the speaker seems, the story he tells packs a real emotional and moral punch. But the genuine interest it generates is in the diction, the dialogue, the characters, the plot, the tone, and so on. In other words, this story is a piece of *literature*—a piece of writing in which our main interest is in the *words as words* and in the ways they are skillfully put together. One needn't know or care that the author was "born in Santo Domingo, Dominican Republic, in 1968, emigrated to New Jersey in 1974, and now lives in Boston" (304). All that matters is that he can *write*.

Much the same might be said about other "immigrant" authors included in *Sudden Fiction Latino*. Besides the stories by Díaz and Alarcón, especially impressive (or so it seems to me) are the stories by Cantú, Gilb, Urrea, and Veiga. And then there is also the story by Judith Ortíz Cofer.

Judith Ortíz Cofer

Cofer's story is titled "Volar" [in English, "To Fly"]. In this often-reprinted tale, the narrator is looking back on herself as a twelve-year-old girl who "was an avid consumer of comic books—*Supergirl* being my favorite" (Cofer, "Volar" 219). She recounts her secret fantasies, at that time, of becoming and kind of supergirl herself. As she climbed, in her dreams, to the roof of her urban apartment building, she imagined a magical transformation: her legs would lengthen, her arms would harden, and her hair would grow blonde and straight. "Of course, I would add the bonus of breasts, but not too large; Supergirl had to be aerodynamic" (219). Finally, at the top of the building, fifty-stories high, she would (in her fantasy) jump "into the black lake of the sky" (220). The story is almost worth reading for that last vivid phrase alone, but there is much else to admire about Cofer's writing here. Thus, Cofer credibly gets "inside the head" of her protagonist, effectively presenting her point of view by writing as a twelve-year-old might speak.

At the same time, the protagonist is obviously not taking her younger self nearly as seriously as her younger self once did. The "voice" of the story blends naïveté and maturity; the narrator gently mocks her earlier self, even as she recalls that self with affection. Already, then, the story is more complex than it might have been. Yet this is also a character to whom most adults can relate—a character appealing partly because her dreams were so innocently unrealistic. On one level, the story is about the immature fantasies of a girl on the cusp of adolescence and eventual adulthood; on another level, the story is about the loss of innocence almost all people suffer as they grow older. Reality, after all, soon reasserts itself, for this girl and for all of us.

When the girl awakened, she would find herself "back in my body: my tight curls still clinging to my head, skinny arms and legs and flat chest unchanged" (220). Simply listen to the sounds of these words to hear the skill of Cofer's phrasing: "**b**ack in m**y b**ody: m**y** t**i**ght curls still c**l**i**n**ging to my head, ski**nn**y arms and legs and flat **ch**est un**ch**anged." Note how the comma balances clauses of roughly equal length and comparable structure, and note how effectively listing is used in the final half of the sentence, with the longest item in the list placed last. Anyone could describe pretty much the same details in similar language, but only an artist as skilled as Cofer could arrange these precise words with such intuitive skill.

Yet the story also offers riches besides the riches of phrasing (crucial as those are); it also develops, in its second half, an impressive deepening of tone and implication. This added depth is all the more impressive in a story so short. After the young girl awakens, she hears her mother and father talking together in the kitchen, as they did every morning. While the father talks about events in the neighborhood, the mother tries to shift the topic to a possible visit—a possible flight—back to their homeland of Puerto Rico. Suddenly, then, the title of the story gains an added dimension. Both the girl and her mother dream about flying. But as the mother looks out the kitchen window, she sees only the next building, a foot or two away. Before coming to get the girl of out bed, the mother would "sigh deeply and say the same thing the view from her kitchen window always inspired"—a deeply ironic word—her to say: "*Ay, si yo pudiera volar*" [Oh, if (only) I could fly].

That one final phrase not only ties everything together, but also opens out into a wealth of possible implications. Suddenly we see the connections between the girl's fantasies and the mother's dreams. Suddenly the distances between mother and daughter, adult and adolescent, significantly narrow. The girl can vividly fantasize about flying; the mother knows that her dreams of flight are impossible. The girl can fantasize about leaping into the "black lake of the sky"; the mother can only stare at a brick wall. A story that had begun as an apparently somewhat whimsical reminiscence abruptly gains psychological, sociological, cultural, and moral depth. The final sentence takes the spotlight off the daughter and instead illuminates the limited, limiting life of the mother and of the family in general. Even the fact that the mother speaks in Spanish is important: that detail implies how close she still is, historically, culturally, and psychologically, to her Puerto Rican homeland. In roughly a thousand words, Cofer manages to alter the tone of the story from simple to profound and from comic to nearly tragic, and she shifts our attention from the individual fantasies of a single girl to the archetypal yearnings and frustrations of humans in general.

Just as impressive, in its own ways, is an even shorter short story by Cofer. This one is titled "Give Us This Day." In this tale, a fifteen-year-old girl is suddenly summoned by phone to meet her Spanish-speaking mother at a hospital where the girl's father has been taken. He has been seriously injured in a fall from a building.

The girl is needed because *she* can speak English and can thus help her mother understand the doctors and nurses (and vice versa). To get to the hospital the girl must walk down dark, dangerous streets; she risks being attacked, raped, or even killed. We never learn, by the end of the story, whether she makes the trip safely. All we know is her steely determination to proceed.

The stunningly effective technique Cofer uses in this story involves a constant alternation between English and Spanish. This method runs throughout the tale and is already present in its first two sentences: "*Había una vez*, a girl, a *quinceañera*, who one night learns the power of fear, of *el terror*. Her father has fallen or jumped from the roof of *un edificio*" (Cofer, "Give" 59). The opening phrase can be translated as "Once upon a time," so that this highly realistic story also takes on the tone of a dark fairy tale involving an archetypically dangerous journey. That journey takes place not, as in most fairy tales, through a terrifying forest but this time through a kind of looming urban jungle. Cofer adds even more interest and mystery to the story by leaving open the possibility that the girl's father has jumped from the building. Thus, while the girl worries for her own safety as she walks down dangerous, thug-filled streets, we wonder if she is putting her own life at risk to help a man who may have tried to commit suicide.

The repeated shifting back and forth between Spanish and English is effective in numerous ways. For one thing, this technique is obviously relevant to the theme of bilingualism, which is not merely discussed in this story but quite literally *enacted*. We get to *feel* what it must be like to *be* this girl, perceiving the world from two distinct, but mutually reinforcing, cross-pollenating perspectives. Rather than simply trying to describe the girl's psychology, Cofer makes us actually share it. Usually the meanings of the Spanish words can be inferred from their contexts, and sometimes the narrator translates or elaborates upon the meanings for us, as when she uses "fear" side-by-side with "*el terror*." But the word "*terror*" sounds, in English, far more literally terrifying than "fear." So the story's phrasing is enriched by this kind of double-usage. Rarely do the Spanish words seem superfluous. The word "*edificio*," for instance, somehow suggests a building taller and more imposing than does the simple word "building," which immediately follows it. The story thus illustrates how bilingualism can enrich one's perceptions of the world while also, in some ways, creating confusion. Readers get to experience how it feels to be both limited in and freed by one's language. Thus, when we come to a reference to the mother's "*lagrimas*," the meaning of the word is not as immediately apparent as the meaning of "*el terror*" was. So we have to go to a translator—much as the mother and doctors do—to understand that "*lagrimas*" means "tears." Cofer could have made the story much easier for English-speakers to comprehend, but by forcing them to rely on dictionaries or digital translators, she makes them understand (without preaching) the constraints non-English–speaking minorities experience every day.

In this story, as in much of her other work, Cofer is alert to subtle details of phrasing. Thus the narrator refers, with effective alliteration, to a "street of strangers." Later, crime symbolically hides "behind a pile of trash." Danger is memorably described as sounding "like a starved cat, or like *una pareja* of lovers struggling behind a dumpster." Cofer uses various briefly mentioned details to summon up whole social and familial worlds. We sense at once the girl's frustrations with her family, but also her love for her mother and her love for (but also fear of) her father. In one especially effective passage, the girl walks past "*Drogaditos. Asesinos. Vecinos*"—drug addicts, killers, neighbors. That final word—neighbors—catches us completely by surprise. The sentence would have a significantly different effect if "*Vecinos*" had come first in the list. If that arrangement had been the case, we would have sensed the girl moving from the familiar, to the somewhat dangerous, to the very dangerous. In the present listing, however, the girl moves from the dangerous, to the very dangerous, to the not dangerous at all. The unpredictability of the final word raises several possibilities. Is the girl's imagination exaggerating the danger she faces? Is the narrator suggesting that in this area drug addicts and killers are also neighbors? Even so brief a passage as this three-word sequence gives us much to ponder.

The story's final sentences are especially powerful:

> She cannot be assaulted, raped, or killed, for she must get to the hospital to speak English for her parents. She possesses *el santo ingles*, and she carries it like a gun, like a chalice. She wears it like a hairshirt, like a bulletproof vest. *Father in Heaven, give us this our daily English*. She feels powerful as *una santa*, as *una asesina*. Anyone who sees her knows nothing can touch her. Fear and anger propel her through the dark. She must get there to translate her mother's *angustia*, and to help name her father's pain. (Coffer 59)

This passage is effective for numerous reasons. First, despite the girl's conviction and determination, we know that she can *indeed* be assaulted, raped, and killed. The "for" in the first quoted sentence suggests logical inevitability, but in the very act of doing so, it undermines the certainty it implies. Later sentences dizzyingly alternate between comfortable religious consolation, on the one hand, and brutal, crude realism on the other. Thus "chalice" is juxtaposed with "gun," "hairshirt" with "bulletproof vest," "*una santa*" with "*una asesina*." The narrator juxtaposes two opposed kinds of human existence—the holy and the homicidal—in much the same way that she also juxtaposes Spanish and English. In both ways, the story takes us inside the painfully divided mind and experience of the isolated but loving, nervous but determined girl, who is full of both fear *and* anger. We admire her heroic determination, but worry about her safety. She is both literally and figuratively surrounded by darkness—concerned about her father, her mother, and herself, but filled with courage precisely because of her concern. It hardly seems an accident that the final word of this very effective piece of "sudden fiction" is "pain."

A different kind of writer would have given the story a more definitive conclusion. A maudlin writer would have shown the girl arriving safely at the hospital. A melodramatic writer would have shown her, in the final sentences, being attacked. Cofer, a highly talented writer, instead leaves the girl in suspended animation, walking forward without ever (at least in our experience of the narrative) reaching her goal. The story stops as abruptly as it began.

It ends, as it opened, with a focus on her connections with her mother and father. Cofer resists the temptation to provide a neat, tidy resolution, one way or another. Instead, she masterfully leaves us hanging.

Yes, the story suggests interesting ideas about the relations between Anglo and Hispanic cultures. Yes, it might be interesting to feminists for presenting the vulnerability, but also the strength, of a resolute young woman. Yes, the narrative implies a good deal about life in dangerous urban areas, and it also makes us wonder what social, cultural, and/or psychological conditions might tempt a husband and father to possibly—just possibly—step deliberately off a building and potentially kill himself. But none of these matters would matter much at all if the story were not skillfully crafted and exceedingly well written. The story's status as *literature* makes all the other questions worth considering. *Viva el formalismo!*

Works Cited or Consulted

Alarcón, Daniel. "The Visitor." *Sudden Fiction Latino: Short-Short Stories from the United States and Latin America.* Ed. Robert Shapard, et al. New York: Norton, 2010. 213–18.

Bogel, Fredric V. *New Formalist Criticism: Theory and Practice.* New York: Palgrave Macmillan, 2013.

Cofer, Judith Ortíz. "Give Us This Day." *The North American Review* 293.3–4 (2008): 59.

_____. "Volar." *Sudden Fiction Latino: Short-Short Stories from the United States and Latin America.* Ed. Robert Shapard, et al. New York: Norton, 2010. 219–221.

Díaz, Junot. "Alma." *Sudden Fiction Latino: Short-Short Stories from the United States and Latin America.* Ed. Robert Shapard, et al. New York: Norton, 2010. 39–42.

Cohen, Stephen, ed. *Shakespeare and Historical Formalism.* Burlington, VT: Ashgate, 2007.

Eagleton, Terry. *How to Read Literature.* New Haven, CT: Yale UP, 2013.

Fish, Stanley. *How to Write a Sentence: And How to Read One.* New York: Harper, 2011.

Ortega, Julio. "Epilogue: Migrations." *Sudden Fiction Latino: Short-Short Stories from the United States and Latin America.* Ed. Robert Shapard, et al. New York: Norton, 2010. 289–96.

Sanborn, Geoffrey & Samuel Otter, eds. *Melville and Aesthetics.* New York: Palgrave Macmillan, 2011.

Shapard, Robert, James Thomas, & Ray Gonzalez, eds. *Sudden Fiction Latino: Short-Short Stories from the United States and Latin America.* New York: Norton, 2010.

Theile, Verena & Linda Tredennick, eds. *New Formalisms and Literary Theory.* New York: Palgrave Macmillan, 2013.

Valenzuela, Luisa. "Introduction: A Smuggler's Sack." *Sudden Fiction Latino: Short-Short Stories from the United States and Latin America.* Ed. Robert Shapard, et al. New York: Norton, 2010. 17–21.

Forbidden Desires: Interracial Relationships in Chimamanda Ngozi Adichie and Jhumpa Lahiri's Short Fiction

Anupama Arora

Chimamanda Ngozi Adichie and Jhumpa Lahiri are undoubtedly two of the most prominent and acclaimed contemporary women writers in the United States today. They have both won major awards—the Pulitzer and the Guggenheim for Lahiri and the Orange Broadband and the MacArthur for Adichie—and have published novels and short fiction that have been on best-seller lists. Their work—which straddles the lines between postcolonial, diaspora, and American studies—has already been anthologized and become part of the academic curriculum. In her short story collections, *Interpreter of Maladies* (1999) and *Unaccustomed Earth* (2008), Lahiri provides a sensitive portrait of the post-1965 middle-class Bengali Hindu Indian American diaspora, while, in the many stories of her collection, *The Thing Around Your Neck* (2009), Adichie casts an astute eye on the experiences of recent Nigerian migrants in the United States.[1] It is no surprise that both have excelled as short fiction writers. In his introduction to *The Short Story*, Paul March-Russell notes that, "Increasingly, it seems that dislocation, rather than locality, has become the dominant trait of the short story" (148), and, indeed, both Adichie and Lahiri's short fiction focuses on the dislocation—physical, emotional or psychological, and cultural—that accompanies migration and navigating the sociocultural landscape of the new home.

Among other thematic overlaps, both Adichie's and Lahiri's works also feature intimate or romantic interracial relationships, desire, or marriages—a theme that has a long history in immigrant and/or ethnic American literature.[2] This essay focuses on these twenty-first century women writers' portrayal of relationships of this type in *The Thing Around Your Neck* and *Unaccustomed Earth*. As I shall here demonstrate, Adichie centers issues of power and privilege and the fetishization of racial difference in her depictions of interracial desire and romance. In contrast, racial difference is almost a non-issue in Lahiri's stories; indeed, though interracial romantic relationships are present in a majority of the stories, they are deftly sidelined in order to foreground the inter- and intra-generational tensions within the Indian American family and the (un)belongings of second-generation diasporics.[3] As the two writers engage this time, Lahiri and Adichie are able to offer, each in her own way, their critique of societal injunctions or dictates, and shed light on how the past history and legacy of colonial and transnational/cultural contact continues to impinge on the intimate/personal realm in the present.[4]

The Thing Around Your Neck is Adichie's first short story collection, with the rest of her body of work consisting of three novels: *Purple Hibiscus* (2003), *Half of a Yellow Sun* (2006), and *Americanah* (2013). There are twelve stories in this eclectic and yet coherent collection; half of its stories are set in the US, while in the other half, the US is variously felt as an influence. For instance, while the setting of "Ghosts" is Nigeria and while its plot revolves around a retired mathematics professor's memories of the Biafran War and its aftermath, the story makes frequent references to the man's daughter, a physician in the US. In another Nigeria-set story, "The American Embassy," a traumatized woman, who has lost her husband and four-year-old child in a General Abacha regime clampdown, now waits in the long lines of applicants for visas outside the US Embassy in Lagos. "The Shivering" plays itself out primarily in a housing complex at Princeton University, where international students, including Nigerian students, live. And lastly, in stories such as "The Arrangers of Marriage" and "Imitation," Adichie explores the disquiet and alienation of Nigerian migrant-wives in their American settings and circumstances. I will focus on two stories from the collection, "The Thing Around Your Neck" and "Jumping Monkey Hill"—one set in the US, the other in South Africa—fictions whose subjects include and focus on interracial desire, primarily the desire of a bourgeois white male for a Nigerian female.

In contrast to Adichie, who first won recognition for her novels set in Nigeria, Lahiri gained prominence primarily as a short story writer of the Indian immigrant/diasporic experience when her first collection, *Interpreter of Maladies*, won the Pulitzer Prize for Fiction and the Hemingway Foundation/PEN Award in 2000. She has since published two novels—*The Namesake* (2004) and *The Lowland* (2013)—and another short story collection, *Unaccustomed Earth* (2008). In all her work, Lahiri has been concerned with mapping the Indian American diaspora. *Unaccustomed Earth* contains eight stories. The collection is organized into two parts: the first part consists of five stories, while the second part is a triptych of three interrelated stories told through the alternating points of view of two Indian Americans, Hema and Kaushik, characters whose lives intertwine as both children and adults. The five stories of the collection's first part, meanwhile, profile second-generation Indian Americans at various phases of their adult lives and their looking back—ruefully, conflictedly, nostalgically—on their immigrant parents' lessons and legacies. I will focus on these five stories—all of which feature interracial relationships in their narratival sidelines.

Negotiating Belonging

Lahiri's stories "Unaccustomed Earth," "Hell-Heaven," "A Choice of Accommodations," and "Only Goodness" all show second-generation Indian Americans in romantic relationships and marriages with white partners. However, these interracial marriages are not the main focus in any of the stories. In her matter-of-fact and reticent treatment of these unions, Lahiri seems to suggest that interracial marriages should be treated as commonplace in twenty-first century US. For Lahiri's diasporic characters, the choice of a Euro-American mate/spouse is not a fraught act. This contrasts with Asian American male writers (such as Carlos Bulosan, David Mura, Ved Mehta) of previous decades whose works fetishize white female American bodies, whose male protagonists' romantic possession of white partners symbolizes control, reassurance, and assimilation for the Asian American male.[5]

The title story, "Unaccustomed Earth" is framed by a retired Indian immigrant father's visit to his daughter in Seattle.[6] The daughter, Ruma, born and raised in the US, has been married for ten years to a white American named Adam. The story focuses on the anguished feelings of this diasporic daughter, a woman who misses her late mother, and who tries to navigate her feelings towards her father, whom she has always thought of as distant. The main source of tension in the story is this father-daughter relationship. We only get a brief glimpse into Adam and Ruma's relationship and marriage, through Ruma's memories and her phone conversations with Adam who is traveling while her father visits. All we learn of the spouses' relationship, past and present, is that since her mother's death, Ruma has felt alienated from Adam, who seems less capable of understanding the loss of a parent than she can. This incapacity troubles her. Also, Adam is perplexed by her insistent discontent. These tensions—in some regards universal, though, too, inflected in this instance by Adam's and Ruma's specific ethnic differences— are of lesser consequence in the fiction than are Ruma's and her father's evolving relationship.

Similarly, the prime focus in "A Choice of Accommodations" is a second-generation Indian American son's sense of abandonment by the parents who enrolled him years ago in a boarding school in Massachusetts and then returned to India (Lahiri 89); secondary, though not unimportant, is the light shed by the story on his relationship with his Euro-American wife. In "Only Goodness," the main plot revolves around Sudha's unraveling relationship with her alcoholic younger brother, Rahul, to which her own interracial marriage with Roger (an Englishman) and Rahul's relationship with Elena, a white American single mother, is subordinated. And in "Hell-Heaven," it is the immigrant woman's loneliness and the mother-daughter relationship that takes center stage, while the dynamics of a secondary Indian American character's relationship with his white girlfriend and later wife are traced with less detail in the story's subplot.

Still, though, the stories keep the characters' interracial relationships in the background and though the characters themselves are nonchalant about their interracial relationships, the stories tell us, too, that first generation Indian American parents were sternly opposed to their children's interracial relationships. The attitude of the Indian families toward these mixed marriages reveals the insularity of the immigrant community as well as their investment in cultural perpetuity. Without fail, all the immigrant parents in these stories forbid their children to marry outside their community and ethnicity. This Indian community is invested in preserving their culture. Insisting on "loving the same" and marrying within their own culture, this community reveals its ethnonationalism. Indeed, one strength of Lahiri's stories lies in her long and hard inward glance at the aspirations and desires of these immigrant Indians as they confront the longings of their diasporic children. In these stories, almost as if in spite of the first-generation Indian parents' injunction to marry within the community, all the second-generation offspring rebel to marry (or have romantic relationships) with non-Bengalis, non-Indians, and non-South Asians. These interracial relationships thus disrupt the immigrant community's need to reproduce itself, in its own image.

As we see, the diasporic offsprings' exogamous marriages are a cause of pain for the immigrant parents, even though they later come to terms with these marriages. In "Unaccustomed Earth," Ruma remembers how her mother "had done everything in her power to talk Ruma out of marrying Adam, saying that he would divorce her, that in the end, he would want an American girl" (Lahiri 26). The tragic irony is that the immigrant Indian mother does not understand that her daughter, too, is an *American* girl. In "Hell-Heaven," Usha, the second-generation diasporic daughter, remembers how her mother disproved of the marriage of their friend Pranab Kaku with the white American Deborah, anticipating their eventual divorce. Usha remembers that after the marriage with Deborah, when Pranab Kaku stops socializing with the Bengalis, it is Deborah who is blamed for his severing of ties with the ethnic community:

Their absences were attributed, by my parents and their circle, to Deborah, and it was universally agreed that she had stripped Pranab

Kaku not only of his origins but his independence. She was the enemy, he was her prey, and their example was invoked as a warning, and as vindication, that mixed marriages were a doomed enterprise. (Lahiri 75)

Ironically, while this mixed marriage ends up being doomed, it does not fail due to tension because of ethno-racial difference or because of the American woman's betrayal; rather, it is Pranab Kaku who commits adultery and falls in love with a married Bengali woman, leaving Deborah after twenty-three years of marriage. In the story "Only Goodness," too, it is not ethno-racial differences between the Indian American woman and the Englishman Roger that cause a rift between them; rather, the strain in their relationship comes from Sudha's younger brother's alcoholism, which she had kept a secret from her husband. This problem almost leads him to drown the couple's infant son when he's babysitting him.

Exemplary, too, of the first-generation Indian American parents' ethnocentric attitude is that of Amit's parents in "A Choice of Accommodations." Their disappointment with their son's white American fiancée, Megan, exposes the elitist snobbery of the globetrotting transnational elite. We learn that Amit Sarkar's parents—accruers of global cultural and economic capital—had been unhappy with Amit's marriage not only because Megan was not Bengali, but because her "ordinary background had displeased" them (Lahiri 95). The parents disprove of Megan's plain and middle-class origins: her father is a policeman, and her mother a kindergarten teacher.

In addition, in "A Choice of Accommodations," as in "Nobody's Business" and "Hell-Heaven," Lahiri also presents triangulated relationships, a device that allows her to further illuminate something of the immigrant and diasporic experience and existence, such as the melancholic yearnings of Indian Americans, or the gendered experiences of migration or the different gendered burdens placed on/felt by diasporic males and females.

"A Choice of Accommodations" focuses on the moment when Amit and Megan attend the wedding of Pam Borden, the daughter of the headmaster from Amit's boarding school days. This occasion involves a return to his adolescent years and the beginnings of his adult life in the US; also, the return invokes in him his haunted sense of his parents' desertion and Pam's rejection. We learn that, when Amit was a teen, the headmaster's family had become a sort of surrogate family to him after his parents had left for India when he was in ninth grade. Also, we learn that Amit and Pam have some additional history; Amit had once felt a strong, unrequited love for Pam. For Amit, this relationship comes to signify his place (or sense of displacement) in the US, an America of which he is a part, and yet from which he feels apart.

We gather from Amit's musings that, for Pam, he can never be anything other than one of the lonely foreign boys that her family invites for Thanksgiving dinner. She cannot imagine a romantic relationship with him. When Amit, drunk at a college party—during the time that they both attended Columbia University—makes a pass at Pam, touching her, she lets him do it and then pulls away. "She had indulged him, just as her family had indulged him once a year in their home, offering a piece of herself and then shutting the door" (Lahiri 100). She seems to always have the upper hand in their friendship and almost treats him like a child whom she indulges. For Amit, Pam and her family represent an America that is friendly but distant, and their reaching out and withdrawing only intensifies his sense of un-fulfillment. Amit remembers that it was Pam who had first initiated contact when they were both in college and that it was she who had "called him in that same ambassadorial way her parents had, even though New York City, and the world of college, was as foreign to her as it was to him" (99). Amit's description of Pam as an "ambassador" is telling. Could Pam calling on Amit as an ambassador (of the US presumably) imply that she remains the official representative of the country, while Amit remains the foreigner in need, someone whom she will help navigate America? Amit's feelings are reminiscent of those of Gogol, Lahiri's protagonist from *The Namesake*, who, when staying briefly at a Chelsea brownstone that belongs to the parents of his white girlfriend Maxine, "cannot help but be aware of having assimilated into a milieu that willingly makes room for him but in ways that leave him feeling perpetually childlike, in need of tutoring, grateful for the opportunities he has been given" (Song 170).

On the upside, Amit's present-moment attendance at Pam's marriage causes him to reflect on his own marriage to Megan. It is not surprising to find out that Amit is the one who has been questioning their love, marriage, and parenting, in contrast to Megan, whose belief in the relationship is solid and "unshakeable." The story ends with Megan and Amit rekindling their marriage in a moment of connection through having clandestine sex in a dorm room, an act that could be read as having cathartic significance, implying a new beginning as Amit might finally shed some of that baggage (of abandonment, betrayal, alienation) that he carries from his adolescent years.

If the diasporic son Amit's dissatisfaction is a central theme in this previous story, then "Hell-Heaven" sheds light on loneliness of an immigrant wife and parent through the portrayal of triangulated relationships. The adult narrator Usha remembers how, when she was a child, Pranab Kaku, an older Bengali Indian student at MIT, inserted himself into their family's life like a breath of fresh air, and how her lonely mother fell in love with him, though she never articulated this love. The narrator remembers the happy times that she, her mother, and Pranab Kaku would spend together while her father was at work. However this dynamic changes once Deborah, a white American philosophy student at Radcliffe, enters Pranab Kaku's life. The seven-year old narrator remembers becoming "part of a new triangle" as she now goes on car-rides with the two of them (Lahiri 70). In this story, Lahiri underscores the gendered experience of migration, where the immigrant woman-wife (who usually arrives in the US through an arranged marriage and does not work outside the home) has to confront isolation and homesickness.

"Nobody's Business" depicts multiple interrelated, interracial romantic triangles. In the story, the three-year relationship between a young Indian American woman named Sang (Sangeeta) with Farouk, an Egyptian academic at Harvard who likes to be called Freddy, unravels after she finds out that he has been cheating on her all along with another woman (a white Canadian woman named Deirdre). This denouement is brought about by the interference of Sang's roommate Paul, a white American PhD student of literature— from whose perspective the story is told—who is creepily infatuated with her and monitors all her romantic moves and relationships.

Both Farouk and Paul are not portrayed as ideal suitors for Sang. Farouk gets little narrative sympathy in the story. The reader learns that Sang does his laundry, buys his groceries, and orders tiles for the remodeling of his kitchen. Farouk comes across as cruel, controlling, exploitative, emotionally abusive, and a cheat. In her reading of this story, Rajini Srikanth finds Lahiri's portrayal of Farouk troubling, especially within the context of the post 9/11 demonization of the Arab male. Srikanth argues that Lahiri uses Farouk to "strengthen the links between Indian Americans and white Americans. His character becomes the instrument through which the Indian American female gets a necessary education in reality and the white American male is enabled to play the role of rescuer" (Srikanth 67). While I agree that Lahiri portrays Farouk as "unpalatable" and unattractive, Lahiri hardly portrays Paul as a hero. Paul is unimpressive and passive. His only moment of action is when he punches Farouk and dislocates his shoulder. In some ways, we could see Paul engaging in his own white male rescue fantasy—of saving the brown woman from another brown man, to paraphrase Gayatri Spivak's oft-cited idea. But, like Farouk, Paul too is self-absorbed and almost stalker-like in his curiosity about Sang's personal and love life. And the story leaves us wondering if his intervention/interference has caused more harm than good, and whether he becomes a pawn for Deirdre, who manipulates him to get rid of Sang in Farouk's life.

In addition, in the end, it is Sang who suffers the most and whose attempt to live life on her own terms is thwarted. Her sexual choices should've been "nobody's business." It is likely that she will be forced to return to the paternal home, where we can imagine that she will have to conform to her parents' demands for an arranged marriage. In her thoughtful analysis, Susan Koshy locates the "political valence" of Lahiri's work in the "devastating critique of the new immigrant family as a vehicle for the reproduction of human capital and cultural identity" (355). Koshy reads this story, as well as others in *Unaccustomed Earth*, as an example of how Lahiri reinscribes "the intergenerational narrative as filial gothic" to illustrate the psychic costs of the immigrants' investment in economic mobility and the model minority narrative. The interracial relationships and marriages become means through which the second generation rebels against this immigrant parental exhortation/ extortion to fulfill their aspirations, preserve and reproduce cultural authenticity, and maintain pure diasporic cultural continuity.

Navigating Racial Difference

In comparison to Lahiri's stories, Adichie insists on the inflections of ethno-racial differences on interracial relationships. In both "The Thing Around Your Neck" and "Jumping Monkey Hill," she casts an honest and unflinching look at love and desire across racial and national lines. In both stories, she critiques the "intense, consuming" gaze of the white male (British and American) upon the black female as an object of sexual desirability and availability (Adichie 121). She explores how racial fantasy and sexual desire are intertwined and also how there is no escape from the colonial baggage and historical racial scripts inherent in interracial desire.

The title story, "The Thing Around Your Neck," set in Maine and Connecticut, revolves around the relationship between Akunna, a twenty-two-year-old Nigerian migrant female and an unnamed white male—a college senior at an American state university—in his late twenties. The story is riddled with both the pressures and the possibilities that coexist in this interracial relationship.

The story begins with Akunna's arrival from Lagos at her uncle's house in a "small white town in Maine" (Adichie 115). Akunna is the lucky winner of the US visa lottery that this distant "uncle" (not related by blood) had applied for on behalf of all his family members. During her short stay at her uncle's house and the small town, she learns the dubious mechanisms by which America manages racial diversity and multiculturalism. Her uncle tells her that his company gives him many incentives because they are "desperately trying to look diverse. They included a photo of him in every brochure, even those that had nothing to do with his unit" (116). In turn, he has made his peace with living "in an all-white town" (116). At the community college that Akunna briefly attends, the questions she is asked and the assumptions that are made about her—how she knows English; if Africans have real houses; if she'd seen a car before arriving in America—reveal the students' "mixture of ignorance and arrogance" (116). However, it is only after the uncle makes a sexual pass at Akunna that she leaves the house. From this insular and isolated town in Maine, she moves undesignedly to another small town in Connecticut. Here she finds work as a waitress in a restaurant run by an immigrant named Juan who hires her because of his assumption that "all immigrants work hard" (117). It is also here that she meets the white male college student and begins a relationship with him.

Initially wary of—but also curious about—the young white man, Akunna finally capitulates to his friendly overtures when he persists. Also, she admits him into her life as a bulwark against the loneliness that gnaws at her. When she first meets him, while she is surprised at his knowledge of Africa, she is suspicious and ready to dismiss him, as she wants "to feel disdain [...] because white people who liked Africa too much and those who liked Africa too little were the same—condescending" (Adichie 120). But, as she warms up to him, she also feels the loneliness—which has wrapped itself like a noose around her neck—slowly dissolve: "The thing that wrapped itself around your neck, that nearly choked you before you fell asleep, started to loosen, to let go" (125). Their companionship promises hope and human connection in Akunna's bleak immigrant life, even as the baggage of intersecting differences threatens to weigh it down.

Their relationship brings to the fore Akunna's realization of the gulf of differences—class, race, and nationality—between her and her partner, a gulf to which he remains oblivious. Akunna is uneasy about how little he recognizes or acknowledges his socioeconomic and white American privilege, such as the fact that his wealthy Boston grandfather has left a trust fund for him, or that he can take time off from college to travel to Africa and Asia "to discover himself." Also, it disconcerts her that he does not notice how they are perceived as an interracial couple. Indeed, he is often startled by Akunna's keen sensitivity to these differences. When Akunna calls him out on his fetishization of the poor Third World native and says that he is "wrong to call only the poor Indians in Bombay the real Indians," he gets upset (Adichie 125). Again, when Akunna says that she does "not want him to go to Nigeria, to add it to the list of countries where he went to gawk at the lives of poor people who could never gawk back at *his* life," he is uncomprehending (124–25). Blind to his privilege of mobility, he can only stare at Akunna blankly when she is angry or upset. As a working-class black female migrant who remits money home to Lagos to her mother (who works as a cleaner) and her father (who is a taxi driver), she is only too painfully aware of all that he takes for granted.

Further, it is Akunna who notices how their appearance in public as a couple evokes a variety of strained responses, suggesting that others view this intimacy as something unnatural:

> You knew by people's reactions that you two were abnormal—the way the nasty ones were too nasty and the nice ones too nice. The old white men and women who muttered and glared at him, the black men who shook their heads at you, the black women whose pitying eyes bemoaned your lack of self-esteem, your self-loathing. Or the black women who smiled swift solidarity smiles; the black men who tried too hard to forgive you, saying a too-obvious hi to him; the white men and women who said, 'What a good-looking pair' too brightly, too loudly, as though to prove their own open-mindedness to themselves. (Adichie 125)

As these reactions suggest, while there is some open-mindedness toward cross-racial desire/romance, such romance continues to invite censure and is seen as transgressive by some in both the dominant and minority communities. Even in the twenty-first century, these matches still remain vexed and evoke anxiety. This is of course also a story of Akunna's experience of becoming racialized as Black in America; though a Nigerian migrant, within the visual optics of race, on the street, she is simply Black. Unfortunately, as she quickly surmises, her presence in public alongside a white man inevitably resonates within the long, complex, and haunted history of black-white desire and the various meanings attached to such desire in American history and culture.

In "Jumping Monkey Hill," the desire of Edward Campbell—an older, white, British, Oxford-trained Africanist—for Ujunwa, a young Nigerian woman and aspiring writer, comes under scrutiny. The setting of the story is an African Writers workshop held in a resort in Cape Town, South Africa. Campbell, the organizer of this workshop, not only fetishizes the body of the African women, but also seeks to possess and own their stories. The story delineates the power dynamic between the white male and African (female) writer within the context of neocolonial and neoliberal realities, where the metropole or the global North continues to be the arbiter or arbitrator of taste and success for the African writer. Through her depiction of Ujunwa's efforts to write as an independent human being, Adichie underscores the asymmetrical power relations between the global North and the global South.

Campbell represents the imperative and will to knowledge of the West to write Africa in a particular way, in a way that seeks to affirm an always already known idea of the continent. He imposes his own notion of what should constitute the true subject of African literature on the African participants at the workshop, suggesting how the image and representation of Africa continues to be mediated by institutions and conventions from the outside. As Madhu Krishnan writes, "Writing Africa, from its incipient moments, has never been an innocent task, nor has it been one free from a broader interpellation into a global system of inequity in representation and its attendant distribution of power" (15). In Adichie's story, we see how the workshop (funded by the British Council Arts Foundation) becomes one such institution. In one instance, when a Senegalese woman at the workshop reads out a draft of her autobiographical story of coming out as a lesbian to her parents, Campbell refuses to see it as an authentic African story, asserting that "homosexual stories of this sort weren't reflective of Africa," and asking "This may indeed be the year 2000, but how African is it for a person to tell her family that she is homosexual?" (Adichie 108). Tellingly, Campbell calls Ujunwa's story "implausible" and dismisses it as "agenda writing" (114). He refuses to believe that a young Nigerian woman desperately in need of work, as is the protagonist of Ujunwa's workshop story, would walk out of a job situation, even one that demands that she prostitute herself; and he even refuses to see the job as unequivocally exploitative, seeing it instead as nothing more nor less than an exchange of commodities. The irony and hypocrisy is that Campbell himself has an "agenda," since he only promotes writing about gender non-specific, black-on-black atrocities (dictators, coups, killings) as the legitimate subjects of African literature. The additional irony is that Ujunwa's story is hardly fiction, but, instead, a barely veiled autobiographical narration of her confrontation with blatant sexism during her own search for jobs in Lagos. Obtuse concerning realities such as these, Campbell constantly seeks to exert his control, in an entitled manner, over the stories being told by the African participants in the workshop.

In the same vein, Campbell also feels that he has the license to gaze at the bodies of the African women at the workshop. This sort of consuming erotic desire of the white man for the black woman is embedded in colonial history. Campbell feels that he has the freedom to tell the Senegalese woman that "he had dreamed of her naked navel" (Adichie 111). He similarly looks at Ujunwa with such naked desire that even the other workshop participants notice it. For her part, Ujunwa hated "the way he always looked at her chest rather than her face, the way his eyes climbed all over her" (109). If, in Lagos, Ujunwa had to fend off the unwelcome advances of potential male bosses, at the workshop, she faces off with a lascivious white man who ogles with impunity. Concomitantly, Ujunwa is patronized by Campbell. When she disagrees with his feedback on a story, "he look[s] at Ujunwa the way one would look at a child who refused to keep still in church" (108). Campbell sees Ujunwa through the prism of racial Otherness—paternalistically as the child-like native and as the accessible and hypersexualized Black woman.

In conclusion, through their short fiction, Lahiri and Adichie offer a rich glimpse into the realities of immigration and transnational encounters in the twenty-first century. While Adichie illuminates the difficulty of navigating and bridging differences of race and geography in cross-racial love and desire, Lahiri depicts interracial relationships and marriages—and biracial children and families—as commonplace and as highlighting the constantly shifting outlines of the United States as a multiracial/multicultural society of global citizens whose affective (un)belongings traverse histories and geographies.

Notes

1. The Immigration and Nationality Act of 1965 reopened immigration from Asia, especially for skilled immigrants, ending the race-based restrictions of the 1924 Act. Most Nigerian migrants, in contrast, have arrived in the United States since the 1990s.

2. For instance, see the work of early twentieth-century writers such as the Jewish American Anzia Yezierska and the Eurasian American Sui Sin Far, as well as mid-to-late twentieth-century writers such as the Indian American Ved Mehta and Japanese American David Mura, among others.

3. I use "first generation" to refer to the immigrant parents, who migrated from elsewhere, and "second-generation" or "diasporic" to refer to the US-born or -raised children of these immigrants.

4. Adichie and Lahiri explore the theme of interracial desire in their novels too. See, for instance, Gogol's relationship with Maxine and Moushumi's with Graham in *The Namesake*; and in *The Lowland*, there's Subhash with Holly and Elise, Gauri and Lorna, and Drew and Bela. Adichie's *Half of a Yellow Sun* features Kainene's relationship with the Englishman Richard, and in *Americanah*, Ifemelu dates the white American Curt.

5. For a discussion, see Chu, Lee, and Ma.

6. Lahiri borrows the phrase "unaccustomed earth" from Nathaniel Hawthorne's famous "The Custom House" preface to his novel, *The Scarlet Letter*, to explore the theme of displacement and transplantation of roots. For a discussion of this Hawthornian connection, see essays by Bilbro, Koshy, and Srikanth.

Works Cited

Adichie, Chimamanda Ngozi. *The Thing Around Your Neck*. New York: Anchor Books, 2009.

Bilbro, Jeffrey. "Lahiri's Hawthornian Roots: Art and Tradition in 'Hema and Kaushik.'" *Critique: Studies in Contemporary Fiction* 54 (2013): 380–394.

Chu, Patricia P. *Assimilating Asians: Gendered Strategies of Authorship in Asian America*. Durham & London: Duke UP, 2000.

Koshy, Susan. "Neoliberal Family Matters." *American Literary History* 25.2 (Summer 2013): 344–380.

Krishnan, Madhu. "Negotiating Africa Now." *Transition* 113 (2014): 11–24.

Lahiri, Jhumpa. *Unaccustomed Earth*. New York & Toronto: Knopf, 2008.

Lee, Rachel C. *The Americas of Asian American Literature: Gendered Fictions of Nation and Transnation*. Princeton, NJ: Princeton UP, 1999.

Ma, Sheng-mei. *Immigrant Subjectivities in Asian American and Asian Diaspora Literatures*. Albany: State U of New York P, 1998.

March-Russell, Paul. *The Short Story: An Introduction*. Edinburgh, UK: Edinburgh UP, 2009.

Song, Min Hyoung. *The Children of 1965: On Writing, and Not Writing, as an Asian American*. Durham & London: Duke UP, 2013.

Srikanth, Rajini. "What Lies Beneath: Lahiri's Brand of Desirable Difference in *Unaccustomed Earth*." *Naming Jhumpa Lahiri: Canons and Controversies*. Eds. Lavina Dhingra & Floyd Cheung. Lanham, MD: Lexington Books, 2012. 51–71.

CRITICAL
READINGS

Divinity and Ekphrasis: DeLillo's Short Fiction, 1990 to 2015_____

John Paul Russo

Don DeLillo has worked only sporadically in short fiction and, excepting pieces that he incorporated into his novels, has published only seventeen stories from 1960 to the present, or about one every three years. By contrast, Hemingway brought out *The First Forty-Nine Stories* in mid-career (he was 39). From 1990 to the present, DeLillo has published five stories—"The Angel Esmeralda," "Baader-Meinhof," "Midnight in Dostoevsky," "Hammer and Sickle," "The Starveling"—so few that when in 2011 he collected his stories in *The Angel Esmeralda*, he had to reach back to 1979 to make a book, no hefty volume at that (213 pp.). This is DeLillo's first collection of short fiction (he is 79). Further, his choice of the title story, "The Angel Esmeralda" (1994), is something of a genre pretender in that it had already been incorporated into a longer work, *Underworld*, in 1997. Still, in their bibliography, Gardner and Nel keep this story in the short fiction category because of the revisions that the author had made in its transition from stand-alone fiction to novel segment.

"The Angel Esmeralda" epitomizes many of the writer's central themes, from the media, spectacle, and consumer culture, to fear and violence, discipline, and redemption. The story is set among the ethnic neighborhoods of the Bronx, where DeLillo grew up and attended a Jesuit high school and Jesuit Fordham University. The elderly and fiercely idealistic Sister Edgar and the young, practical Sister Grace perform errands of mercy into the most run-down sections of the Bronx to deliver food and medicine. The nuns are a study in generational contrast: Sister Edgar insists on wearing the ancient habit, recites the Baltimore Catechism as litany, and detects signs of moral decay in bad grammar, misspelling, and dirt: a man with cancer wants to kiss her "latexed hands" (*A* 84). (Sister Edgar has a touch of Christopher Durang's bossy Sister Mary Ignatius.)

Secular in dress, Sister Grace is almost as secular in outlook, less imaginative than her counterpart, though no less courageous. On their missions into the slums of the 1990s, a far cry from the vibrant heyday of these communities in the 1920s and 30s, the nuns encounter sickness of every kind, as well as drugs, hunger, AIDS, cocaine babies, and more. One sentence could be their Homeric epithet—for they are heroines—as they make their rounds: "They rode the elevators and walked down the long passageways." They visit the diabetic amputee, the two blind women who share a seeing-eye dog, the five small children on a bed being minded by a ten-year-old, and many others who survive in flats without heat, lights, or water (*A* 83–85; *U*, 245).

The nuns are assisted by Ismael Muñoz, a muralist, and the street kids whom he organizes for car-spotting (abandoned cars can be sold for scrap to buy groceries) and graffiti-writing. One of DeLillo's many surrogate artists (Kavaldo 153), Ismael spray-paints a memorial angel on a tenement wall every time a child dies in the neighborhood; "angels in blue and pink covered roughly half the high slab," with the name and cause of death beneath: "TB, AIDS, beatings, drive-by shootings, blood disorders, measles, general neglect and abandonment at birth, left in dumpster, forgot in car, left in Glad bag Xmas eve" (*A* 76; *U* 235). The nuns inquire after a twelve-year-old homeless child, Esmeralda Lopez, who eludes their every effort to find her. In the second half of the story, the nuns learn that Esmeralda was raped and thrown from a roof, probably where she had been sleeping (this half of the story figures prominently in the climax of *Underworld*). The savage brutality of the crime stuns even this hard-bitten neighborhood.

Soon after Ismael paints the newest angel on the wall, word spreads about a strange apparition in the "bottommost" Bronx, a point of ultimacy, amid "industrial desolation that breaks your heart with its fretful Depression beauty" (*A* 94). There, a billboard advertising Minute Maid Orange juice is unevenly lighted owing to broken or unreplaced bulbs. The ad features "a vast cascade of orange juice pouring diagonally from top right into a goblet"—not a glass, a goblet—"that was handheld at lower left" by a "perfectly formed" female hand (*A* 96). Each night, at eight minute intervals, the headlights of a commuter train sweep across the "dimmest" part of the billboard so that, for a split second in flashing light, the face of the murdered girl, appears above a misty lake, probably the effect of an undersheet from a previous ad showing through. Esmeralda's apparition overwhelms a dozen women who "whooped and sobbed, a spirit, a godsbreath passing through the crowd" (*A* 98). Standing among the Charismatics, and beneath the Minute Maid's "rainbow of bounteous juice," Sister Edgar experiences its "verifying force," its "animating spirit" (*A* 99; *U* 819). With each passing night the frenzied crowds grow larger, like the cult scene in Fellini's *La Dolce Vita* (a possible influence). While Sister Grace deplores such "tabloid superstition" and refuses to participate in a "spectacle of bad taste," Sister Edgar sternly admonishes her with Pope Gregory I's "Don't pray to pictures, pray to saints" (*A* 96; *U* 819). She believes in the possibility of a miracle and defends the billboard picture with its "flowing," "pouring" juice, which is a sign of God's sanctifying grace (*A* 96, 98, 100; *U* 820). She joins in universal prayer: "Pour forth we beseech Thee, O Lord, Thy grace" (*A* 102; *U* 816). The billboard ad is eventually changed and the media circus ends. In *Underworld*, the media reports may be dialed up on a new website: *miraculum.com*.

The story is among the strongest expressions of DeLillo's immanentist frame of mind, Italian American Catholicism combines the concept of a single transcendent deity with the belief in the local presence or immanence of the divine, often through intermediaries, within everyday life. Although God is the *mysterium tremendum*, he reveals himself in the sacraments, ritual, and the Church, the saints and holy people, works of mercy, prayer, festa, food, nature at large, and the "quotidian" (*U* 542). This blend of transcendence and immanence may be contrasted with strict Calvinist Protestantism, which holds that God "participates in the universe he created and controls it but is in no way incorporated in it" (Swanson 2). Immanence with its affinities to Greco-Roman and Old Italic paganism assigns enormous authority to the artistic image. For the southern Italian (DeLillo's family had emigrated from Molise), the divine expresses itself in and through the object; devotional pictures, statues of local saints (some not officially recognized), rosaries, ex-votos, yard and roadside shrines (*edicole*), crèches, frescoes, colorful processions, all attest to the fact that "Italian Catholics are drawn to activities with a strong emphasis upon the concrete and the visible" (Carroll 69); "the invisible is known through the visible" (Praz 414). The physical and moral universe is crisscrossed by innumerable correspondences, linking God as the Absolute to the God of pantheistic participation. One of the lessons of immanentism, one that substantiates DeLillo's Aquinian outlook, is that "everything is connected" (*U* 131, 289, 408, 776, 825, 826). If you cannot fathom the meaning, think hard and wait and think harder because "everything connects in the end" (*U* 465). In such analogical thinking, any one thing in the natural world may potentially illuminate some other thing, and the object participates to varying degrees "in the vast hierarchy of being which reaches to God" (Ross 290).

Given his religious and cultural grounding, DeLillo works in the incarnationist (spirit made flesh) mode, which, to a greater or lesser degree, informs one segment of his fictional world. The smallest details in "The Angel Esmeralda" are integrated within the overall web of correspondences. The train's headlight is a secularized version of divine *lumen*. As in St. Bonaventure's mystical theology, DeLillo treats light as both a physical and metaphysical entity, the "original metaphor for spiritual realities" (Eco 46, 50). In the advertisement, the "goblet" continuously filling with or pouring out bright orange (golden?) juice is the Cup or Grail, which is the plenitude of grace or "food-supplying talisman" originally associated with the female and "reproductive energy" (West 73–74). Painted high up, "angel" Esmeralda ascends the kind of wall from which she had been thrown. She is now the "Minute Maid," the intercessor quick to the rescue of lost souls because she was a runner, a "running fool" (*A* 92), like Erasmus's Christ the Fool. She now wears the finest footwear, "a pair of white Air Jordans," which recall Christ baptized in the waters of the River Jordan (she was painted in pink and "aqua" pants: "water"). The innocent child is linked to the purity of heavenly "air" reinforced by the "white" color, and the name of a champion,

Michael Jordan, who jumped so high it seemed he could fly (like an airline, Air Jordan). Ismael employs an old hand-powered hoist to dangle an assistant, who can paint the epitaph: "PETECTED IN HEAVEN" as she was unprotected on earth, abandoned by her mother, an "addict" (*A* 82). It is, comments Ismael, "without a letter misspell" (*sic*) (*A* 93)—not quite, much to Sister Edgar's dismay— and in the style of "the great gone era of wildstyle graffiti" (*A* 92, 93). Ismael's assistant is "Juano," *Johnny*, John the Baptist, the "voice of one crying in the wilderness" (John 1:23). The newborn "left in Glad bag Xmas eve" (*A* 76: *U* 235), possibly exposed to die, is another image of the Christ Child, whose traces of gladness have been x'd out in a darkening world. A common consumer item, the Glad bag of Santa Claus will not bring good tidings this Christmas. In his poem "The Bag," George Herbert likens Christ's spear wound to a post-bag carried on the side in which one puts letters to God.

Spanish for emerald, the Hispanic Esmeralda is possessed of a jewel of great price, her ever-living soul. In medieval symbology, the color green signifies both nature and hope (cf., the "green cloth at Verona," Dante, *Inf.* XV: 122). "Emerald" appears as an English word only once in the story and in the sections of *Underworld* where the revised story appears. There, it symbolizes the resolution of chance and design within an evolutionary perspective. The "spurt of blank matter chances to make an emerald planet" or a "dying star," life or death, amid the inscrutable "serenity of immense design" (*A* 93; *U* 817): spirit, nature, hope.

When DeLillo revised "The Angel Esmeralda" for *Underworld*, he expanded upon his notion of the sacred by adding a sentence: "Among the hardest cases in the tenement corridors, Sister Grace believed the proof of God's creativity eddied from the fact that you could not surmise the life, even remotely, of his humblest shut-in" (*U* 246). The abject tenement dwellers challenge Grace's imaginative empathy under extreme conditions ("hardest," "humblest"), so that she intimates the plenitude of the sacred. God bestows "grace" upon the nun, true to her name, in her effortful attempts to "surmise," to make the imaginative leap and narrow the distance between herself and the abject. An eddy is a contrary, disruptive motion within a current: the whirling of the spirit against its resistance, the non-spirit, Coleridge's "eddying of her [Nature's] living soul" ("Ode: To Dejection"). The contraries of analogy are near/remote, humble/exalted, shut-in/boundless, death/creation. "Something in me comes alive when I come into this area," said Sister Marty, a South Bronx aid worker interviewed by Robert Orsi, "I feel God's presence more strongly here than anywhere else" (1). The divine analogue for this spiritual action traces to the book of Matthew. The Lord addresses the righteous at the Last Judgment: "I was a stranger and you welcomed me, I was naked and you gave me clothing, I was sick and you took care of me." When the righteous do not recollect seeing the Lord in their works of charity, He replies, "Truly I tell you, just as you did it to one of the least of these, you did it to me" (24:35–40).

Although DeLillo did not employ the incarnationist mode directly in the other stories of *The Angel Esmeralda*, it remained a resource to which he could repair as the occasion demanded. One of the most impressive of the late stories, sharing the use of ekphrasis (literary description of a work of art) with "The Angel Esmeralda," is "Baader-Meinhof." The title refers to Gerhard Richter's cycle of fifteen paintings, *October 18, 1977* (1988), which are based on newspaper and police photographs of members of the Baader-Meinhof gang or Red Army Faction (RAF). This left-wing group had terrorized Germany beginning in the 1970s and had provoked a national crisis of conscience, similar to what happened in Italy during the same period with the Brigate Rosse (Red Brigades). DeLillo could have seen the Baader-Meinhof cycle in 1990, when it was on tour in the United States; or in 1995, when MoMA purchased the cycle for a reported $3 million dollars; or, most likely, in 2000–2001 when the museum held its *Open Ends* millennial exhibition. "Baader-Meinhof" appeared in the *New Yorker* on April 1, 2002, in the midst of a fourth exhibition, MoMA's major retrospective of Richter's works. In the wake of 9/11, his cycle had gathered new resonance and reawakened intense controversy; by the time DeLillo's story appeared, Richter's series was being hailed as one of the masterpieces of Western art since 1945.

On October 18, 1977, in what became known as the German Autumn, convicted terrorists Andreas Baader and Gudrun Ensslin were found dead, and Jan-Carl Raspe lay dying, in their cells at Stammheim Prison near Stuttgart (Raspe would die later the same day). Ulrike Meinhof, a fourth RAF member, had hanged herself in prison in May 1976. While the official explanation for the deaths was suicide, conspiracy theories proliferated, suggesting that they were murdered by the German state police. The RAF never came forth with such a theory, and it is thought more likely that the group had orchestrated a suicide pact (another gang member had tried and failed to kill herself). Richter himself believed in the pact, which was meant to create just the kind of sensation and mythologizing that unfolded. His black-and-white "photopaintings" include two of Baader lying dead in his cell; one of his bookcases; another of his phonograph, in which he had possibly hidden a gun; one of Meinhof as a young woman and three of her dead, in profile, after being taken down, with a rope around her neck; two of Raspe being arrested; Ensslin's body hanging from a rope; three pictures of Ensslin (one smiling); and *Funeral*, a genre piece of nineteenth-century history painting; the burial of Baader, Ensslin, and Raspe surrounded by throngs of people. Instead of grainy or shiny photorealism, however, Richter had characteristically "blurred" or "slurred" his images, making them deliberately hard to see (and fathom): one cannot make out *anything* in the grayish *Arrest* group without knowing the story. But all the paintings appear as if one were trying to view and make sense of "a landscape or a murder through a car window smeared with rain" (Jones 2).

Richter's cycle has prompted widely divergent responses from its debut in Germany in 1988, when it left many in a state of shock or disgust. At the time, the RAF was still active, and it seemed impossible to treat the paintings outside of their political and ideological context. Richter was accused of neutrality, exploitation, aestheticism, sympathy, and even forgiveness for Marxist terrorists with a record of assassination and murder. Sophie Schwartz attacked the "puzzling timidity" and insincerity of his approach: "the quality most evident in Richter's treatment of these still disturbing images is a dark and totally staged pathos" (qtd. in Storr 31). With the passage of time, the cycle continued to draw fire. In 1995, Hilton Kramer subjected the MoMA board of directors to withering irony, mocking the purchase of the cycle as "liberal guilt among the affluent": "those selected for kidnapping and assassination—people prominent in business, finance, and public life—were, in fact, a lot like the kind of people who serve on the board of the Museum of Modern Art" (5). Reviewing the Richter retrospective in 2002 for the *New Republic*, Jed Perl lambasted a "bullshit artist masquerading as a painter": "Saint Gerhard of the Sorrows of Painting," a "phony Kafka," a "counterfeit crisis," a "deprivation chic" (1), and so forth.

In defense of the cycle, MoMA curator Robert Storr argued that Richter had never intended to choose sides in the ideological debate or forge a "third way": "by virtue of its very lack of polemical intent, the Baader-Meinhof cycle *re*politicizes the controversy surrounding the RAF, by redefining the parameters of a deadlocked debate and shifting it away from fixed polarities" (Storr 130), i.e., the RAF vs. the German state. This approach situates the moral content of the cycle in an area of ambiguity: "by picturing doubt he had made the jagged cracks and spiderweb fissures in supposedly monolithic blocks of public opinion" (130). Taking a stance closest to Richter's is James Jones: "these paintings treat their subjects as human beings, to be mourned and, if possible, understood;" "Richter's paintings are uncannily prophetic because they are about the limits of empathy and understanding, and the terrible mystery of those who side with death" (2). (One recalls that the "limits of empathy" border on the sacred in "The Angel Esmeralda.") Karin Crawford reaches for an empathic understanding of wasted youth; the "presumed truth resid[es] in the validity of one's emotional response, the validity and understanding of a human(ist) response to the events Richter captures in his cycle" (211–212). Wendy Lesser sets aside the various contexts and positions and defends leaving these enigmatic paintings to the viewer:

> They do not ask us to condemn or to forgive. They do not defend any
> particular political perspective . . . . They do not even represent the

artist's viewpoint, because viewpoint itself is one of the things they are questioning. They ask us to stand in front of them and contemplate what we think, what we feel, even as they quietly cut the ground out from under us" (Lesser 11).

Lesser's title, "Richter's Masterpiece," gives the judgment that resulted from her contemplation.

In "Baader-Mainhof," DeLillo refers to ten of the fifteen paintings, passing from one group to another, as his two characters comment upon them. Terror, conspiracy, and assassination had been explored in one of DeLillo's most widely read and esteemed novels, *Libra*, on Lee Harvey Oswald. What new was there to say?

The first of the story's three scenes takes place in the MoMA gallery in which *October 18, 1977* is being shown (DeLillo's *Point Omega* [2010] opens in MoMA's sixth-floor gallery). For the third straight day, a divorced and unemployed young woman has returned to the exhibition. "Alone for a time," she is seated in the middle of the room facing the paintings. Wendy Lesser recalls the empty rooms where she saw the cycle in Berlin. Was the subject matter or its treatment so disturbing as to scare away the public? I remember the same emptiness at the Rothko Chapel in Houston, where the large canvasses of black and of black hued with deep purple initially had a profoundly chilling effect, even as they brought one forward to the edge of mysticism. The emptiness and loneliness became a part of the experience for me. Richter's disturbing photopaintings do not scare DeLillo's protagonist; rather, they attract her to the point of obsession, possibly even identification with the two subjects who are of the same gender and age. She feels as if she were "keeping watch over the body of a relative or a friend" in a "mortuary chapel" (*A* 106), in sum, as if she were in mourning.

Using free indirect discourse, slipping back and forth between third-person and first-person narration, DeLillo reads the woman's thoughts as she compares the three nearly similar paintings of Ulrike Meinhof lying dead with the rope around her neck: "nuances of obscurity and pall, a detail clearer here and there, the slurred mouth in one painting appearing nearly natural elsewhere" (*A* 106).

Intrigued and baffled, she cannot find a satisfactory narrative for her observations, and so, she concludes: "unsystematic." She is on the right track: Richter did not specify that the paintings be shown in any particular order: "invariable" is the word that guides their installation. The tendency to treat them chronologically, from Ulrike as a lively young person to *Funeral*, can only be arbitrary. Richter is saying: here are the brute facts, make your own sense of the story (Buchloh 100).

In the midst of her contemplative viewing, a man interrupts her. He has been hovering in the background from the suspenseful first sentence (a perfect example of what Aristotle means by a "beginning"): "She knew there was someone else in the room . . . a faint displacement of air" (*A* 105). An unemployed financial analyst, he does not come to museums to see art, but to pick up women. His opening line, "Why do you think he did it this way?" is typical of him, an open-ended question seeking a definite answer. The women's responses are just as typically evasive: "I don't know" (five times in two pages), followed by suggestive possibilities. Quick to judge, he continues, "They committed suicide. Or the state killed them." It is either one thing or the other: syntactically, the period after the word "suicide" allows for a pause between two paratactic sentences. She replies, "I don't know." She assumes that they were murdered (*A* 108): after all, the translated titles of two paintings, *Man Shot Down 1* implies that someone shot Baader; however, Richter's German title is *Erschossener* ("*Man, Shot Dead*") (Buchloh 98), a term that does not eliminate suicide as a possibility. When the analyst insists it must have been a suicide pact, she takes her cue from the paintings and lifts the issue to another plane: "Maybe that's even worse in a way. It's so much sadder. There's so much sadness in these pictures" (*A* 106). Note her tentativeness in "Maybe," "even," "in a way"; even the word "worse" is a comparative on a sliding scale. DeLillo's ear was never better than in these late stories. Linda Kauffman writes that DeLillo must have researched Richter's exhibition catalogue because he does favor Richter's interpretation of the case, leaning to the suicide pact, but remaining open, moving beyond into the essential "horror." "Their [the dead gang members'] presence is the horror and the hard-to-bear refusal to answer, to explain, to give an opinion" (Richter qtd. in Kaufmann 4). This "refusal . . . to give an opinion" well describes the woman's response.

To give one more example, the man says that Gudrun is "smiling" in one painting, the "clearest image in the room" (*A* 107): he wants clarity and definitiveness—from a Richter painting, no less, where even clarity is ironized! "I don't know if that's a smile," she responds, then probes the three paintings and decides that Richter has painted three nuanced possibilities from *maybe* in one direction to *probably* not in the other: "maybe smiling, smiling and probably not smiling" (*A* 107). Though she does not want intentionally to exasperate the man, she has that effect, and that effect may ultimately be therapeutic. Perhaps one needs "special training" to look at such difficult art, he observes, concluding that she must be a "grad student." "I can't tell the persons apart," he remarks, presumably because of all the blurring. "Yes, you can," she says with Jamesean economy, "Just look. You have to look" (*A* 107).

DeLillo probably knew that, in a 1989 interview, Richter had affirmed his belief that the RAF was "primarily a women's movement." Women like Meinhof and Ensslin "made a much bigger impression on me than the men" (Richter 130). He registers his gendered response in various ways, chief of which is that eight of the ten paintings with human subjects in the cycle are of women. Crawford adopts this line of interpretation; Meinhof and Gudrun are "victims" of their ideology (208). Charity Scribner concurs, noting that Volker Schlöndorf and Heinrich Böll "invoke *Antigone*" (51) in their assessment of the RAF women. At the same time, as Scribner comments, Richter's ideas of RAF women are "signals of a radical feminism that could have been, but never was," having been "derailed by the armed struggle" (51).

In DeLillo's "Baader-Meinhof," one sees the world through the woman's eye, outward and inward. She concentrates on the paintings of Ulrike and Gudrun. She is aware of the fact that she thinks of Meinhof by her first name Ulrike, which is a sign of familiarity, while she thinks of Andreas Baader by both names, which implies formality and distance. In the snack bar, she smiles at the man even while the after-image of Ulrike's rope burn is still in her mind. She even imitates some of Gudrun's poses. Crawford argues that "DeLillo's gendered response to Richter's paintings enacts the ambiguity at the core of Richter's challenge to the viewer to move beyond ideology" (226). The woman's empathy with Ulrike and Gudrun, and ultimately her feeling of helplessness, make her vulnerable to an aggressive male: "the story unfolds to show how the opposing responses of the man and the woman establish a power differential between them that is potentially dangerous for the woman" (Crawford 226). At the same time, the woman's empathy expands her range of feeling and understanding, is itself a power. Three days of return visits have paid off in her sensitive readings of these enigmatic works of art. Her knowledge will return as power.

On the first day, she had not noticed the cross in *Funeral*. On the second day, she saw it, "striking once she'd found it," "a tree perhaps, in the rough shape of a cross" (*A* 108). In the heavily slurred background, it could easily be mistaken for a tree. But it *is* a tree, "a bare tree, a dead tree" (*A* 108–109) which in late October would be barren of leaves, "a spindly trunk with a single branch remaining, or two branches forming a transverse piece near the top of the trunk" (*A* 109). It is highly unlikely that there would be any reason for a real cross amid the clump of trees. Was the cross in the original photograph, she asks? No, it was not a cross; but there was a tree with cross branches that Richter painted or "smeared" ever so slightly to look more like a cross. In an example of spiritual immanence, she reads the tree as a transformed symbol of the Crucifixion. Historically, trees were the original gibbets, as in Sir Walter Raleigh's "gallows tree" ("To His Son"). The cross symbolism is appropriate in a painting of three convicted terrorists (in fact, I see three crosses in the clump of trees). This "dead" tree brings in the association of the Crucifixion and martyrdom, a German Golgotha. Richter was accused of heroizing and making martyrs of the gang members (Kramer 5). It is perhaps sufficient to say he humanized them, which is DeLillo's own position.

Richter places the tree/cross in a position of strength, "at the top of the painting, just left of center" (*A* 108). Writing of Germanic qualities in painting from Dürer to Arnold Böcklin, Heinrich Wölfflin comments that, as opposed to the centeredness typical of classical art, German art is more faithful to the rules of nature than the rules of formal (Italian) art; it rejects "the tectonic and regular structure as inadequate" (109). Thus, the cross in Grünewald's *Isenheim Altarpiece* is off-center. It is also to the left, that is, on Christ's right hand, the sign of salvation. The vast milling crowd in Richter's *Funeral* is invested with the "painterly indistinctness" (*A* 21) and "free rhythmicality" (*A* 87) of German art; "there is free form which cannot be apprehended, it is true, in terms of laws, but which nevertheless is not the same as formlessness" (*A* 87). The compelling movement of the scene has the character of a spontaneous, "sudden event" (*A* 107)—unclassical at the least, if not anticlassical. Richter's smearing technique can be said to bring the tendency of "painterly indistinctness" in German art to its logical conclusion.

In the meantime the man confesses that "I don't feel anything" from looking at the paintings and asks her what she feels (*A* 109). For the fifth time, she says "I don't know. It's complicated," and "I think I feel helpless. These paintings make me feel how helpless a person can be" (*A* 109). The statement mystifies him, so she adds: "I am here because I love the paintings." She admits at first she was "confused" by them "and still am a little. But I know I love the paintings now." She loves them also because she has come to unite feeling and understanding. She cannot articulate this response, hard won through her thinking and imaginative absorption. Here she reaches the climax of her interpretation: making the cross explicit in *Funeral* is Richter's imparting "an element of forgiveness," his way of saying that the terrorists are not "beyond forgiveness" (*A* 109). Just as Sister Edgar grows nearer to God in approaching the helpless poor, so too the woman in "Baader-Meinhoff" moves through the experience of the paintings towards forgiveness. The cross symbolizes both death (gibbet, the barren October scene) and new life (forgiveness). She does not want to discuss the cross with him, lest his unimaginative empiricism raise doubts about her own still fragile interpretation of the cross. In any case, he must find his own interpretation.

The scene shifts to a snack bar. After-images of the paintings haunt her, while he ponders how to break a much-needed job interview so that he can go back with her to her apartment. The man's story now develops, revealing vulnerability of his own: Prufrock 2000, down to iambic pentameter: "I shave. I smile. My life is living hell" (*A* 110). He says this of course off-handedly; perhaps his smile is ambiguous, too. Still, his frankness encourages her own, and it is only when the subject returns to the paintings that he is lost and virtually repeats himself: "No color. No meaning" (*A* 110). She now has much to say conclusively about the paintings: "It [the terrorism] was wrong but it wasn't blind or empty"; it "had meaning." The Baader-Meinhof gang members did not sit on the fence. The artist sought to convey the totality of their experience and then ask why it had to end with "Everybody dead" (*A* 110). While she pursues the deeper motives, he jokes defensively, "You teach art to handicapped children." Indeed, he is emotionally handicapped. In response to his question, her face wears a "grudging smile" (*A* 110), while Gudrun is "probably not smiling" (*A* 107).

A few questions about rents, neighborhoods, and stolen bikes lead in to the final scene in her tiny apartment with no view: she has lost her perspective. He asks her to "be friends," his manner of saying to "make love." Why else would she allow him into her room, in the middle of the afternoon, a perfect stranger whose name she does not even know? Admitting her "mistake," she says abruptly, "I want you to leave." He remarks that she is like "someone convalescing" (*A* 114) and that she should follow her original instinct in inviting him to her apartment. Since he will not leave at once, she retreats to the bathroom: like Gudrun, "she walked along the wall, head down, a person marching blindly" (*A* 116). She hears him masturbating on her bed, then, in shame, speaking through the bathroom door, "barely audible, close to a moan": "Forgive me" (*A* 117). He has transgressed; can she forgive him? After he leaves, shocked back into reality, she curses him; "Bastard." It will be difficult to forgive him, as she appears to have forgiven the dead terrorists.

The brief coda acts like a frame. The next morning she returns to the museum. "He was alone in the gallery, seated on the bench in the middle of the room" (*A* 118), his back to the entrance. The words are almost exactly those by which she was introduced. Just as she felt she was in a mortuary, he is studying *Funeral*, "the largest by far, and maybe most breathtaking [of the cycle], the one with the coffins and cross" (*A* 118). DeLillo has postponed this encomium until the end. The painting exemplifies the negative sublime, with its size, power, obscurity, terror,—and, under aesthetic conditions, "'frenzied' death" (Sertoli 124), literally "breathtaking." Instead of empowering the ego, the jagged, "unpleasant" negative sublime exhausts it, to the loss of self. The man undergoes such feelings as he proceeds from his aggressiveness and lack of insight: he has now become absorbed in the paintings and is perhaps capable of understanding their message. Now she is standing behind him—will she forgive him?

Works Cited

Buchloh, Benjamin H. D. "A Note on Gerhard Richter's *October 18, 1977*." *October* 48 (Spring 1989): 88–109.

Carroll, Michael P. *Veiled Threats: The Logic of Popular Catholicism in Italy*. Baltimore: Johns Hopkins UP, 1996.

Crawford, Karin L. "Gender and Terror in Gerhard Richter's *October 18, 1977* and Don DeLillo's 'Baader-Meinhof.'" *New German Critique* 107 (Summer 2009): 207–230.

DeLillo, Don. *The Angel Esmeralda: Nine Stories*. New York: Scribner. 2011. Cited as *A* in text.

_____. *Underworld*. New York: Scribner, 1997. Cited as *U* in text.

Durang, Christopher. *Twenty-Seven Short Plays*. Hanover, NH: Smith & Kraus, 1995.

Eco, Umberto. *Art and Beauty in the Middle Ages*. Trans. Hugh Bredin. New Haven, CT: Yale UP, 2002.

Gardner, Curt & Phil Nel. "A DeLillo Bibliography." *Don DeLillo's America*. Curt Gardner, 5 Oct. 2015. Web. 10 Oct. 2015. <http://www.perival.com/delillo/ddbiblio.html>.

Jones, Jonathan. "What's the Biggest Show in New York? Paintings of Terrorists." *The Guardian*. Guardian News and Media Limited, 25 Apr. 2002. Web. 10 Oct. 2015. <http://www.theguardian.com/culture/2002/apr/25/artsfeatures>.

Kauffman, Linda S. "The Wake of Terror: Don DeLillo's 'In the Ruins of the Future,' 'Baader-Meinhof,' and *Falling Man*." *Modern Film Studies* 54.2 (Autumn 2008): 353–377.

Lesser, Wendy. "Richter's Masterpiece." *Three Penny Review* (Fall 2012). Web. 10 Oct. 2015. <https://www.threepennyreview.com/samples/lesser_f12.html>.

Menand, Louis. "Market Report" [Review of *Mao II* by Don DeLillo]. *Critical Essays on Don DeLillo*. Eds. Hugh Ruppersburg & Tim Engles. New York: G.K. Hall, 2000.

Orsi, Robert A., ed. *Gods of the City: Religion and the American Urban Landscape*. Bloomington: Indiana UP, 1999.

Perl, Jed. "Saint Gerhard and the Sorrows of Painting." *New Republic* (1 April 2002).

Praz, Mario. *The Hero in Eclipse in Victorian Fiction*. Oxford: Oxford UP, 1969.

Richter, Gerhard. "Gerhard Richter: *18. Oktober 1977*." Interview with Jan Thorn-Prikker. *Parkett* 19 (1989): 124–65.

Ross, Malcolm MacKenzie. "Ruskin, Hooker, and 'the Christian Theoria.'" *Essays in English Literature from the Renaissance to the Victorian Age Presented to A.S.P. Woodhouse*. Ed. Millar MacLure & F.W. Watt. Toronto: Toronto UP, 1964. 283–303.

Russo, John Paul. "DeLillo: Italian American Catholic Writer." *Altreitalie* 25 (2002): 4–29.

Scribner, Charity. *After the Red Army Faction: Gender, Culture, and Militancy*. New York: Columbia, 2015.

Sertoli, Giuseppe. *The Johns Hopkins Guide to Literary Theory & Criticism*. Ed. Michael Groden & Martin Kreiswirth. Baltimore, MD: Johns Hopkins UP, 1994.

Swanson, Guy E. *Religion and Regime: A Sociological Account of the Reformation*. Ann Arbor: U of Michigan P, 1967.

Storr, Robert. *Gerhard Richter: 'October 18, 1977.'* New York: Museum of Modern Art, 2000.

Wölfflin, Heinrich. *The Sense of Form in Art: A Comparative Psychological Study.* 1931. Trans. Alice Muehsam & Norma A. Shatan. New York: Chelsea, 1958.

Somewhat Queer Triangles: Yiyun Li's "The Princess of Nebraska" and "Gold Boy, Emerald Girl"

King-Kok Cheung

Yiyun Li's "The Princess of Nebraska" and "Gold Boy, Emerald Girl" reveal the pressure on Chinese gays and lesbians to lead compromised lives so as to create the semblance of heterosexual families and to avoid the homophobic gaze of their larger societies. The suspense in reading these two stories lies in ferreting out the secrets and pains the characters try to hide from one another and even from themselves. What haunts all the principal characters is their palpable solitude. Unlike the fiction by early Chinese immigrants and Asian immigrants generally, this story no longer presents the United States primarily as a land of economic opportunity. In "The Princess of Nebraska," the United States provides a refuge from homophobic persecution, but the gay refugee must marry a lesbian in order to emigrate. In "Gold Boy, Emerald Girl," a gay immigrant actually chooses to return to China after being disenchanted by a succession of noncommittal relationships in North America (including New York, Montreal, Vancouver, and San Francisco). The choices made by the characters also reflect their negotiation between interdependence, the predominant ethos in China, and independence, the spirit of the New World. Whether in the US or in China, a heterosexual union is assumed to be the only solution to an unconventional love triangle, in which a person is loved by both a man and a woman.[1]

"The Princess of Nebraska"

"The Princess of Nebraska" is told from the alternate perspectives of Sasha, a twenty-one-year-old exchange student planning to have an abortion, and Boshen, a thirty-eight-year-old physician who has been repeatedly harassed for his sexual orientation and gay activism in China. In Beijing, both Boshen and Sasha have fallen in love with Yang, an eighteen-year-old *Nan Dan* (a male actor who plays female roles in Peking opera) expelled from the Peking Opera School after he is seen with his lover. Yang seems unable to love anyone but himself after being jilted by his first lover, but he agrees to live with Boshen when the latter promises to help him get back on stage. But then Boshen himself is expelled from Beijing for his AIDS activism. During his absence, Sasha is impregnated by Yang during a one-night stand. Boshen soon smuggles himself to the US through a sham marriage to a newly naturalized lesbian. Sasha, too, leaves for graduate school in Omaha, Nebraska. Unable to persuade Yang to leave China with her, Sasha (now four months pregnant) intends to have an abortion. The story opens with a meeting between Boshen and Sasha in Chicago, where she plans to have the operation. Boshen, however, tries to talk her into keeping Yang's child. They stay for a Christmas parade that evening, during which Sasha seems to experience a change of heart.

The story juxtaposes life in China and life in the US. As a gay doctor, Boshen has had a checkered career in China. At thirty-eight, "he felt he had achieved less than he had failed" (Li, "Princess" 71). He is asked to leave the hospital in his hometown after he has established the first counseling hotline for homosexuals. In Beijing, he falls madly in love with Yang, and they live together. Working as a gay activist, Boshen is visited by the secret police and put under surveillance, for "in the post-Tiananmen era, talk of any kind of human rights was dangerous" (71). Then he is banished from Beijing and put under house arrest in his hometown for corresponding with a Western reporter concerning a potential AIDS epidemic; to earn his freedom, he must publish a written confession of his "wrongdoing" (69). The move to the US, an opportunity that Boshen has landed under the pretense of a false marriage, also poses challenges. He goes from being a physician to a helper to a Sichuan chef in a Chinese restaurant. By the end of the story, he and Sasha are entertaining another spurious marriage, between Yang and Sasha, so that her child can have a legitimate father.

Yang is similarly branded on account of his sexual orientation. Trained as a female impersonator in Peking opera, he had lived in the opera school until he turned seventeen, when he was expelled after being seen with his lover. Boshen meets Yang for the first time when the actor, after being deserted by his first lover, becomes a prostitute, a "*money boy* interested only in selling" (Li, "Princess" 72). After Boshen takes him in, Yang fits into "the quiet life like the most virtuous woman he had played on stage," animating Boshen's mundane life: "Yang's voice splitting the waterfall, the bath curtain, the door, and the rest of the dull world like a silver knife. At those moments Boshen was overwhelmed by gratitude— he was not the only one to have been touched by the boy's beauty, but he was the one to guard and nurture it" (73–74). Hence Boshen's promise to help Yang perform again. But the singer is skeptical. "*An empty promise of a man keeps a woman's heart full*," Yang recites (73). The prevalence of conventional gender norms is evident in these passages. Even a gay couple continues to gauge one another according to heterosexual norms.

Even more conventional is Sasha, a straight woman who considers homosexuality to be a deviation. Sasha undergoes several about-face changes in the course of the story. At first, she finds Yang vain and disparages him and his admirers, including Boshen. Yet she is quite vain herself. She believes she is the first person in Yang's life who is immune to his charm and thinks "he must be following her around because of that. It pleased her" (Li, "Princess" 78). All set to leave for American graduate school in a month, she does not expect to fall in love: "It was pointless to start a relationship now. Besides, how smart was it to date a boy who loved no one but himself?" (78). But Sasha underestimates Yang's allure and soon falls in love despite her intention to the contrary. She tries to persuade Yang to go with her to the US after they watch the movie *Pretty Woman* (starring Julia Roberts): "Everything could happen there. A prostitute becomes a princess; a crow turns into a swan overnight" (81). They spend a night in a small hotel and Sasha tries to talk Yang into leaving China with her again the next morning:

> "Come to America with me," she said. "We'll be the prince and the princess of Nebraska."
> "I was not trained to play a prince," Yang said.

"The script is changed," Sasha said. "From today on." (Li, "Princess" 85)

This passage at once reveals the performativity of gender and Sasha's refusal to acknowledge its fluidity.[2] Notwithstanding her strong personality, Sasha is mired in the conventional mores of mainstream Chinese society, which considers homosexuality to be an aberration that can be "corrected," a script that can be easily altered. She blames Peking opera for "corrupting" Yang, attributing his sexual orientation to his training as a female impersonator. She asks Boshen, who, in her mind, is also to blame:

> Why was there *Nan Dan* in the Peking opera in the first place? *Men loved him because he was playing a woman; women loved him because he was a man playing....* Why else do you want so much to put him back on the stage? .... He didn't have to be a man playing a woman—I thought I would make him understand. But what did I end up with? (Li, "Princess" 89–90, emphasis original)

Watching the Christmas parade on Michigan Avenue, Sasha marvels at the American youth: "They looked so young and carefree, these Americans.... They were born to be themselves, naïve and contented with their naivety" (Li, "Princess" 78). Implicitly, these American youngsters are contrasted with the three Chinese characters, who must derail their intrinsic selves to abide by societal norms. Feeling burdened by her pregnancy, Sasha intends to have an abortion to free herself from the past and from maternity, looking forward to the moment when she is "ready to move on" (69). She believes that "moving on" is an American concept that suits her well, a phrase that calls forth the image of "stapling her Chinese life, one staple after another around the pages until they became one solid block that nobody would be able to open and read. She would have a fresh page then, for her American life" (69). America is thus associated with turning a new page, a fresh beginning; China, with the past and confinement. Sasha wishes to forget the past and start afresh.

However, Sasha, who has felt no affection for the baby growing inside her thus far, experiences its first stirrings during the parade: "A tap, and then another one, gentle and tentative, the first greeting that Sasha had wished she would never have to answer, but it seemed impossible, once it happened, not to hope for more" (Li, "Princess" 90). The ending suggests that she is about to change her mind:

> Sasha held her breath and waited for more of the baby's messages. America was a good country, she thought, a right place to be born into, even though the baby had come at a wrong time. Everything was possible in America, she thought, and imagined a baby possessing the beauty of her father but happier, and luckier. Sasha smiled, but then when the baby moved again, she burst into tears. Being a mother must be the saddest yet the most hopeful thing in the world, falling into a love that, once started, would never end. (Li, "Princess" 91)

Gish Jen, building on the work of cultural psychologists, has expounded two different models of self-construal in a collection of essays entitled *Tiger Writing*: "The first—the 'independent,' individualistic self—stresses uniqueness, defines itself via inherent attributes such as its traits, abilities, values, and preferences, and tends to see things in isolation. The second—the 'interdependent,' collectivist self—stresses commonality, defines itself via its place, roles, loyalties, and duties, and tends to see things in context" (Jen 7). Jen associates the first with American culture and the second with Chinese culture, though she is quick to add that between these two lies "a continuum along which most people are located" (7). Sasha's inclination to keep the baby, though prompted by her sense that the US is a "good country," shows her choice for "interdependence" over "independence."

Even though Sasha is buoyed by the prospect of autonomy, she is tugged, palpably, by kinship. The prospect of "falling into a love that…would never end" is the opposite of what she regards as the American predilection of "moving on." To be sure, being in the US is what has brought about her change of heart. She knows that her child would not be under the kind of social surveillance to which Boshen and Yang have been subjected in the home country. But the freedom in the US, at least at the time of the story, is still limited. If Sasha wants the child to have a legitimate father, she must either marry Yang, the gay biological father, or allow Boshen, another gay man, to be the adoptive father. Or the three can stay together. But the "three-member family" Boshen has in mind would constitute yet another one of the kind of compromises that he has made previously on account of heteronormative constraint: "what right did he have to talk about options, when the decisions he had made for his life were all compromises? He was in love with a boy twenty years younger, and he thought he could make a difference in the boy's life. In the end, he was the one to marry a woman and leave" (Li, "Princess" 71). Furthermore, Sasha would have to settle for a nominal marriage, not unlike the one depicted at the end of the next story.

"Gold Boy, Emerald Girl"
Like "The Princess of Nebraska," "Gold Boy, Emerald Girl" opens with a meeting between the two main characters, Hanfeng, a forty-four-year-old man, and Siyu, a thirty-eight-year-old woman. The story is told from their alternate points of view. The two are meeting at the behest of Professor Dai, Hanfeng's mother who, at seventy-one, plays matchmaker for her son by encouraging him to marry Siyu, her former student and a frequent companion since. At first, Hanfeng seems the only homosexual character in the story. But it gradually dawns on the reader that Professor Dai, Hanfeng's mother, and Siyu, her former student (and his prospective wife), are far from straight as well.

In this story, the US is no longer the only country of opportunity and not even the preferred abode for Hanfeng. When he tells his colleagues in San Francisco about his plan to move back to China for good, "they had joked about moving with him and becoming the forty-niners of the new gold rush" (Li, "Gold" 207). The joke suggests that immigration across the Pacific has become two-way, that economic opportunity may be even greater in China. But that is not the reason for Hanfeng's return: "His mother was getting old, he explained to his friends; the thought that he, too, was no longer a young man in need of adventures he kept to himself" (207). He also leaves unsaid the fact that all his stateside relationships have failed to last. His return may also be seen as the prioritizing of interdependence—the obligation to take care of an elderly mother—over independence.

Although Hanfeng can come out of the closet in North America, he is unable to form a long-term relationship. Like Yang in the previous story, he was reluctant initially to commit himself after his first love abandoned him (twenty-three at the time) for a woman, just before his departure for the US:

> America, at first glance, seemed a happy enough place, and when his friend called with the news of his engagement, Hanfeng sought out companions. All he wanted was to have some fun, he replied when more was asked of him...But eventually the reply came back to taunt him: I thought we would have some fun and that's all, his last love had said, a Chinese boy, a new immigrant ... whom Hanfeng had helped support through college. (Li, "Gold" 212–213)

The passage suggests that it is not easy for Hanfeng to sustain a gay relationship in the US, not only because of his psychological resistance earlier, but also because of the American penchant for just "having fun." Li has elsewhere associated such a mentality with the US, where everyone she met seemed to expect her to have fun: "What a strange country, I thought, where fun...seemed mandatory" (Li, "Clean"). In Hangfeng's case, the phrase is linked ironically with lovesickness. Hanfeng has been jilted at least twice. Just as he left for America after the first heartbreak, when having fun was his self-defense against further injury, he returns to China after the last, when his lover has had enough fun.

This theme of love and betrayal recurs across two generations. Hanfeng's father died in an accident when Hanfeng was only two and Professor Dai never remarries. The couple was so handsome that, at their wedding, they were described as gold boy and emerald girl "for their matching good looks" (Li, "Gold" 216). The phrase derives from a famous Chinese reference to the pair of male and female icons accompanying the statue of Guanyin in many temples. Thus it seems rather strange to compliment the groom and bride that way because these icons are chaste.[3] The marriage turns out to be an unhappy one, evidenced in the advice Professor Dai offers Siyu:

> [Siyu] shouldn't get married if it was not what she wanted.... You could feel trapped by the wrong man.... You would have to wish for his death every day of your marriage...but once the wish was granted by a miracle, you would never be free of your own cruelty. Siyu listened, knowing that the older woman was talking about herself. (Li, "Gold" 220)

Although Hanfeng's father had died in "an accident that no one could be blamed for," Siyu senses the others' "disapproval of Professor Dai, as if she were partially responsible for the unfair fate that befell the man"; the dead husband, on the other hand, "was always praised as the gentlest person" (Li, "Gold" 216). Given the blameless character of Hanfeng's father, at least in public eye, one may surmise that the marriage was unhappy because it was sexually unfulfilling, at least for Professor Dai, whose sexual orientation is open to question.

This hunch about Professor Dai is reinforced when Hanfeng relates a visit from a woman from a southern province when he was ten:

> An unannounced visit, he could tell, when his mother had returned home in the evening and found him shelling peas alongside the guest.... The woman, who had told Hanfeng that she was a very old friend of his mother's and was planning to stay with them for a week, left the next morning.... Still, the image of the woman's face, pale at the sight of his mother, and her hands, which let the peas fall into the pile of shells, stayed with Hanfeng. He could not pinpoint when he understood that there had been betrayals between the two friends. (Li, "Gold" 218–219)

Since Hanfeng has informed the reader earlier that he can always tell what is on his mother's mind, he is probably right in detecting reciprocal betrayals. In "The Princess of Nebraska," Boshen's marriage to a naturalized lesbian friend is judged to be "an unforgivable betrayal, in Sasha's and Yang's eyes alike" (80). A similar betrayal of homoerotic love by heterosexual union(s) might have occurred in Professor Dai's past.

Professor Dai is not the only one with a secret, however. Siyu, for whom many women have tried in vain to be her matchmaker, also harbors a clandestine desire. When her devoted father remarries, she decides to leave his new family alone: "He did not need her to complicate his life," she tells him, agreeing only to have a "monthly lunch" with him as their only way of sustaining their filiation. She knows that to others she must have come across as "ungrateful and coldhearted," but "how could she stay in his sight when she was going through her life with a reckless speed known only to herself, all because of a love she could not explain and did not have the right to claim in the first place?" She adds that were people to know her secret, they would interpret it as her yearning for a mother, "but Siyu did not believe that things would have turned out any differently had she had a mother" (Li, "Gold" 217–218). Although Siyu never names the object of her secret love, Professor Dai is undoubtedly the older woman in question. While a female student's infatuation with an older male professor is all too common, hardly requiring explanation, a similar crush on a professor of the same sex beggars description, understanding, and acceptance in a heteronormative society. At best, it would be seen as a search for a surrogate mother, an assumption Siyu pointedly refutes.

The attraction Siyu feels for Professor Dai seems at once erotic and platonic, as obsessive as any heterosexual passion, evidenced by her getting up at six every morning as a student to ensure seeing the professor as she parked her bike (Li, "Gold" 206) and by her turning down all invitations during holidays on the odd chance that her mentor should call. Because she could not predict when the older woman would be so inclined, for two decades, Siyu tried to "keep herself uncommitted, which meant that most of the holidays she spent alone" (204). Such behavior of putting herself "on hold" and reserving all her time for one person is again not untypical of straight women in love, but in this instance the beloved is of the same sex.

While a romance between an elderly man and a much younger woman is commonplace, and while a relationship between an older and a much younger man (as between Boshen and Yang) is not noteworthy, attraction between an older woman and a much younger one is, as Siyu implies, unspeakable and, therefore, unspoken. Even Professor Dai might have been unaware of Siyu's crush on her at first. Since Siyu has seen photos of handsome Hanfeng in Professor Dai's apartment, the older woman might have assumed early on that the student wants to befriend her so as to be close to her son. When Professor Dai finally tries to arrange a marriage between Siyu and Hanfeng, Siyu herself wonders if the matchmaking has come "as a result of a beguiling impression she had left of her interest in a good-looking bachelor" (Li, "Gold" 211). The word "beguiling" is sufficient, however, to indicate the absence in her of any romantic interest in the son. The reader is soon told explicitly that "it was not the thought of the boy that had made her wait on the bench outside the biology building in the mornings during college; nor was he the reason she continued to befriend Professor Dai in a manner allowed by the older woman" (217–218). Then what's the reason?

The ending of this story, like that of "The Princess of Nebraska," is infused with tempered poignancy:

[Siyu] had remained unmarried for Professor Dai… and she would, with her blessing, become a married woman. She would not wish for her husband's death, as his mother had, because the marriage, arranged as it was, would still be a love marriage. Siyu had wished to be a companion for Professor Dai in her old age, and her wish would now be granted, an unexpected gift from a stingy life. (Li, "Gold" 221)

Although neither Siyu nor Hanfeng loves the other in an amatory way, they both care deeply for Professor Dai, who has allowed all three of them to cohabit without raising societal eye brows, an arrangement Siyu considers to be a "gift from a stingy life." Professor Dai indeed has been sparing in her affection, but as in most of Li's fiction, those who seem most niggardly with their emotions, Yang and Hanfeng included, have usually been badly hurt by a previous lover. Perhaps Professor Dai is no exception, as the encounter with the woman from the Southern province intimates. Like Hanfeng, and as he has suspected, the mother might have been betrayed in the past. Both of them now find a loyal companion in Siyu, but the three will likely continue to maintain a discrete distance from one another: "They were lonely and sad people, all three of them and they would not make one another less sad, but they could, with great care, make a world that would accommodate their loneliness" (Li, "Gold" 221). Like Professor Dai and her husband, Hanfeng and Siyu will be another gold boy and emerald girl, who must lead sexually unfulfilling lives, as hard and cold as gold and emerald, but they will remain together.

The two stories by Li underscore the constraints of gender norms and the social pressure not only on gays and lesbians, but also on women and men who do not conform to patriarchal codes of masculinity and femininity. Li refers so often to the hostile gaze of society that it seems a ubiquitous regulative force, which may further explain the aloofness of just about all the principal characters (perhaps with the exception of Boshen), who lead rather "stingy" lives. Yang is kicked out of the Peking opera school on being seen with his gay lover. Boshen is sacked by his hospital and later expelled from Beijing and put under house arrest in his hometown for being a gay activist.

Both lesbians and gays, as well as single and professionally driven women, are constantly subject to unrelenting social scrutiny. Professor Dai, who used to spend most of her time studying animals, was seen as deviant; a similar obsession in a male zoology professor would most likely be commended as professional dedication. After retirement she is ridiculed for her dedication to learning the piano, instead of doing what other women her age do—"taking morning walks with a companion, gossiping and bargaining at the marketplace, watching soap operas in the afternoon" (Li, "Gold" 208). On seeing his aged mother perform in front of a mocking audience, Hanfeng reflects:

His mother had always been a headstrong woman…. Still, seeing her through *other people's eyes*, Hanfeng realized that all that made her who she was—the decades of solitude in her widowhood, her coldness to the *prying eyes of people* who tried to mask their nosiness with friendliness, and her faith in the notion of living one's own life without having to go out of one's way for other people—could be deemed pointless and laughable" (Li, "Gold" 209–210; my emphasis).

Hanfeng feels that, now that he is becoming a parent to his mother, it is incumbent upon him to protect her "from the hostility of the world" (Li, "Gold" 209).[4]

Siyu likewise has been considered eccentric by others for various reasons. These include the distance she keeps from her father, her passion for Charles Dickens, and her status as a single (albeit good-looking) woman, not to mention her unspoken love for a matron. She is aware of how she is judged unfilial "in the eyes of old neighbors and family friends" (Li, "Gold" 217). She relates that ever since she turned twenty, neighbors and acquaintances have tried to find a husband for her, but "with those men"—and presumably with any man—she has known "from the beginning that she would not bother trying to impress them. Over the years, she had developed a reputation as unmatchable" (207). That matters of personal intimacy should be translated into communal reputation bespeaks the staking out of private lives.

The characters themselves reiterate heteronormative mores and assess one another accordingly, notwithstanding their own nonconformity. Sasha disparages Boshen as "the type of man as fussy as an old hen" (Li, "Princess" 70). She looks askance at Yang for being a kept man: "Go back to the man who keeps you if this is not a place for a princess like you" (83). She blames Peking opera for Yang's sexual orientation, but does not scruple to assume the masculine role in their relationship: "She called him 'my little *Nan Dan*,' and that was what he was to her, a boy destined to play a woman's part. She paged him often, and invited him to movies and walks in the park. She made decisions for them both, and he let her" (77). Yang, who has internalized public prejudice toward AIDS, denigrates Boshen's effort to raise awareness and to staunch the epidemic: "Why are you concerned with that dirty disease?" (74). When Sasha asks Yang to go with her to America, he tells her that "nothing humiliates a man more than living as a parasite on his woman" (88). (Yet Yang has no compunction about living off Boshen.) Boshen can only think of using matrimony and paternity—the trappings of patriarchy—to lure Yang to the US. He tells Sasha: "If you could marry Yang, he would be here in no time" (80). Even Hanfeng, a gay bachelor of forty-two who should know better, wonders why Siyu, four years younger and "beautiful in an unassuming way," has remained single (Li, "Gold" 206). "I imagine for the obvious reason of not having felt the need to get married," his mother interjects. But Professor Dai does not venture the less obvious answer—that Siyu prefers her to any male companion. The behavior of all the characters attests to the power of official discourse and social pressures.

Although the US is presented as a country of relative tolerance, where anything seems possible and permissible, the American Dream remains elusive for many, and individual freedom is sometimes attained at the expense of companionship. Sasha tells Yang that a crow can become a swan in America, but the reality for many Chinese emigrants is closer to the experience of Boshen—a physician turned chef's assistant. The New World is also depicted as a place of instant gratification, where relationships are often transient and individualistic pursuit sometimes translates as a lack of commitment. Sasha, who at first welcomes the American concept of "moving on," and Hanfeng, who for some time indulges in the American proclivity for "having fun," have in the end chosen a lasting relationship over immediate pleasure, interdependence over independence. "Freedom is like restaurant food," Hanfeng tells an old friend in California, "one can lose one's appetite for even the best restaurants" (Li, "Gold" 208). In his mind, he may be also linking his flings in North America to restaurant food, none of which offers the comfort, familiarity, and personal touch of a home-cooked meal, even when that home is devoid of sexual intimacy.

Siyu tries to envisage herself in her new residence as nominal wife: "the room which served as a piano studio for Professor Dai would be converted into the third bedroom.... She could see herself standing by the window and listening to Hanfeng and Professor Dai play four-hand, and she could see the day when she would replace Professor Dai on the piano bench, her husband patient with her inexperienced fingers" (Li, "Gold" 221). She definitely sees her marriage with Hanfeng as a permanent one, lasting beyond Professor Dai's passing. For her "the love for his mother that they could share with no one else" is a sufficient reason to attach herself to Hanfeng: "he as a son who had once left but had now returned, she who had not left and would never leave" (221). Despite the unconventional sexual orientations of the three principals, they hail from a culture that puts great stock in interdependence, including filial obligation; the domestic arrangement they settle for at the end reflects the cultural ethos. Without an appreciation for the solace of kinship, of abiding companionship, it would be difficult to understand Hanfeng's relinquishment of sexual freedom in North America for compromised domesticity in China.

Furthermore, as "The Princess of Nebraska" indicates, there are still legal and social sanctions and discrimination against homosexuality stateside. Boshen has come to the US under the guise of a heterosexual marriage, and he wants Yang's child to have a legitimate father through another union of convenience, between Yang and Sasha: "Yang could choose to live with either of them... they could—the three of them—bring up the baby together.... If only he knew how to make Sasha love Yang again" (Li, "Princess" 90). As Sasha suspects from the beginning, "Whatever interest [Boshen] had in the baby was stupid and selfish" (71). The *ménage a trois* Boshen tries to engineer is obviously unfair to Sasha. He wants Sasha to love Yang enough to marry him so that Yang can come to the US, so that Yang can be his lover again.

Whether in China or in America, a heterosexual union is envisioned as the only resolution to the love triangle in each story. Yet Boshen has described his earlier marriage to a lesbian as "an unforgivable betrayal" (Li, "Princess" 80). If Yang marries Sasha so as to give her unborn child a legitimate father, he will betray Boshen in turn. If the three decide to cohabit, Sasha may end up as the "jade girl," the lovelorn spouse. The only long-term love Sasha conjures up by the end of the story is not with a spouse, but with her own child. Professor Dai, to spare her gay son and possibly lesbian protégé a fate similar to her own—one fraught with loneliness and subject to the critical gaze of the world—has knowingly matched the two young persons linked only by their love for her. The dispassionate marriages entertained at the end of the two stories are not of the "happily ever after" ilk, but are, perhaps, to borrow the title of Yiyun Li's latest novel, "kinder than solitude."

Notes

1. See also Ha Jin, "The Bridegroom," which features a marriage between a gay man and a homely woman.

2. The theme of gender fluidity is introduced earlier when Yang reminds Sasha of "a statue of Kuanyin, the male Buddha in a female body" (76).

3. In fact, one of the most famous Cantonese movies, *Princess Chang Ping*《帝女花》, is about how the Gold Boy and Emerald Girl are punished for being erotically attracted to each other; they must do penance by being reincarnated into human beings who suffer lovesickness unto death.

4. Like Hisaye Yamamoto's eponymous character in "The Legend of Miss Sasagawara," a strong professional woman, especially one who does not gossip in accordance with gender norms, is looked at askance as eccentric and temperamental, if not outright insane by a community living in close quarters.

Works Cited

Jen, Gish. *Tiger Writing: Art, Culture, and the Interdependent Self.* Cambridge, MA: Harvard UP, 2013.

Ha Jin, "The Bridegroom." *The Bridegroom: Stories*. New York: Random House, 2000. 89–115.

Li, Yiyun. "A Clean Well-Lighted Place." *New Yorker.* Condé Nast, 18 Apr. 2011. Web. 20 May 2015. <http://www.newyorker.com/magazine/2011/04/18/a-clean-well-lighted-place>.

_____. "Gold Boy, Emerald Girl." *Gold Boy, Emerald Girl.* New York: Random House, 2010. 204–221.

_____. "The Princess of Nebraska." *A Thousand Years of Good Prayers*. New York: Harper Perennial, 2006. 68–91.

Yamamoto, Hisaye. "The Legend of Miss Sasagawara." *Seventeen Syllables and Other Stories*. Rev. & exp. ed. New Brunswick, NJ: Rutgers UP, 2001. 20–33.

The Migrant Writes: A Reading of Ha Jin's Short Fiction Collections *Under the Red Flag* and *A Good Fall*_____

Te-hsing Shan

An Extraordinary Immigrant Writer

As an immigrant writer who decided to leave his home country (China) behind after the Tiananmen Massacre in 1989 and to write in English in his adopted country (the United States), Ha Jin exemplifies two types of betrayal described in his collection of essays, *The Writer as Migrant*: "physical absence from his native country" and "the ultimate betrayal . . . to choose to write in another language" (Jin, *Writer* 31). While difficult, his situation provided him with a critical distance from which to observe both his home country and his adopted country and to channel his observations into creative writings.

To date, Jin has published in his adopted language, English, three collections of poems, seven novels, four short story collections, and one collection of essays.[1] Moreover, he has won a number of prestigious awards, including the Flannery O'Connor Award for Short Fiction (for *Under the Red Flag*, 1996); the PEN/Hemingway Award (for *Ocean of Words*, 1997); the National Book Award (for *Waiting*, 1999); the PEN/Faulkner Award (for *Waiting*, 2000 and *War Trash*, 2005); and the Asian American Literary Award (for *The Bridegroom*, 2001). His latest novel, *A Map of Betrayal* (2014), was a *Christian Science Monitor* Best Book of the Year. In recognition of his literary achievements, he was elected a fellow of the American Academy of Arts and Sciences (2006) and a fellow of the American Academy of Arts and Letters (2014). Winning these awards and honors would be extraordinary for a native speaker, which makes winning them all the more remarkable for a person who only started to learn English by listening to radio broadcasts at age nineteen and did not receive any formal training in English until he entered Heilongjiang University in 1976.

After receiving his master's degree in English and American literature from Shandong University, he left for the US in 1985 and obtained his PhD in English and American literature from Brandeis University in 1992. With so many works and awards to his credit, Jin has accomplished a level of acceptance and acclaim that usually takes immigrants three generations to achieve. As the protagonist of his novel, *A Free Life*, Wu Nan understands, "[u]sually the first generation drudged to feed and shelter themselves and their families . . . . Their children . . . would have different kinds of dreams and ambitions, going to college and becoming professionals and 'real Americans'" (Jin, *Free* 418–19). Finally, the third generation, building on the foundations laid by the previous generations, may try their hands at arts and literature.

A close examination of Jin's literary corpus reveals that all his earlier works focus on subjects related to China and that it was not until 2007, twenty-two years after he had arrived in the US, that he finally published his first novel about the Chinese American community, *A Free Life*. Two years later, *A Good Fall*, his only short story collection about new Chinese immigrants in Flushing, Queens, New York, was published. The present essay will read *A Good Fall* alongside *Under the Red Flag* (1997), his collection of eleven stories centering on Dismount Fort, a small town in Northeastern China, in order to demonstrate Jin's artistic representations of his homeland and his adopted country as a migrant writing in a language other than his mother tongue. A translingual and cross-cultural perspective is adopted here to do better justice to Jin as a Chinese American writer.[2]

Under the Red Flag

The title *Under the Red Flag* suggests that this collection is about people and events in China under the Communist regime or, to be exact, China during the Cultural Revolution. In his preface to the Chinese version, Jin offers important information, which helps us better understand the background of, and motivation for, this book. According to him, Dismount Fort is modeled after Liangjiadian, a small town in Jin County, Liaoning Province in northeastern China, where he spent almost all his childhood because his father was a commissar of a communications battalion there in the early 1960s (Jin, *Guang* 6). Although "I made up some place names and street names and incorporated some events from other places in order to make these stories rich and solid" (5), he insists, "[t]his is a real book, for none of the events is fabricated. As a writer, all I did was to reorganize characters and details and put them in Dismount Fort and nearby villages" (6). The reason for writing this book was "to preserve on paper some people and events which once existed, however cruel or warm they might be" (6).

Moreover, Jin discloses how this collection was inspired by Anglophone writers:

> Structurally speaking, *Under the Red Flag* was deeply influenced by James Joyce's *Dubliners* and Sherwood Anderson's *Winesburg, Ohio*: all the stories happened in the same place; some people appeared in different stories; each single story serves the function of supporting others; and *all these stories constitute an ethnographic moral history*. Nevertheless, *Under the Red Flag* writes not only about a place, but about a period. (Jin, *Guang* 6, emphasis added)

Therefore, the characters "White Cat" and "Bare Hips" appear in "In Broad Daylight" and "Emperor," and Zu Ming, "the head of the town police" (Jin, *Under* 98), in "Emperor" and "Again, the Spring Breeze Blew," a writing strategy that helps to string the stories together. By focusing on the people and events in a small town of northeastern China in the late 1960s and early 1970s, the author offers his representations and critiques of the Cultural Revolution.

The expression "an ethnographic moral history" is reminiscent of Joyce's statement about *Dubliners*: "My intention was to write a chapter of the moral history of my country and I chose Dublin for the scene because that city seemed to me the centre of paralysis" (Joyce 83). Despite this thematic similarity and the aforementioned structural influence, there are some significant differences between Joyce and Jin. Instead of writing about a central city, Jin opts for a small town in a faraway area to show how pervasive such paralysis might be. Moreover, the world in *Under the Red Flag* is much more violent, chaotic, and absurd. In other words, as exiles, both Joyce and Jin utilize geographical and psychological distance to more objectively observe and critically reflect on their home countries. While Joyce uses English to write about a central city dominated politically, economically, and culturally, for centuries, by the British people, Jin employs his hard-won second language to describe a small town as an epitome of "what millions of the mainland Chinese had experienced" (Jin, *Guang* 7). By writing this way, Jin joins the literary tradition established by Joseph Conrad and Vladimir Nabokov and tries to carve out a niche of his own.[3]

This information provides a convenient entry point to the place and the period described in *Under the Red Flag*. The Chinese name of this place, *Xiemating*, means "A Pavilion for Horses to Rest," a title rich in local color and ancient associations. Dismount Fort is described as "a place where troops made a brief stop for rest during their maneuvers in ancient times as well as a preparatory place for the Korean campaigns" (Jin, *Guang* 140). On the other hand, other details—including Chairman Mao's badges, the Little Red Book, Red Guards, revolutionary songs, slogans, and public persecutions—all indicate that the period represented is the Cultural Revolution, a period when human nature was put to severe test.

While a couple of characters appear in different stories, the most prominent presence is none other than Chairman Mao himself, who, with his mysterious aura, was both the target of blind worship and allegiance as well as a powerful and convenient tool for getting rid of one's opponents. By means of all-pervasive thought control and a tight-knit web of surveillance, Mao became the Big Brother whose presence was felt everywhere, either in the form of a badge, button, portrait, red book, revolutionary slogans and songs, or in the living embodiment of the frenzied Red Guards. Anything against Mao or, worse still, anything that could be interpreted as deviating from the orthodox, was to be punished.

Prominent themes of *Under the Red Flag* include sex, poverty, hunger, and distorted love. For instance, "In Broad Daylight" tells how the townspeople paraded and publicly persecuted Mu Ying, "the Old Whore" (Jin, *Under* 1), because, though married to a kind person who had saved her, she had slept with three other men in exchange for money. In "New Arrival," Jin describes how Jia Cheng had an extramarital relationship because his wife, whom he had bought out [for he paid money to buy her out] from a brothel, could not give birth to a child. In "Taking a Husband" (132–53), Hong Chen and her mother cry out as if "all [their] property was gone" (144), for of the two young men competing for her affection, the one whom she had passed over had been promoted to the commune's vice-chairmanship. More absurd is "Man to Be" (17–30), in which an old husband invites five militia men to "sleep" with (in fact, to gang rape) his young wife in order to "teach her a lesson so she will stop seducing other men and be a chaste woman in the future" (21). Ironically, among the songs the militia sing on their way to victimize the young wife are revolutionary ones, such as "Our Navigation Depends on the Great Helmsman" and "Without the Communist Party There Would Be No New China" (22).

All these stories are set during the period when Mao was worshiped as the great helmsman and supreme leader of China. His words, badges, statues, and whatnots carried highest authority and could be wielded as dreadful weapons. Human nature was distorted by the cult of personality, blind patriotism, blood-thirst, and sheer self-protection. Among the most violent manifestations of the era was the public persecution of anyone labelled an enemy of the people for breaking party rules or showing the slightest sign of contempt for Mao. For instance, Li Wan, the wealthy retired military doctor in "The Richest Man," becomes a target for popular violence after he accidentally breaks a Chairman Mao button and then discards it in a trash heap (Jin, *Under* 70). For this, he is immediately condemned as a "Current Counterrevolutionary" (71). Even his past patriotic acts, such as mailing food coupons to Chairman Mao during the great famine, are reinterpreted to his detriment, as if they say to Mao: "Look, we are all starving because of your leadership" (74). Overnight, his property is confiscated, he is sent to "Sea Nest Village to be reformed" (75), and compelled to serve as a barefoot doctor for five years without pay. In "A Decade," a young teacher at an elementary school is condemned and sent to the countryside for reform because, among other things, students in her Chinese class regard her interpretation of a metaphor in Mao's letter to the Albanian Communist Party as "not only wrong but reactionary. How dare she change Chairman Mao's meaning!" (204).

In these stories, all things personal are related to the collective and the national. In "Taking a Husband," when Hong Chen chooses Pang Hai as her husband, the latter, though elated, maintains a low profile, for his expected promotion is still in process. At this "critical juncture of his official career," the first thought that comes to him is to maintain a low profile and to keep "firmly in mind Chairman's Mao's instruction: 'We must always be modest and prudent and must, so to speak, tuck our tails between our legs'" (Jin, *Under* 139). The wedding is held on October 1, National Day (145), and the songs the newlyweds sing at the banquet are "The East Is Red, the Sun Is Rising" and "Happy, We Must Not Forget the Communist Party" (146).

Mao's omnipresence probably finds its best expression in "Resurrection." Before the brigade leaders' initial interrogation of him about his adultery, Lu Han hears "a droning sound made by a few flies," which reminds him of a few lines from Chairman Mao's poem "On our small planet / A few flies bang on walls / Buzzing, moaning, sobbing" (Jin, *Under* 171–72). This sound somehow symbolizes his own plight. The subsequent interrogation is conducted in front of Mao's portrait (172). When Lu Han decides to leave home, what comes to mind are another few lines from Mao. Even thinking about becoming a beggar in Beijing, he still laments, "It's too bad that Chairman Mao doesn't inspect Red Guards anymore, or I'd see his glorious face and his stalwart body on the gate tower as well" (185).

As his oral confession of the details of his extramarital relationship is insufficient to satisfy the voyeuristic brigade leaders, they demand from him a written confession of no less than one hundred pages. Seeing that there is no way to meet this impossible demand, he decides to run away. However, his attempts to become a monk and a beggar are thwarted when he cannot produce any valid official papers. After being returned to his hometown and facing a still more severe interrogation, Lu Han, in desperation, takes a pair of large scissors and cuts off his scrotum and testicles.

Everything changes after this shocking act of self-castration: his adultery is forgiven by the townspeople; his wife returns with their son, "determined to be a model wife" (Jin, *Under* 194); he is elected by the villagers as "an exemplary commune member" (196); and even Secretary Zhao, who earlier interrogated him, encourages him "to write an application for Party membership, which Lu was, of course, delighted to do." Consequently, "a new, normal life" (196). Symbolically, this suggests that to survive and to thrive in an oppressive society, one has to undergo self-castration and sacrifice self-dignity. In an interview with me, Jin said he regards "Resurrection" as his favorite short story, for it "carries to the extreme the tradition established by Lu Xun's 'The True Story of Ah Q'" (146).

Although the whole collection abounds in sarcasm and presents the dark side of human nature, Jin leaves some room for redemption. For instance, he depicts the selfless loving care of the childless couple to the son of a military officer in "New Arrival"; the true feelings of the final reunion of the newlyweds whose wedding banquet is disrupted by the jealous loser in this game of love in "Taking a Husband;" Lanlan's heart-felt gratitude to the first anonymous reporter whose coverage of her bravery brings her good fortune in "Again, the Spring Breeze Blew"; and a narrative poem telling the story of an old Red Guard who, having repented of his past wrongdoings, comes to take care of his teacher, allowing the old man to die "with gratitude" (Jin, *Under* 198) in "A Decade." These details show that human nature, though under severe strain during political turmoil, nonetheless has a chance to reassert itself. All in all, these stories confirm Frederic Jameson's argument about third-world texts as national allegories and his statement that "the story of the private individual destiny is always an allegory of the embattled situation of the public third-world culture and society" (69).

By presenting stories focusing on Dismount Fort, Jin offers a kaleidoscopic view of the daily life of the townspeople, who, under the Chinese Communist rule during the Cultural Revolution, seem to have become "grotesques," to borrow Anderson's description of the people in *Winesburg, Ohio*. As the book title suggests, anything, no matter how absurd, could happen under the red flag. However, what remains of humanity still offers a chance for rebirth. Reflecting on these people and their stories from a distant country in his adopted language, Jin exposes a chapter of the ethnographic moral history of his native town to a much larger world.

A Good Fall

While *Under the Red Flag* describes a remote town in China in the crucible of the Cultural Revolution, *A Good Fall* tells stories about newly arrived Chinese immigrants in Flushing, the second largest Chinatown in New York. Jin took pains to translate the whole work into Chinese singlehandedly because he firmly believes in the universality and translatability of literature (Jin, *Luo* 6) and would like to find a temporary resting place in his mother tongue to alleviate the nostalgia he feels for his home country (7). In an interview with Dwight Garner, Jin says, "perhaps I can make sense of it [America] from a different angle, from an immigrant's perspective." The opening paragraph of his preface to the Chinese version of *A Good Fall* provides the following background information:

> For years I had been thinking about writing a short story collection about the immigrant life, but I had no idea about the location of these stories. In early February, 2005, I was invited by the *World Journal* [the largest Chinese newspaper in North America] to attend a conference at the city center of Flushing. On that first visit I saw the bustling streets and a large number of Chinese immigrants, mostly from mainland China and Taiwan. They took their roots here and began their new life. I was very much moved by the prosperous street scenes and thought that many American towns must have started like this. So I decided to put all my stories in Flushing. . . . Altogether, I visited there about twenty times. Now Flushing has already been the new Chinatown of New York, so *A Good Fall* can be seen as stories of the new Chinatown. (Jin, *Luo* 5)

In writing *A Good Fall*, Jin, who used to write about subjects related to mainland China, seeks to highlight the significance of the lives of humble, newly arrived Chinatown immigrants. He asks rhetorically, "Why can't a new immigrant in Chinatown deserve the same artistic treatment of that 'Great China'?" (Jin, *Luo* 6) To him, an artist should be able to "demonstrate a complex and turbulent life by way of humble human lives" (Jin, *Luo* 6).

In contrast to the old Cantonese-speaking Chinatown immigrants in Lower Manhattan, many new immigrants came to Flushing after the reform and opening-up of the People's Republic of China in the early 1980s. Chun-jen Chen observes that "*A Good Fall* shows influences from Joyce's *Dubliners* and Anderson's *Winesburg, Ohio*, as a collection of short stories that both provide a picture of an era while ethnographically telling a moral history" (71).

Drastically different from Jin's previous works on China, this collection of twelve stories presents a spectrum of Chinese immigrants with professors and realtors at one end and laborers and sex workers at the other. To them, the US is both a land of opportunity, where they can pursue their dreams, and a threatening land, especially to those who do not have a good command of English. Their stories reveal different facets of the Chinese American diasporic community: the personal histories of the immigrants, their hopes and fears, struggles and frustrations, success and failure, their American Dream and nightmare, and, not the least of these, the cultural clashes of the home country and the host country.

Traditional Chinese values, such as filial piety, come under threat in the US. A case in point is the old Chinese couple in "Children as Enemies," who sell all their property in China and move to the new continent to be with their son, "a bridge engineer pulling in almost six figures a year" (Jin, *Good Fall* 85). However, conflicts between the old couple and their daughter-in-law and their grandchildren are so intense that they find "[i]n America it feels as if the older you are, the more inferior you grow" (80). Unable to bridge the generational and cultural gap that sets them apart from their daughter-in-law and grandchildren and dissatisfied with their son, who is "henpecked and indulgent with the kids" (85), they finally decide to move into a one-bedroom apartment their son rents for them. The story ends with the old man's realization that "[t]his is America, where we must learn self-reliance and mind our own business" (86).

On the other hand, "In the Crossfire" shows the son, Tian Chu, caught between his mother, Meifen, and his wife, Connie Liu. Already an American citizen, Chu works in a floundering company that will soon begin laying off employees. The young couple's life is disrupted by Meifen, who comes from China to visit her son for half a year. Knowing no English, she spends much of her time at home and finds fault (and quarrels with) her daughter-in-law in the very first week. Unable to dispel the hostility between the two most important women in his life, Chu decides to resign from his post "for family reasons" (Jin, *Good Fall* 110), though he is not among the people slated to be laid off. The son's drastic move makes his mother realize the great "stress and insecurity in America" (116) and so decides to return to China earlier than she had intended.

The sense of insecurity is not limited to those who are not proficient in English. "An English Professor" tells the story of a Chinese assistant professor with a Harvard PhD who writes an incorrect word in the materials submitted for tenure evaluation. Obsessed with what seems to him an unforgivable mistake, he goes to apply for other jobs as a newspaper editor and as a salesman for a publishing company. Eventually, his fear of rejection proves unfounded, and he is so overjoyed with his promotion and tenure that he seems to have "lost his mind" (Jin, *Good Fall* 154).

On the other hand, the US remains, in Ha Jin's fiction, a land of opportunity. The characters in the aforementioned stories most likely would not have become a bridge engineer, an accountant, or an English professor had they not moved to the US. It is a country where Chinese immigrants can hold to their ideals, like the composer in "A Composer and His Parakeets" or the PhD student of American history who acts contrary to his parents' will in "Choice." The US is so attractive that in "Shame," a visiting professor—an Americanist and translator at a prestigious university in China— decides to become an illegal alien and work as a dishwasher in a

Chinese restaurant so that he might earn money to send back to his sick wife in China.

"The Beauty" provides a good example of how America is a promised land for people seeking to leave the past behind and start a new life. Dan Feng, a handsome realtor, marries a beautiful woman, Gina. Yet their daughter is so ugly that he suspects Fooming Yu might be the real father and even hires a private detective to investigate. In the face of her husband's suspicion, Gina confesses that she was acquainted with Yu in their native village in China. Yu knew that Gina used to be very ugly, and he threatened to tell her secret to her husband. She confides that after she came to the US, she underwent "a series of plastic surgeries" (Jin, *Good Fall* 44–45) and changed her name from Lai Hsu, "arrived lately" (46), to a stylish American name. With a new face and a new name, she starts a new life, "the best thing America gave me" (45). Consequently, she is able to marry this handsome and prosperous realtor. Interestingly, it turns out that Feng was a Chinese Communist Party member who gave up his "membership publicly in 1989," which made him "a clean man in this country" (47), and became naturalized, "no longer a deportable foreigner" (48). If Gina and Feng had not come to the US, they would not have had found these opportunities to start their new lives. Significantly, the Chinese title of the story, *meijen*, is a pun in translation, meaning both "a beauty" and "an American" (*meiguojen*), for both statuses are possible only in the US.

The US' status as a land of both opportunity and danger is probably best presented in the title story "A Good Fall." A monk from Tianjin, China, Ganchin bribes "the elders in charge of international exchanges" (Jin, *Good Fall* 222) at his monastery to become a martial arts teacher at a Buddhist temple in New York, which promises a monthly salary of $1,500 for three years. However, he is exploited by the temple master and paid nothing. Worse, he is fired when he is unable to teach due to illness, and his passport expires. "An illegal alien, a lawbreaker" (222) with no money and no English except "thank you" and "good-bye" (234), he regrets that "[h]e'd been misled by the people who bragged about the opportunity found in American and wouldn't reveal the hardship they'd gone through here. . . . Silly, how silly" (232). Desperate, he jumps off a five-story building to kill himself. Yet his martial arts abilities save him, for, because he had the skills of a kungfu teacher, "[h]is body instinctively adjusted itself" (239). With one leg broken, he was hospitalized and appeared on the news in Chinese communities across North America. With offers of help from many hands, he recovers his health, retains an attorney to sue the head monk for damages, and is offered a number of legal avenues to avoid deportation, for "[t]his is America . . . a land ruled by law" (240). The story ends on a happy note.

In his preface to the Chinese translation, Jin admits that a number of the stories in *A Good Fall* are based on events known to many people. To him, "all these are news and the task of a writer is to turn news into literature, making it into eternal news" (Jin, *Luo* 5). An investigation into the English and Chinese titles of the stories reveals that Jin is a master of irony. As he mentioned elsewhere, "a good fall" alludes to "the fortunate fall" in John Milton's *Paradise Lost*, and many other twists and turns are to be found in this story. To being with, Ganchin is fortunate enough to come to the US, albeit through bribery. Then, his good luck turns bad when he falls into an inhuman underside of New York society. Unable to overcome his bad fortune, he tries to end his life by jumping out a window and not only survives, but finds unexpected good fortune, and, thus, "a good fall."

The Chinese title, "*luodi*" means "landing" or "falling to the ground." This expression may also refer to the changing identity of the Chinese in the US. For example, "*luodi shenggen*" means "taking roots where you are," in contrast to "*luoye guigen*" ("falling leaves returning to their roots").[4] When Ganchin is frustrated with his life in the US, he considers returning to China, like a falling leaf returning to its roots. When this wish is frustrated, he attempts to kill himself with a long fall to the ground, but instead the fall brings him good fortune, allowing him to "take root" and discover the true promise of the US.

In *A Good Fall*, Jin describes the newly arrived immigrants of Flushing, many of whom used to live under the red flag. Their lives in the adopted country demonstrate that the US abounds in opportunity as well as dangers and offers chances and challenges alike for the immigrants. By turning their stories into literature, the author presents the everyday lives of those immigrants, which constitutes a chapter in the moral history of the diasporic Chinese community in Flushing.

Jin's Good Fall

Written ten years apart, *Under the Red Flag* and *A Good Fall* indicate how Jin's literary concerns have grown, with his subject shifting from life in China to that in the US. Keenly aware of the plight of a migrant writer trying to excel in an adopted language, Jin quotes Nabokov's confession that "to write in English was a 'private tragedy,'" for "he [Nabokov] had to give the prime years of his creative life to English, a language in which he never felt at home" (Jin, *Writer* 57). However, with his talent, diligence, and perseverance, this writer of Russian descent eventually excelled in English and became a literary maestro in his adopted language.

Following the literary tradition established by Conrad and Nabokov, Jin confronts similar challenges. In answering why he decided to write in English, Jin's succinct answer is "for survival," which carries both practical and existential meanings: "practical" because it was difficult for him as a PhD-holder in English literature to obtain a teaching position at an American university, so writing appeared to be a way to make a living; and "existential" because if he wanted to be a true artist and avoid censorship, English would be his only choice. He is able to see both the negative and positive sides of his choice. He admits, "On various occasions, I have said that choosing to write in English is my personal tragedy" (Jin, *Luo* 6), but he is also quick to recognize that, besides allowing him to avoid censorship, "writing in English does make me independent and strong and gives me an additional chance, namely, to find readers in another language" (Jin, *Luo* 6).

Writing as a migrant in the US, Jin makes good use of his diasporic position and bilingual resources and strives to write about things that he would not have been able to write about and publish in his home country. Offering interesting stories and vivid characters, both *Under the Red Flag* and *A Good Fall* demonstrate Jin's effort and talent in presenting the ethnographic moral histories in different locales and periods—from the Chinese natives in Dismount Fort in northeastern China during the Cultural Revolution in the late 1960s and early 1970s, to the Chinese immigrants in Flushing, New York, in the US after China's Reform and Opening-Up Policy in the early 1980s.

In *The Writer as Migrant*, a combination of critical insights and personal experiences, Jin constantly reflects upon his own situation by drawing examples from different literary traditions. To him, Nabokov is "a supreme example of how to adapt writing to the circumstances of displacement, how to imagine and attain an intimate relationship with his mother tongue, and how to face an oppressive regime with contempt, artistic integrity, and individual dignity" (Jin, *Writer* 57). This evaluation is not abstract theorization, but a reflection of his own experiences as a writer in the US, an impossible dream if he had not decided to leave his motherland behind and had not chosen to write in English. Through great effort, he has successfully turned his private tragedy into a most welcome public contribution. His various writings, their reception, and the many prestigious awards and honors he has received all provide strong proof of his own good fall.

Notes

1. All his works have been translated into Chinese and published in Taiwan. However, because he is a dissident in the eyes of the PRC government, almost all of his works have been banned in mainland China. Moreover, he has not been allowed to visit his homeland since he first left China in 1985.

2. In my interview with him, I asked, "How would you identify yourself—a first-generation Chinese American writer writing in English, a Chinese-American writer with a hyphen, an overseas Chinese writer, a Chinese writer in exile, a writer of the Chinese diaspora, an immigrant writer, or just a writer?" He answered, "A Chinese American writer. Of course, a writer in my situation can

have several hats, and I don't mind wearing more than one" (Shan 154–55).

3. In *The Writer as Migrant*, Jin discusses Conrad's and Nabokov's different styles and contributions to the English language. To him, any writers "who have adopted English . . . are all related to Conrad one way or another" (44) and "[a]fter Nabokov, who can say nonnative writers cannot crack jokes in English?" (51) While following their tradition, Jin strives to make his unique contributions by bringing in linguistic characteristics of the Chinese language, as he argues in "In Defense of Foreignness."

4. For a detailed discussion of the five types of Chinese identity in the United States, including "*luodi shenggen*" and "*luoye guigen*," see Wang, 198–211. Although this categorization is convenient, it must be pointed out that people may change their identity under different circumstances, as Ganchin's case shows.

Works Cited

Anderson, Sherwood. "The Book of the Grotesque." *Winesburg, Ohio.* 1919. New York: Dover, 1995. 1–3.

Chen, Chun-jen. "'The Best Thing America Gave Me': Diasporic Memory and Creative Nostalgia in *A Good Fall.*" *Studies in Modern Fiction* (2014): 53–78.

Garner, Dwight. "Ha Jin's Cultural Revolution." *New York Times Magazine* (Feb 6, 2000): 6+.

Jameson, Fredric. "Third-World Literature in the Era of Multinational Capitalism." *Social Text* 15 (1986): 65–88.

Jin, Ha. *A Free Life.* New York: Pantheon, 2007.

_____. *A Good Fall.* New York: Pantheon, 2009.

_____. "In Defense of Foreignness." *The Routledge Handbook of World Englishes.* Ed. Andy Kirkpatrick. New York: Routledge, 2010. 461–70.

_____. "Preface." *Luodi* (*A Good Fall*). Taipei: China Times, 2010. 5–7.

_____. "Preface." *Guangtianhuari* (*Under the Red Flag*). Taipei: China Times, 2000. 5–7.

_____. *Under the Red Flag.* Hanover, NH: Zoland, 1999.

_____. *The Writer as Migrant*. Chicago: U of Chicago P, 2008.

Joyce, James. *Selected Letters of James Joyce*. Ed. Richard Ellmann. New York: Viking Press, 1975.

Shan, Te-hsing. "In the Ocean of Words: An Interview with Ha Jin." *Tamkang Review* 38.2 (2008): 135–57.

Wang, L. Ling-chi. "Roots and the Changing Identity of the Chinese in the United States." Ed. Wei-ming Tu. *The Living Tree: The Changing Meaning of Being Chinese Today*. Stanford: Stanford UP, 1994. 185–212.

"Even the dead make noises:" Silence and Language in Ernesto Quiñonez's Stories_____

Bridget Kevane

Ernesto Quiñonez, born in 1969, of an Ecuadorian father and a Puerto Rican mother, is best known for his dynamic portraits of New York City's Spanish Harlem, *el barrio*, in his two novels *Bodega Dreams* (2000) and *Chango's Fire* (2004), as well as in his short stories. Quiñonez's own childhood was spent in *el barrio* and all of his fiction is firmly rooted in this neighborhood's gritty and yet vibrant streets. The *barrio* he describes is, in equal measure, a place of despair and hope, a place of the community's failures and successes. In working within this favored geographical space, Quiñonez renders *el barrio* and its mostly Puerto Rican inhabitants as an emergent, distinct cultural and political entity. Spanish Harlem is not only a physical space, but also an emotional collective infused by social isolation, prejudice, and the struggle for a meaningful identity. His fiction offers a portrait of important historical and cultural moments as well as a depiction of the current struggles and challenges facing the Puerto Rican community in Manhattan's Upper East Side. "It's basically a fact," Quiñonez says in an interview about his first novel, "that a lot of Latino issues [in the United States] go uncovered, especially in neighborhoods like Spanish Harlem. They get totally ignored. I want the world to know that they exist. I wanted to show that this is a neighborhood that is vibrant and a big cultural force in New York City and that you can't keep ignoring us, we're part of the United States" (Wiegand).

Accompanying Quiñonez's themes of collective identity and social isolation is a pointed focus on the mechanics of language and silence. His novels reveal a constant tension between language and silence, between babble and muteness, as his main characters attempt to overcome a sense of hopelessness. Indeed, language or, more specifically, the urgent need for a different linguistic representation of the Puerto Rican experience in *el barrio*, constitutes the visionary grand finale, the crescendo, of *Bodega Dreams*. Only a new language can save the community: "Don't you see what's happening?" asks Willie Bodega, then continues, "A new language means a new race. Spanglish is the future. It's a new language being born out of the ashes of two cultures clashing with each other" (Quiñonez, *Bodega* 212).

Language and silence also play a critical role in Quiñonez's lesser-known fiction, his short stories. This essay hopes to introduce readers to some of his stories—"Graffiti Monk" (2004), "Taina's Song" (2011), and "The First Book of the Sinner" (2011)—and analyze how they expand upon the writer's linguistic, literary project for Spanish Harlem. As in his novels, these stories' protagonists grapple with the insufficiencies that they both experience and discover in the language handed to them. The protagonists yearn to find a different mode of expression, one that can accurately convey their unique bilingual and bicultural experience, and convey, too, the bitterness and frustration of their social and political disenfranchisement.

What are the risks of language and silence, asks Quiñonez? When do his characters suffer from the inadequacy of language, from an exhaustion with the verbal? When, in other words, do they "retreat from the word?"[1] And where do they find the utopic impulse for a new language or an active, even politicized, silence? This essay hopes to provide some answers to these questions by offering a close reading of these stories.

Before turning to the stories, however, it is useful to highlight several commonalities in Quiñonez's fiction. The geographical location is present-day Spanish Harlem and the fiction is typically narrated in first person. The narrators and protagonists are young disenfranchised Puerto Rican men, who are at odds with their surroundings mostly because they perceive the changes in their neighborhood as culturally destructive.[2] The changes wrought by the process of gentrification, the economic and social transformation of the *barrio*, provoke anger, disillusionment, and cultural angst in the main characters.[3] Such changes also temporarily paralyze them from undertaking any positive action or from moving forward.

Aside from writing against gentrification and aside from offering language and silence as alternative strategies for salvation, Quiñonez also continually produces an intimate portrait of the young male Puerto Rican who is cynical, indifferent, or drifting—a near-criminal or a lost soul. The author bears witness to a lost generation of young male Puerto Ricans and their penchant for self-destructiveness. But there is also always a message of hope and expectation that the community will *seguir pa'lante* (continue moving forward).

As the *barrio* becomes transformed by wealthy outsiders, the community is compromised emotionally and economically; it loses dignity, pride, and social capital. For, as Quiñonez reminds readers, there is a long and important history of Puerto Rican culture in the *barrio*, a culture that is the essential glue of the community. He pays homage to many of the Puerto Rican pioneers and luminaries, including writers like Pedro Pietri or social movements like the Young Lords, to remind readers what is at stake if the community passively watches from the sidelines. The community risks losing its unique cultural past, a past that can replenish future generations. In fact, on many levels, Quinónez's fiction is part of an answer, a solution, a resistance, to the larger social silencing that takes place during gentrification. His characters come to understand on a visceral level the risks of being pushed out, from living in poverty, from being neglected as a throwaway people. Spanish Harlem is a battleground, but it is also a site of transformation. The protagonists' progression from crisis and disillusionment to transformation and redemption contains a message for the future, a message of hope. Both novels, as critic Sean Moiles points out, end with a celebratory and syncretic message emphasizing Spanglish and Santería, a message that hinges on a syncretism, a combination of languages, of faiths, of identities, of communities (127–130).

But another major theme that appears in Quiñonez's fiction is language. More specifically, Quñonez explores the limits of language and the contours of silence, a nonverbal form of language. He seems obsessed with language, with wringing it out, in order to find something innovative and different that is capable of better capturing life experience in the *barrio*. He revisits the positive and negative roles language and silence play in the lives of his characters in Spanish Harlem, characters who feel, as Quiñonez says, that they have been failed as citizens of the United States. "Why is it," Quiñonez asks in an interview, "that we keep failing the residents of inner city ghettos?" ("Author Q & A").

Language also keeps failing. Or, more precisely, language fails because it has become incapable of capturing and articulating the experience of Puerto Ricans, of redeeming their history and culture, their collective community, in Spanish Harlem. It always falls short; it falls on deaf ears; even the characters themselves complain. It doesn't create opportunity, but rather dead ends. Thus the writer's focus on language reveals a desire, a longing for a different immigrant future. If a new lexicon, phonology, vocabulary can be created, perhaps a new future can be created—one that eliminates teenage pregnancy, prison, isolation, and personal dead ends.

Examples of this same thinking abound in his short fiction. In "The First Book of the Sinner," the protagonist craves the language, the words, and the concepts the 'reverend' articulates while teaching prisoners about the larger world and its philosophies. In "Taina's Song," a teenage pregnancy casts shame upon a family that, in turn, leads them to a world of "monk-like silence." Finally, in "Graffiti Monk," language is a multi-layered platform that includes criminalized art (graffiti), music (Blondie), philosophy (Kierkegaard), and the spiritual awakening provided by *The Tibetan Book of the Dead*.

Why all this focus on language? Because Quiñonez's short fiction characters, like his novels' protagonists, are explicit in how it fails them: "I wanted to find a new language," the narrator of "The First Book" says, "A new way of speaking . . . . I needed a language that made me feel worthy of being human, and most of all I wanted a language that told the world I was now another person" (178). Surrounded by bleak environments, the projects or prison, the streets of burnt-out buildings, or by stifling institutions like the prison system or a religious institution, the characters feel an exhaustion directly linked to the restrictions of English syntax.

They are, therefore, searching, sometimes without knowing it, for innovative articulations to better capture their experiences. Spanglish, graffiti art, silence, music, song, slang, innovative words and concepts—all push the boundaries of the normative and reach closer to adequate expression for them. As Quiñonez says, Spanglish is "not two languages that chop each other up, but words that don't exist in either language" (Wiegand). And those words that don't exist are better at expressing the soul of Puerto Ricans in Spanish Harlem.

*   *   *

"Taina's Song," a stand-alone story as well as part of Quiñonez's novel in progress, is the story of thirteen-year-old Taina Flores's [OR Flores'] pregnancy. Taina and her mother, Sister Flores, are members of the evangelical Jehovah's Witness community, for whom intercourse and pregnancy out of wedlock are sins and considered heinous crimes against the church. When Taina becomes pregnant, the daughter (or mother, it is not clear) tells the elders of Kingdom Hall that the pregnancy is the result of an immaculate conception. "It had worked for the Virgin Mary," the narrator tells us. So why not for Taina? (Quiñonez, "Taina's Song" 70).

For weeks, the mother and daughter are subjected to a grueling interrogation about her pregnancy. The mother is accused of not protecting the daughter's most precious commodities, her virginity and her honor. Eventually the church decides not to believe them. At that point, the mother hurls curses at the elders, and it is this—the cursing, the showering of taboo language—that forces the elders to excommunicate mother and daughter. "Sister Flores cursed at the elders in the street. Sister Flores spewed out so many curses it was as if she was exorcising the anger felt by all the women in the third world" (Quiñonez, "Taina's Song" 70–71). She curses the men who "play us like dominoes . . . with no love at all" and asks "Donde esta el amor de Dios [sic]?" (71). [Translation: Where is the love of God? Or Where is God's love?] For this, for disrespecting the "men appointed by the Holy Spirit," the mother and daughter are exiled from "the truth" (71).

Here, there is a progression toward complete silence, a movement in stages: Before the silence, there is the curse. Before the curse, there is interrogation by the elders. After the cursing, there is gossip, a linguistic chorus of voices, of "they saids": "They said Sister Flores was to blame," "They said Sister Flores should have known better," "They said Sister Flores had been the worst of mothers." And "They said it was shame that had turned these two women to become like monks." (Quiñonez, "Taina's Song" 71).

When the wall of shame encloses them, the narrator, a fifteen-year-old whose name is not revealed, decides to voice a different story, to question the elders of the church, to rewrite the events, to believe a different truth. When the narrator, curious, but also compassionate, ventures to Taina's building and presses his ear against their apartment door, he only *hears* complete silence. The neighbor, who also has been listening at the door, tells the narrator that no sounds emerge from their apartment. They are silenced even more than the dead, for, as she says, "Even the dead make noises" (Quiñonez, "Taina's Song" 72).

The narrator at first fantasizes about a different outcome for Taina. He imagines a biblical miracle story for Taina, a "glorious vision," in which the faithful from all over the world would make a pilgrimage to Spanish Harlem to catch a glimpse of the pregnant virgin (Quiñonez, "Taina's Song" 72). The narrator, in his imagined alternative story, says that "In El Barrio, the word, the story, had already spread" and would lead to a babble in the newspapers, like *El Vocero*, or TV stations, like *Telemundo*, and more. "But this didn't happen," the narrator tells us. "The story of the pregnant virgin didn't catch on . . . . Instead everyone believed in the unfortunate shame that had befallen upon Taina" (72).

Soon, however, it becomes apparent that Taina's pregnancy is a rape—that a man who had been preying on young girls in the neighborhood, a man who "would bargain shop for women on the street, like one shops for a dress or shoes" (Quiñonez, "Taina's Song" 72), was the father of her child.

Still, despite the narrator's failure to imagine the story accurately, he chooses to believe the miracle story. He chooses miracle over crime, and he chooses *story*, the language of invention, over reality. But above all, he chooses to believe Taina's story out of respect (and infatuation) because no one has purchase on the one truth. Then, because he chooses to believe, he, too, is ostracized by his peers and by the church. But his silence is an active silence, it is a choice rooted in himself and in his belief that shaming is an unacceptable punishment. In fact, the narrator says that what might have been perceived as a burden might also be perceived as a burden or sacrifice that is transformed into a gift: "The burden, says the narrator, "became a gift and I didn't care because I began behaving as the two women were. I had joined their way of dealing with a world of unbelievers. I had embraced silence" (Quiñonez, "Taina's Song" 74).

The story, then, directs a pointed critique at the failings of institutional religion, of gender roles, of the *barrio*, and so on. However, the story also fits within the parameters of Quiñonez's project on language. As the narrator chooses to believe Taina's story, he also chooses to envelop himself in silence, in the absence of words. His silence stands as a powerful indictment against the verbiage of a strict religious code or *barrio* gossip or the double standard of gender roles. The narrator's silence suggests that when confronted by an inadequate narrative, like the one dictating Taina's life, there is still a choice. In this case, the choice is to reject the verbal and adopt silence. For if a story cannot be corroborated, explicated, or even forgiven in the sphere of the verbal, then what better way to remain faithful to it and to honor it than through silence?

If in "Taina's Song" the story moves from chatter to muteness, in "The First Book of the Sinner," it moves in the opposite direction. The narrator, Miguel, a young man who has been in and out of prison since he was sixteen, struggles to break his learned habit of silence. "The only language I have ever known," he says, "is that of silence. Silence protects you when you're inside. Silence, because no one inside respects physical strength . . . Different or with nothing to take from you but your useless silence" (Quiñonez, "First Book" 177). But Miguel had already become accustomed to the language of silence even before prison. As a young boy in Spanish Harlem, he worked at cultivating his silence, along with a "stone face" because even outside of prison the non-verbal works as a protective shield against the trappings of his environment.

Now, however, Miguel wants to change. And to change, he believes he has to learn a new language: "I needed a language that made me feel worthy of being human, and most of all I wanted a language that told the world I was now another person" (Quiñonez, "First Book" 178). When a teacher, nicknamed "the reverend" and, later, "the sucker," begins to offer classes, Miguel feels renewed hope that he will be able to use the reverend's language to construct a "worthy" self. The "reverend" inspires and offers the prisoners everything: "Western philosophy, esoteric religions, pragmatic existentialism, comparative economics, literature, and here's a kicker—spelling." He teaches them about writers such as Jean-Jacques Rousseau, Søren Kierkegaard, Thomas Merton, Sigmund Freud, Che Guevara, and Frantz Fanon, including the last's theory of the colonization and subjugation of mind and body. "History," he tells his student prisoners, "is not a collection of facts. . . . History starts when we begin to free ourselves from limitations and start to argue" (180). Miguel loves it all, but he especially loves all the big words, such as "context and relativity." "I'd say them to myself rolling off my mind like tongue twisters" (179). As he repeats the words to himself, he begins to dream and imagine the things he will say outside of prison, things like "The most revolutionary thing to be these days is articulate" (179). These articulations, as well as the ideas behind them, will aid in the creation of a worthy human being. In short, the reverend's rhetoric seduces Miguel into believing that his salvation lies in adopting the twists and turns of the language offered by the reverend.

Miguel's habit of silence, however, prevents him from speaking out loud. Whereas before, silence prevented him from being killed, now, he says, "It killed me to stay quiet" (Quiñonez, "First Book" 179). Despite the fact that he mentally responds and argues with the reverend, he is unable to utter a single word out loud. When the reverend finally approaches Miguel directly with a book, he says, "The first thing if you want to learn a new language, Miguel, is to stop cursing inside your mind" (181). As in "Taina's Song," swearing, another linguistic mode altogether, plays an important role here. In the former, it is ultimately responsible for the mother's and daughter's permanent imprisonment or exile from their religious and social community. Here the reverend, imitating Frantz Fanon's ideas about the oppressed or colonized mind, believes that swearing is responsible for Miguel's silence. In other words, the reverend believes that Miguel curses in his mind because he does not believe in himself and has adopted the "colonizer's" belief that he is inferior, subordinate. If he can untangle himself from cursing, he will have a voice. But for Miguel, swearing has more currency, more psychological charge, than simply being a reflection of his self-worth or lack thereof. It is the linguistic tool he wields against the reverend. This final scene returns the reader to the beginning of the story by revealing how and why the teacher comes to be called both the "reverend" and "the sucker," nouns that conjure contradictory images, one positive and one negative. As Miguel takes the book, he observes his teacher's hands and discovers that they are the hands "of someone who has lived off someone else's labor. Hands that only old money rich people, or men who have a sugar mommy at home, have—soft, white, dove hands" (Quiñonez, "First Book" 181). The teacher is not who he pretends he is. He is a con artist, a magician, a Wizard of Oz. Miguel, who might be considered the sucker for being drawn to the teacher's mesmerizing verbal rhetoric, deftly ascribes the word to the teacher because the real sucker is the teacher for believing that he could transform Miguel and the other prisoners, for believing that his words would empower them. The title "Reverend" is meant sardonically as well; instead of revering the teacher, Miguel mocks the teacher because, in the end, this teacher-sucker-reverend is a con artist whose flowery rhetoric and knowledge remain at a superficial level far removed from reality as Miguel knows and understands it. Miguel can discriminate between the theories, such as those of Freud or Merton, Thoreau or Mao, and the harsh realities of daily life within the walls of the prison.

And yet ironically, Miguel is only able to become worthy, at least in his own eyes, because of the reverend's lessons. The knowledge and language that the teacher provides are also the knowledge and language that Miguel uses to narrate the story we read and, finally, to reject the teacher: "I didn't take the book because, though I wanted his language, I wanted his language so bad, I also knew that that place is full of magicians, full of men like him" (Quiñonez, "First Book" 182).

"Graffiti Monk," the earliest story out of the four analyzed here, offers the most explicit manifesto about language and silence and the clearest sense of urgency in considering the non-verbal as a legitimate, indeed necessary, form of communication. In this story, Quiñonez's characters find self-expression in a number of forms that range from art, graffiti, music, stories, slang, and innovative uses of words. In explaining the inspiration behind this story, Quiñonez recalls that, while he was watching an MTV music video, the images of a "filthy and broken New York City" created a sense of longing in him, especially for the graffiti artists of the 70s and 80s. Despite the desolate atmosphere of those times, art was made, and it spoke to those in the *barrio* and, if it was on subway trains, to those outside the *barrio*. "We took all that neglect, crime, and poverty," he says, "and turned it into art" (Quiñonez, "Graffiti Monk" 254).

Quiñonez's story, then, recommends a recovery of a significant cultural mode—graffiti—lost to gentrification. When a city builds over the old and brings in the new (including inhabitants), an act of recovery and intervention is required, one that will pay homage and celebrate what has been lost and even deemed to be filth by outsiders. Quiñonez's own act of recovery is the story itself, "Graffiti Monk." It memorializes graffiti as a significant social movement, as well as paying tribute to the neighborhood that was heavily vested in this art form. His narrative creation also commemorates a geographical location that developers and city politicians saw as a cultural wasteland or a "sick neighborhood" (see Quiñonez's essay "The Fires Last Time").

"Graffiti Monk" is the story of two friends, Indio and Hector, who form part of the most popular graffiti crew in Spanish Harlem. Their crew, The Spanish Connection or TSC, is famous because of Indio, "the best graffiti writer in Spanish Harlem" (Quiñonez,

"Graffiti Monk" 233). But when Indio returns from prison, he is a changed person, a nonviolent monk-like individual, who enjoys reading more than tagging or creating new pieces of art. Graffiti, which has always been considered a somewhat destructive act of subversion and defiance, no longer fits within Indio's spiritual philosophy. He refuses to participate in creating any more of it, despite Hector's pleading that he do so. "I reminded him [Indio] of who he was. 'What are you talking about? You're the best. No one can do pieces like you, Indio. . . . Listen, just give it a few weeks, you'll be back with us in no time. We got to reclaim the 6 train, right? Right? The green line, that's ours, right?'" (249–250).

Hector is the protagonist and the narrator of the story. He is, in many ways, Quiñonez's alter-ego. Whereas Indio can give up the practice, Hector cannot because he has found salvation in graffiti art: "This was 1981," he says,

New York City had almost been bankrupt. It was a time when if things broke, they stayed broken. Poor neighborhoods were deserts full of vacant lots. It was a bleak time and I was a teenager stuck in a helpless ghetto. Then graffiti entered my life. To me, graffiti was the ultimate. The beat-up subway lines became an opportunity for me to create something to believe in. (Quiñonez, "Graffiti Monk" 238–239)

Graffiti, according to Hector, is a calling, and the artists are "writers" who risk their lives for the art form. It is, in short, a political, cultural, and spiritual mode of expression.

Hector's progression is toward commemorating his world, *el barrio*. The emotional language that guides him is made up of both nostalgia for the lost art form and a desire to honor it. Indio's progression is toward removing himself from it; he moves toward silence and then, literally, emotional and physical disappearance (he disappears from the *barrio*). At the center of Indio's transformation is an ancient text, *The Tibetan Book of the Dead*, imbued with the language of transcendence, of moving from the earthly to the otherworldly.

Within these two bookends of movement, there are layers of other languages. In particular, there is the unique vocabulary, the verbs and nouns, belonging to the world of graffiti: words such as "crew," "tags," "throw-up," "bomb," "pinched," "bite off," and "scrub" represent a technical and specialized vocabulary that invokes this culture of street and of subway art. There is also the language of books, such as the spiritual philosophical books that Indio reads despite not understanding them: "I don't understand these books," he tells Hector later in the story, "but they fill me up" (Quiñonez, "Graffiti Monk" 252). And there is the art itself, a language that fills Hector: "Nothing brought me more pleasure than to know that strangers were reading my words [his art], seeing my pieces whether they liked it or not . . . I was somebody" (253). And, of course, there is the story that we read.

The story's title, "Grafitti Monk," contains two seemingly irreconcilable nouns. Graffiti, long considered an act of vandalism by city officials and police, for example, is also a form of communication, a shouting of a community's existence to the outside world and to members of different *barrios* or ghettoes across the nation. Monk, in turn, is a spiritual person who usually retreats from the world (and word, often adopting a vow of silence). These nouns are opposites the way "reverend" and "sucker" in "The First Book" can be seen as opposites. They embody the tension between the verbal and the non-verbal that is palpable in all of Quiñonez's fiction.

In the end, says Quiñonez's fiction, the answer to the constraints of normative language can be found in a harmonious merging of sorts, a widening of disparate communicative tools. That is what he celebrates: Spanglish, Santería, graffiti art, conscientious silence. As Hector says,

> Subway graffiti had a short but glorious history. I still say the city blew it. Subway art could have been a tourist attraction. If done right, people would have come from all over the world to see our trains. Another artistic ghetto invention America could've exported like rap music. More beauty from the gutters of NYC. (Quiñonez, "Graffiti Monk" 252–253)

But Hector's dreams of what might have been do not materialize. Nor do the dreams of the narrator of "Taina's Song," who dreams of Taina's story becoming a miracle story, nor those of Miguel in "The

First Book," who dreams of what he will say when released from prison. These several dreams do not materialize. Still, Quiñonez, in his fiction, can dream for us and imagine a new world by depicting characters creating new languages or keeping silent like a monk, through imaginative miracles of Nuyorican immaculate conceptions or through moving art that "strangers" like us will read: "I never understood why Indio turned away from graffiti . . . . Back in those days, fame was the name of the game. 'I saw your tag in Far Rockaway, nice.' And I felt as if I had traveled all five boroughs. I was getting around. I was somebody" (Quiñonez, "Graffiti Monk" 253). For Quiñonez's characters, what matters is "being somebody;" for his readers, it is about knowing that the "somebody" has something to say.

Notes

1. The phrase is taken from George Steiner's seminal book of essays on language and silence.

2. See Ignacio F. Rodeño Iturriaga's article for an interesting study on the elements of the picaresque that appear in Quiñonez's novels.

3. See Sean Moiles and June Dwyer for more on gentrification.

Works Cited

Dwyer, June. "Reimagining the Ethnic Enclave: Gentrification, Rooted Cosmopolitanism, and Ernesto Quiñonez's *Chango's Fire*," *MELUS.* 34. 2 (Summer 2009): 125–139.

Quiñonez, Ernesto. "Author Q & A." *Bodega Dreams Publicity Page.* Penguin Random House, 2015. Web. 11 Oct. 2015. <http://www.penguinrandomhouse.com/books/136934/bodega-dreams-by-ernesto-quinonez/>.

_____. *Bodega Dreams.* New York: Vintage Press, 2000.

_____. *Chango's Fire.* New York: HarperPerennial, 2004.

_____. "The Fires Last Time." *New York Times.* The New York Times Company, 18 Dec. 2005. Web. 20 Jun. 2015. <http://www.nytimes.com/2005/12/18/nyregion/thecity/the-fires-last-time.html?_r=0>.

_____. "The First Book of the Sinner." *En el ojo del huracán: Nueva antología de narradores puertorriqueños*. Eds. Mayra Santos Febres & Ángel Darío Carrero. Columbia: Grupo Editorial Norma, 2011.

_____. "Graffiti Monk." *Lit Riffs Anthology*. Ed. Matthew Miele. New York: Simon & Schuster, 2004.

_____. "Taina's Song." *Gulf Coast* 20.2 (Summer/Fall 2008).

Rodeño Iturriaga, Ignacio F. "Ernesto Quiñonez's Fiction as a Picaresque Narrative" *CENTRO Journal* 20:2. (Fall 2008): 158–173.

Méndez, Susan C. "The Fire Between Them: Religion & Gentrification in Ernesto Quiñonez's *Changó's Fire*." *CENTRO Journal* 23.1 (Spring 2011): 177–195.

Moiles, Sean. "The Politics of Gentrification in Ernesto Quiñonez's Novels." *Critique*. 52.1 (2011): 114–133.

Steiner, George. *Language and Silence: Essays on Language, Literature, and the Inhuman*. New York: Atheneum, 1967.

Wiegand, Chris. "Ernesto Quiñonez: *Bodega Dreams*: Spanglish Stories." *Spike Magazine*. Spike Magazine, 1 Feb. 2001. Web. 15 Jun. 2015. <http://www.spikemagazine.com/0201bodegadreams.php>.

Heroic Insecurity in Junot Díaz's *Drown* and *This Is How You Lose Her*_____

David A. Colón

In June of 2008, soon after his novel *The Brief Wondrous Life of Oscar Wao* (2007) won him the Pulitzer Prize in Fiction, Junot Díaz made a guest appearance on Comedy Central's *The Colbert Report*. The audience applause dies down and Stephen Colbert, in character, begins the studio interview by asking, "Do you just carry this book around as, like, a pickup line? *'Sorry, can me and my Pulitzer Prize buy you ladies a drink?'*" Díaz appears shyly amused, perhaps daunted by appearing before more than a million viewers, equally ready for this kind of roast and not quite sure what to say: smiling, glancing down, wringing his hands. He politely deflects the line of inquiry, to which Colbert adds, "Do it, my man, do it. You will cut a swath through the literate femininity."

This exchange is rich with irony. The central character of *The Brief Wondrous Life of Oscar Wao*, Oscar de León, is an awkward, obese, nerdy Dominican American, who transitions to manhood within a social climate thick with *machismo*—a particularly Latino strain of male chauvinism typified by, above all else, the value of heterosexual male dominance. Only at the very beginning and the very end of the novel does Oscar enjoy any success in romantic pursuit of the opposite sex; the intermediate two decades are fraught with disappointment and disillusionment, largely because Oscar is a character completely at odds with the standards of *machista* masculinity so rife in his milieu. Much of this prevailing machismo is attributable to the character Yunior de las Casas, the principal narrator of *Oscar Wao* and self-proclaimed "biggest player of them all" (186) who becomes Oscar's college roommate and chief confidante. This is the same Yunior as the one in Díaz's first book, *Drown* (1996), a collection of short stories that together form a bildungsroman of Yunior's reckoning with his upbringing as a Latino youth straddling the worlds of the Dominican Republic and New Jersey. *Drown*, too, centers around the tension of a male submerged in a sea of machismo, where Yunior's older brother demonstrates how "to score points with the girls" (33), where his father brings him along to watch television at his mistress's apartment when Yunior is still at an impressionable age. The frank, colloquial, often crass language Díaz employs in his fiction to illustrate the sexist world and mindset of his characters has been the subject of numerous analyses by students, teachers, and critics of his work, both in praise of its candor and in derision of its lack of apology. Thus, when Stephen Colbert gives a sheepish Junot Díaz unsolicited advice on how to mobilize "the literate femininity" by dispatching his Pulitzer Prize into an effective pickup line, the ironies abound: that Díaz, inventor of both Oscar, whose idea of a pickup line is "We'll talk anon!" (*Oscar Wao* 183), and Yunior, proud to brag that he is immune to AIDS (*Drown* 51), would need coaching on the finer points of machismo from a priggish Anglo persona like Stephen Colbert's anchorman character is comedic absurdity at its finest.

But there is a greater subtlety behind Colbert's deadpan provocation. Díaz's exploration of the gamut of Latino masculinity in his fiction is predicated on the vulnerabilities and insecurities— sometimes masked, sometimes buried—of a young man who challenges the rules of the *machista* stereotype. The challenge is twofold, involving gender identity as well as immigrant identity, for Díaz portrays machismo in both its masculinity and its Dominicanness. His masculinities are constructed in the relationships male psyches have with girls and women; his Dominicanness is highlighted by lenses of non-Dominican perspectives: Anglo American, African American, and others, either in characters within the fiction or supposed audiences of the work. By these means, Díaz's fiction questions the premises of machismo, and since machismo is defined by arrogance, fearlessness, appetite, and cruelty, the foil to this drive would be a persona who exhibits opposite traits: self-doubt, reticence, discipline, and kindness. These qualities are blatant in the character of Oscar, but in Díaz's short stories, particularly in his two collections, *Drown* and *This Is How You Lose Her* (2013), the identity of Yunior is more nuanced and conflicted in this regard.

As the primary narrator of *Drown*, *Oscar Wao*, and *This Is How You Lose Her*, Yunior is the connective voice that speaks truth to *machista* power. The opening lines of *This Is How You Lose Her* capture the tension within Yunior's mind: "I'm not a bad guy. I know how that sounds—defensive, unscrupulous—but it's true. I'm like everybody else: weak, full of mistakes, but basically good. Magdalena disagrees though. She considers me a typical Dominican man: a sucio, an asshole" (3). Yunior's pervasive struggle is to deviate from the stereotype he has been nearly powerless to stop from internalizing and the self-reflection on this powerlessness, coupled with an expressed desire to be something different— to be less *machista* and, by extension, less unbridled—leads him to a profound sense of insecurity. Given that it is admirable for a Dominican American male author to place the pivotal ethos of machismo under critical scrutiny, and given how destabilizing the effect is on our inherited sense of Latino masculinity, it is revealing to consider Díaz's fiction through an analysis of heroic insecurity. The insecure hero—an amalgam of courage, shame, pride, and remorse—embodies the struggle that both Díaz and Yunior face in deconstructing the psychosocial structures of male chauvinism and conservative Latino cultural values and, therefore, will be the focus of the analysis of Díaz's short fiction in this essay.

Immaturity and Vulnerability in *Drown*

The opening story of *Drown*, "Ysrael," recalls the childhood summers Yunior spent in the rural enclaves, the "campo" (3), of the Dominican Republic with his brother Rafa. A feel for the tropical setting unfolds in tandem with a morbid curiosity growing into an all-consuming obsession: to see firsthand the disfigured face of a young neighbor named Ysrael. When Ysrael was "a baby a pig had eaten his face off, skinned it like an orange" (Díaz, *Drown* 7), and knowing this, Rafa quickly becomes fixated on finding Ysrael and forcing him to remove his mask. The task won't be easy: as Yunior explains, Ysrael "was about a foot bigger than either of us and looked like he'd been fattened on that supergrain the farmers around Ocoa were giving their stock" (15). Rafa, three years older than Yunior, has taken on the responsibility of toughening up his nine-year-old brother, and while sharing stories of sexual exploits (5–6) and swindling a bus driver out of fares (13) serve this purpose, the biggest lesson of all for Yunior becomes conquering the manchild Ysrael. Ysrael's brute strength and prowess as a wrestler (18) promise to make the mission dangerous, raising the bar of this test of Yunior's machismo.

But Yunior is uncomfortable with the demands Rafa makes of him. Yunior is too immature and thereby too vulnerable to shoulder the load of bravado that Rafa has begun to master. In one moment on the spectrum of Yunior's initiation into *machista* identity, Rafa recounts a series of experiences with girls, a telling peppered with sexual innuendo and juvenile absurdity, and as a captive audience, Yunior realizes how Rafa "was handsome and spoke out of the corner of his mouth. I was too young to understand most of what he said, but I listened to him anyway, in case these things might be useful in the future" (Díaz, *Drown* 6). Such an admission of ignorance about sex and a sensitivity attuned to the charisma of his brother are signs of the holdover of Yunior's pre-*machista* psyche and surely things of which Rafa would disapprove—for "Díaz's male characters... empathy is a dangerous and problematic sentiment" (Riofrio 28). Later in "Ysrael," the boys take a ride, and on the bus, Yunior is suddenly molested by a man feigning to help Yunior wipe away a stain on his shorts (Díaz, *Drown* 12). Afterwards, Yunior succumbs to the stress and weeps. Rafa doesn't hesitate to admonish Yunior for being "a pussy" (13), adding, "You have to get tougher. Crying all the time. Do you think our papi's crying? Do you think that's what he's been doing the last six years?" (14). Their father had left them in Santo Domingo years ago and is living somewhere in the Northeastern US. The exchange reveals that both boys are especially vulnerable to the pressures of *machista* conformity: that they "must create, out of the romanticized vestiges of their imaginations, their own vision of masculinity, a hyper-masculinity hopelessly disconnected to reality and selfish in the way that only adolescent machismo allows" (Riofrio 27). Without a present father, Rafa has assumed a paternal role for Yunior, and thus we discover that Yunior is being fathered by a mere boy imagining what a father should say and do. And to an extent, Yunior in this episode answers the call—he doesn't tell Rafa what happened to him on the bus, perhaps because, at least to some degree, he has gotten the message to take it like a man.

When the boys finally encounter Ysrael, Rafa's and Yunior's respective intentions diverge, even if both intentions initially appear innocuous. Rafa asks Ysrael where the closest "colmado" is to buy his younger brother a soda (Díaz, *Drown* 15), and Yunior compliments Ysrael on his kite-flying skills (16). As the scene develops, Rafa's dialogue is as weighted by disingenuousness as is Yunior's lightened by amiability. Rafa is lying when he insists that drinking the local water would make Yunior sick, and he pretends he cannot find the colmado and needs Ysrael's guidance. However, when Ysrael confides that his father got him his kite in New York, Yunior shouts without pretension, "No shit! Our father's there, too!" (16). Rafa asks Ysrael why he wears a mask as if he doesn't know the reason, but Yunior reveals that he is already aware of Ysrael's interest in wrestling and, at one point, intimately taps Ysrael on the arm to get his attention (18). At the moment when "[t]he mask twitched" and Yunior "realized he was smiling," Rafa smashes the soda bottle on Ysrael's head and knocks him to the ground. Yunior's response is pure shock—"Holy fucking shit" (18)—an indication that this sudden attack was not only one against Ysrael, but also against Yunior's innocence. The reactions of the two brothers to seeing Ysrael's face, once unmasked, are opposite as well: Yunior pleads with his brother to leave, while "Rafa crouched and using only two of his fingers, turned Ysrael's head from side to side" (19).

This opening story establishes several elements of heroic insecurity as key to the makeup of Yunior's character in *Drown*. The love-crushing indifference of machismo extends to every reach of Yunior's existence, but it does not stop him from expressing intermittent sympathies. Similar to how he recognizes Rafa's charm for a brief moment in "Ysrael," Yunior begins the narration of the second story, "Fiesta, 1980" with a portrayal of his father's adulterous habits (Díaz, *Drown* 23) followed by an adoring, if fleeting, tribute to his young mother: "She smelled like herself, like the wind through a tree" (24). Yunior's compassion is at once brave and uncertain; it makes faint flashes between longer descriptions of harsh attitudes that establish this more prevalent atmosphere as essentially the challenge his life must overcome. In "Ysrael," the mischief that Rafa and Yunior involve themselves in moves beyond the matter that boys will be boys and enters the realm of the picaresque, in which bragging, cunning, flouting authority, and flirting with disaster coat the surface of Yunior's persona, underneath which lie core memories of moral failings and emotional defeats.

In the story "Edison, New Jersey," we encounter Yunior as a young man, and by this point in his life, he seems to have mastered— or perhaps been mastered by—the braggadocious style of a full-fledged *machista*. He is employed by a company that sells billiards tables and, on deliveries with his partner Wayne, he welcomes any chance for hijinks: inside customers' homes, he says, "I've been caught roaming around plenty of times but you'd be surprised how quickly someone believes you're looking for the bathroom if you don't jump when you're discovered, if you just say, Hi" (Díaz, *Drown* 123). In the company's showroom, he has made it a habit to "slouch behind the front register and steal" (125). Wayne is married, but more committed to philandering, a suitable replacement to the companionship of Rafa now that Yunior is no longer a child. And as in "Ysrael," in "Edison, New Jersey," Yunior is less than at ease with Wayne's tales of promiscuity, although in the latter story it is not for lack of experience, but rather for a recent, profound breakup with a woman Yunior refers to only as "the girlfriend." Yunior indulges Wayne as Wayne's distant pursuit of a colleague, Charlene, travels its rise and fall, but Yunior's parallel romantic fortunes in this story have a different substance. His inner lament about his failed relationship with the girlfriend spurs an interest in a woman they meet at a customer's house, an attractive young Dominican who might be the maid, but perhaps more. She resents her boss, and, once Yunior speaks with her in Spanish, she asks him to give her a ride back to Washington Heights where her family lives. Yunior obliges. On the way, he lays his hand in her lap, but she is unresponsive (137); after she's gone, Yunior lies to Wayne, covering the fact that she spurned his advance, declaring "[h]omegirl was an animal. I still have the teeth marks" (138).

Even though Yunior in "Edison, New Jersey" is more than twice as old as he is in "Ysrael," his sensitive nature, a mixture of innocence and vulnerability, has not really changed: it is only masked by a fluency he lacked as a boy. The savvy is surface; what we see of Yunior as a man is the evolved product of an impressionable boy once prescient enough to take mental notes "in case these things might be useful in the future," and the things in question are the keys to machismo. But the way he handles his intimate knowledge of machismo undermines its ethos. The story "How to Date a Browngirl, Blackgirl, Whitegirl, or Halfie" places somewhere in the middle of the timeline of Yunior's maturation and thus illustrates the delicate balance Díaz strikes in Yunior's psyche. "How to Date…" is narrated in second-person voice, underscoring its imperative manner, and provides a primer on dating in his hardscrabble neighborhood, "the Terrace." The tone of instructiveness erects a magisterial façade that earns confidence in its attention to detail, but from the very beginning we know this is merely an adolescent speaking:

> Clear the government cheese from the refrigerator. If the girl's from the Terrace stack the boxes behind the milk. If she's from the Park or Society Hill hide the cheese in the cabinet above the oven, way up where she'll never see. Leave yourself a reminder to get it out before morning or your moms will kick your ass. Take down any embarrassing photos of your family in the campo, especially the one with the half-naked kids dragging a goat on a rope leash. The kids are your cousins and by now they're old enough to understand why you're doing what you're doing. (Díaz, *Drown* 143)

The delicate balance in Yunior's psyche is between extremes: extreme courage and extreme fear, extreme confidence and extreme insecurity. Here we have a boy, most likely thirteen, composing his own field manual on how to con middle-school girls into sex, or "at least get a hand job" (Díaz, *Drown* 144). His posturing as an expert belies his multidirectional impotence—his mother might kill him, the neighborhood bully might kill him (146), his date's father might kill him (144–145)—and there are overwhelming odds that, in the end, all of the outlined measures will result in nothing but rejection and low morale (148). There is also the matter of his Dominicanness, which oscillates between asset and liability. In certain situations, "She'll say, I like Spanish guys" (148); in others, she'll correct "your busted-up Spanish" (145). Yunior commands the reader to appreciate the white girl's features, hair, and skin, "because, in truth, you love them more than you love your own" (147). The uncooperative tugging of so many social forces in all directions, with a lonely, sad teenager hopelessly in the middle, generates sympathy, a definitive aspect of a literary hero. A hero also exudes enviable talents or morality, and in Yunior's case, these go hand in hand—his talent is to express the emotional nuances of a Dominican American masculinity that responds to machismo without being entirely of it.

The title story, "Drown," is a full display of virtually all of Yunior's vulnerabilities. Set during the years surrounding his high school graduation, it provides a portrait of his friendship with his peer Beto. Yunior identifies Beto in the opening paragraph as "a pato" (Díaz, *Drown* 91), the Dominican slur for a gay man, insinuating that Beto's homosexuality was a root cause of undoing their relationship. The tone of the story is palpably defeatist: lazy, resigned, melancholic. In the summer, the "heat in the apartments was like something heavy that had come inside to die" (92); in a swimming pool, "everything above is loud and bright, everything below is whispers" (93). The tone is also confessional, with most attention paid to Yunior's relationships with Beto and with his mother, moving back and forth between the two and establishing an emotional parallel. Yunior's mother has lost all *joie de vivre*—"She has discovered the secret to silence: pouring café without a splash, walking between rooms as if gliding on a cushion of felt, crying without a sound" (94). She mourns the loss of her husband, Yunior's father, who is in Florida living with another woman and only calls when in need of money or self-esteem (101). Yunior shares her burden, the absence of his father—and the conspicuous absence of Rafa—a deficit he seems to fill with intimacy from Beto.

At a dramatic pivot in the story, he admits that he had sexual relations with Beto: "Twice. That's it" (Díaz, *Drown* 103). The details of the encounters are sparse, shrouded in *machista* shame, and effectively presented as moments of weakness when he was starved of unconditional, fatherly, and brotherly love. Yunior himself cannot offer much of an explanation as to why he accepted Beto's advances, even if the author Díaz effectively employs foreshadowing. When Yunior was molested on the bus in "Ysrael," it was a disgrace he would not divulge to Rafa, his confidante and guardian, but in "Drown," Yunior divulges his affair with Beto to the reader, an affair that can equally be construed as abuse. Such an increase in candor signals Yunior's heightened sensitivity. It is palpable that the strain on the family of the abandonment by Yunior's father, Ramón, has grown heavy, forecasting the need to narrate Ramón's struggles as an immigrant in the book's final story, "Negocios," in which Ramón is depicted as living in emotional states not completely unlike those of Yunior, whom Díaz has said "lives most of the time terrified" ("Growing the Hell Up" n.p.). Dispersing the terror of shouldering the *machista* burden within an uncertain, emasculating world, Díaz infuses Yunior and Ramón with fears and anxieties that carry over to a later portrayal of the character Ysrael in the story "No Face."

"No Face" is a divergence from the rest of the collection in that Yunior is not present in the story, but it is precisely this parallel to Yunior's isolating experience throughout *Drown* that magnifies the themes of immaturity and vulnerability in establishing the centrality of heroic insecurity. Narrated in a present-tense, third-person voice, "No Face" is a portal to the point of view of Ysrael and the cruel, often inhumane treatment he suffers. A cleaning lady yells "from the kitchen, Stay away from here. Don't you have any shame?" (Díaz, *Drown* 155); a driver shouts insults, accusing him of eating cats (155); a group of boys assault him, threatening him with rape (156). In between these episodes, other characters show him pity, especially a priest named Father Lou, but the kindnesses are not enough to counteract the abject abuse he endures nearly constantly. Ysrael has internalized the voices of his tormentors, reflexively turning down an invitation to watch television with a neighbor (155) and admonishing himself for having a night terror, only to calm down once he "tells himself to be a man" (158). Ysrael is trapped in a stunted state of immaturity even though all signs indicate he is a grown man, or nearly so. He starts his day with pull-ups on a tree branch, "nearly fifty now" (153), and weighs enough to worry Father Lou that he could tip them off their motorcycle if he leans into the turns (158). But Ysrael's tactics with coping with the stress of his disfigurement are childlike; he narrates his actions with exclamations—"FLIGHT" (153), "INVISIBILITY" (155), "STRENGTH" (156)—as if he were playing make-believe, imagining himself a superhero in a comic book. Like Yunior, Ysrael is powerless to withstand the unrelenting pressure that equally pulls him to and repels him from the threshold of masculine dignity, and the more he is subjected to this contradictory force, the more his psyche stretches to hold together an expanding division of self.

Machismo-as-Tragic Flaw in *This Is How You Lose Her*

While *Drown* has the effect of a bildungsroman, *This Is How You Lose Her* is more tragic. It begins with Yunior as an adult dating a woman named Magda and an immediate confession that he has ruined their relationship by being unfaithful, news of which travels to Magda from the other woman Cassandra because "homegirl wrote her a fucking *letter*. And the letter had *details*" (Díaz, *This Is How* 3). The tragic flaw of our hero is initial and blatant and recognizable as a kind of hubris. By his own account, Yunior has desired, respected, even admired Magda, but for uncertain reasons—as uncertain to him as they are to the audience—he has been compelled to cheat. The motivation for Yunior to pursue another woman is portrayed as deriving from little more than the fact that she flirted heavily, and the onset of Yunior's guilt is so immediate that he actually phones Magda while still in bed for the first time with Cassandra (20). If anyone appears confident about knowing the reason behind Yunior's infidelity, it is Magda's friends:

> All of Magda's friends say I cheated because I was Dominican, that all us Dominican men are dogs and can't be trusted. I doubt that I can

speak for all Dominican men but I doubt they can either. From my perspective it wasn't genetics; there were reasons. Causalities. (Díaz, *This Is How* 18–19)

In spite of Yunior asserting that he had his reasons, he doesn't go on to provide any justifiable rationale. His thoughts on the matter have little chance to wander before reaching dead ends; his actions would give Magda's friends no reason for pause. In this opening story ("Magda"), as in the rest of *This Is How You Lose Her*, Yunior maintains a capacity for earning sympathy—if only for a formidable intelligence undermined by the pathetic limits of his self-reflection—that is corrupted by an unrootable tragic flaw: machismo.

The connective telos of "Magda" is the story of a vacation that Yunior takes with her to the Dominican Republic. After her parents and friends have expressed their disdain for him (Díaz, *This Is How* 4) and their respective friends have offered their loyal counsel (4, 7), Yunior and Magda resume their relationship in uncertainty. She becomes more aloof and insensitive to him, and Yunior confides, "I know what she was doing. Making me aware of my precarious position in her life. Like I was not aware" (7). This precariousness is mirrored in Díaz's method of narration; tenses shift from present to past to present continuous to past perfect to future to conditional in unexpected ways, as if the whole of the story consumes his memory, the present moment, and his hopes for the future. The slippages underscore his own lack of confidence as to what really happened and why, a confusion that extends to his decision to go ahead as planned with the trip that they had scheduled long before. Once in the Dominican Republic, he brings her to visit his grandfather (10), but very soon, she conveys that she is bored and would rather be at a beachside resort (12). The rest of the trip is painful to read: their discomfort with each other grows by the hour, and within a day or two, she asks for some space to herself, suggesting that "maybe once a day, you do one thing, I do another" (15).

The two times that Magda exercises her right to alone time, Yunior takes drinks at the bar with a pair of characters named the Vice-President and Bárbaro. In the episode when he first meets

---

them, Yunior claims "I must have the footprint of fresh disaster on my face" (Díaz, *This Is How* 17); the second time, he knows his relationship with Magda is beyond repair, saying "I feel unmoored and don't have a clue what comes next. This is the endgame" (21). Yunior unburdens himself to them, and they play the role of a sympathetic audience. But they are so predisposed to a *machista* outlook that they are powerless to help Yunior recover good judgment. The first bit of advice the Vice-President offers Yunior is that "[j]ealousy is the best way to jump-start a relationship." Yunior then says that Magda smacked him when she first found out about the affair with Cassandra, and in response the Vice-President gives his second bit of advice: "They only hit you…when they care" (18). It is clear that Yunior is seeking something different from the Vice-President and Bárbaro when confiding in them about Magda—a way of being more pliable, less automated, expanding his capacity for honest intimacy—but his lack of inner resources is rendered only more futile in the company of stereotypical *machistas* like the Vice-President and Bárbaro. They are the rhetors of his inarticulate subconscious, a chorus voicing the principles of his self-destructive behavior. In the end, there is no recovering Magda's affection, and no amount of contemplation or remorse can undo the persistent damage of his *machista* ways.

The second story in *This Is How You Lose Her*, "Nilda," adds a profound layer of tragedy to the collection: it shows that when Yunior was in high school, Rafa died of cancer. "Nilda" and the later stories "The Pura Principle" and "Miss Lora" together complete the story of Rafa's demise and, by doing so, intertextually complete the storyline of Rafa set forth in *Drown*. These stories in effect explain the depth of depression that Yunior and his mother were experiencing in the title story of *Drown*, when Yunior turns to Beto for unlikely love, and Mami, once vibrant and giving, has collapsed, sullen and aimless. It is not all because Ramón is away but, as subsequently revealed in *This Is How You Lose Her*, also because Rafa is dead. On a timeline of events, Rafa's death happens shortly before the setting of "Drown": in "The Pura Principle," Yunior notes that he himself "was seventeen and a half" (Díaz, *This Is How* 91). The tragedy of Rafa's young death reverberates throughout the total portrayal of Yunior in all three of Díaz's books. The lessons Yunior learns from Rafa about the ways of men—surrogates for Ramón's failures as a father—all come from their childhood. Yunior never experiences manhood together with his brother, and, as strong as Rafa's influence is on him, Yunior balks at the chance to mature in his masculine outlook and sense of self. The masculinity that Yunior inherits from the teachings of Rafa are frozen in time, a perception of manhood perpetually stuck in boyhood. Yunior observes that, at first, the specter of death had little effect on Rafa's persona:

> Dude had lost eighty pounds to the chemo, looked like a break-dancing ghoul (my brother was the last motherfucker in the Jerz to give up his tracksuit and rope chain), had a back laced with spinal-tap scars, but his swagger was more or less where it had been before the illness: a hundred percent loco. He prided himself on being the neighborhood lunatic, wasn't going to let a little thing like cancer get in the way of his official duties. (Díaz, *This Is How* 93)

That said, in the end, Rafa does change. "The Pura Principle" details Rafa's last romantic relationship with a woman, Pura, and it is clear that Rafa had become a different person: "He was definitely more caballero with Pura than he'd been with his other girls. Opening doors. Talking all polite…A lot of his ex-girls would have died to see this Rafa. This was the Rafa they'd all been waiting for" (Díaz, *This Is How* 105).

But Rafa's judgment is too impaired for this sea change to count as virtue. Despised by both Yunior and Mami, Pura proves to be selfish and conniving, likely the driving force behind Rafa's stealing money and items from their home. A brief lifetime of objectifying and manipulating girls and women leaves Rafa unequipped to choose a deserving partner to treat with generosity. Between *Drown* and *This Is How You Lose Her*, the rise and fall of Rafa parallels Yunior's ongoing predicament: the more he tries to be a real man, the more he suffers indignities. The perverted version of manhood encapsulated by machismo is the tragic flaw that neither Rafa nor

Yunior can escape. The final story of *This Is How You Lose Her*, "The Cheater's Guide to Love," spans six years rife with episodes of self-doubt, depression, envy, and failed relationships. It begins with the lines, "Your girl catches you cheating. (Well, actually she's your fiancée, but hey, in a bit it *so* won't matter.)" (Díaz, *This Is How* 175). It ends with the lines, "you know in your lying cheater's heart that sometimes a start is all we ever get" (213). To the very end, Yunior cannot inspire hope that he will overcome his compulsion for self-sabotage, "retreading the same circuit over and over" through an "active participation in maintaining the terms of [his] own exclusion" (Stringer 114, 113). His last words are those of a person incapable of long-lasting, healthy intimacy. That he can articulate the idea with such honesty and fluidity allow for him to be considered a sort of hero, a pitiable, vulnerable hero.

Works Cited

Díaz, Junot. *Drown*. New York: Riverhead Books, 1996.

_____. "Growing the Hell Up: From Middle Earth to NJ." Interview by Richard Wolinsky. *Guernica: A Magazine of Art and Politics*. Guernica, 2012. Web. 1 Jul. 2015.

_____. *The Brief Wondrous Life of Oscar Wao*. New York: Riverhead Books, 2007.

_____. *This Is How You Lose Her*. New York: Riverhead Books, 2013.

"Junot Díaz." *The Colbert Report*. Comedy Central, 18 Jun. 2008. Web. 1 Jul. 2015.

Riofrio, John. "Situating Latin American Masculinity: Immigration, Empathy, and Emasculation in Junot Díaz's *Drown*." *Atenea* 28.1 (2008): 23–36.

Stringer, Dorothy. "Passing and the State in Junot Díaz's *Drown*." *MELUS* 38.2 (2013): 111–126.

Resignifying Wounds through Silences in Edwidge Danticat's *The Dew Breaker*

Rebecca Fuchs

Sólo los tontos creen que el silencio es un vacío. No está vacío nunca. Y a veces la mejor manera de comunicarse es callando. (Eduardo Galeano)

(Only the simple-minded believe that silence is a vacuum. It is never empty. Sometimes, the best way to communicate is to be silent.—my translation)

The Dew Breaker (2004) by the Haitian American writer Edwidge Danticat consists of nine closely interrelated short stories. Some critics regard the work as a novel (Conwell 221; Kaussen 201; Mehta 8; Parisot 214; Thomas 100; and Kalisa 174). However, in the context of this essay's main topics—trauma and silence—it is more enriching to read the text as a short story cycle. Forrest L. Ingram, who wrote the first critical study on story cycles, defines the genre as "a book of short stories so linked to each other by their author that the reader's successive experience on various levels of the pattern of the whole significantly modifies his experience of each of its component parts" (19). The stories of a cycle can be read independently as well as in their interrelation as one work. In contrast to a story collection or a compilation, the short story cycle is characterized by interdependencies and connections between the stories. In addition to relationships between the characters and plots of one story and another, a short story cycle also offers variations on a theme, all of which the following analysis of *The Dew Breaker* brings out.

In *The Dew Breaker*, each story or story chapter is narrated or reflected by a different character. One of the main interconnections between these single story chapters is the title character and protagonist, a man called 'the Dew Breaker,' to whom all of the other characters are connected in one way or another. A 'dew breaker' in Haitian Creole is a *Tonton Macoute* or bogeyman, a member of the secret police in the service of the dictators François and later his son Jean-Claude Duvalier—also known as Papa Doc and Baby Doc—the successive presidents who operated a violent dictatorial regime in Haiti from 1957 to 1986. For these two despots, the *Tonton Macoutes* killed and tortured people opposed to the regime or suspected of any form of resistance.

By choosing the form of the story cycle, Danticat gives voice to the dew breaker's victims (met in "The Bridal Seamstress"), the children of his victims (met in "Night Talkers"), his family members (in "The Book of the Dead" and "The Book of Miracles"), people affected by the regime's violence (in "The Funeral Singer"), and to the torturer himself (in "The Dew Breaker"). The form, in other words, empowers all of the characters to narrate their own stories. This is significant because, as the psychologist and critic Grada Kilomba explains, narrating one's own story is a political act and a form of liberation from colonial relics, such as the dictatorial violence in Danticat's text. Taking the part of one of the burdened, Kilomba argues that as a describer of one's own history, "... I become the narrator, and the writer of my own reality, the author and the authority on my own history. In this sense, I become the absolute opposition of what the colonial project has predetermined" (12). By unsilencing historical acts of violence, hitherto oppressed people become empowered subjects capable of resisting the historiographic processes of silencing and thus of coming to terms with their traumatizations resulting from these oppressive practices. Therefore, Danticat's story cycle emphasizes the need for ever new negotiations of the lingering effects of historical violence and trauma.

Nevertheless, Danticat is criticized for equipping her characters with too little agency and too much symbolism as well as emotionality. In this vein, the critic Aitor Ibarrola Armendariz writes that Danticat's attempt at "unravelling and constructing a collective past" is characterized by "an emotional involvement which, some would say, verges on the pathological" (33). In this paper, however, the fictional rendering of trauma is regarded as a form of agency expressed in the short story cycle as a multi-voiced chorus. This chorus refrains from proposing one simple truth, but represents the complexity of trauma's different aspects and also offers diverse means of coming to terms with wounds.

Another important consequence of choosing the form of the short story cycle is the emergence of the dew breaker as a bifurcated man who is both a former torturer in the service of the dictatorship in Haiti and a loving father and husband in the United States. Indeed, it was just after killing a prisoner whom he was supposed to release that the dew breaker left Haiti. With Anne, the step-sister of his last victim and the woman who would later become his wife, he secretly moved to the US and named himself M. Bienaimé. In the beginning, Anne is the only person who knows his true identity; their daughter Ka believes her father to be a victim of the dictatorship, since he wears a big scar across his face that he actually received from his last victim, Anne's step-brother. As a consequence of the different views on the dew breaker, the short story cycle as a whole complicates and destabilizes one story's simpler truth. The dew breaker does not merely represent a villain who is entirely evil. Instead, he emerges as a human being with more facets, a man who is also capable of loving his wife and daughter and who is being loved by them in return.

The multi-voiced narrative situation reinforced by the form of the story cycle therefore appropriately expresses the paradoxes and contradictions Danticat deals with in the book: How can a former torturer be a loving father and husband? How can Anne fall in love with her step-brother's murderer? How can their daughter Ka endure the truth about her father? How can the victims go on living? How can the unspeakable—violence and trauma—be expressed in words? Rather than answering all of these questions, this essay shows that the form of the short story cycle permits oppositional entities to persist side by side without reducing complex meanings to simple truths. Instead of telling one coherent and complete story, the story cycle rather leaves gaps and jumps between different characters, settings, plots, and themes. One of these gaps is silence, both as a thematic connector resulting from trauma and as a symbolic act employed by the cycle's characters. The cycle allows for silences if speaking is not possible and thereby emphasizes the complexity of trauma that cannot simply be healed by speaking out aloud. In Danticat's text, silences then become an alternative form of communication that can stand for different phenomena: survival or death, pain or healing, speechlessness or communication.

In her story cycle, Danticat embraces all these seeming contradictions and oppositions and interweaves them in her storytelling. Even if her characters are not completely healed in the end, they find means of survival and of living with their traumas by appropriating silences, as will be demonstrated by my analysis here of the story chapter "Water Child." Beforehand, it would be helpful to reflect upon the tensions between speaking and silence in the context of traumatization and to reflect upon them in brief relation to other of the cycle's stories.

Trauma in *The Dew Breaker*

In most texts about trauma theory, speaking about one's trauma is considered to be the only path to healing. The trauma theorist Cathy Caruth defines a trauma as "an overwhelming experience of sudden or catastrophic events in which the response to the events occurs in the often delayed, uncontrolled repetitive appearance of hallucinations and other intrusive phenomena" (*Unclaimed* 11). In its reaction to such a shock, the psyche develops defense mechanisms, among them silence. One example is Dany in "Night Talkers," who is also Eric's neighbor in "Seven." As a six-year-old boy, Dany witnesses how the dew breaker not only kills his parents, but then also threatens the boy by screaming at him: "Shut up now or I'll shoot you too!" (*DB* 105). The dew breaker does not physically harm Dany. Nevertheless, Dany, both as boy and then later as a man, 'shuts up' emotionally and falls into a traumatized silence as a response to the horror and fear he experienced. In "The Book of the Dead," Ka learns that her father was a dew breaker rather than a victim of the dictatorship, as she previously assumed. She furthermore finds out that her mother has always known this fact without telling her. As a reaction to her parents' betrayal, Ka becomes speechless (cf. *DB* 242).

However, an absolute silence about a traumatic experience keeps the trauma alive and even reinforces its effects. Therefore, it is essential for trauma's victims to develop techniques of communicating their hurt (though, of course, doing so does not guarantee healing). Trauma is a complex phenomenon with both a physical and a psychological dimension. Even after the physical wound has healed, the psychological one often remains.

Another feature of the traumas prevalent in Danticat's story cycle is their range across generations. The dew breaker's victims' memories and the children's imaginations of their parents' sufferings linger as unresolved traumas that limit their lives in various ways. Trauma can be passed on across generations as what the memory theorist Marianne Hirsch calls "postmemory," which she describes as "the relationship of the second generation to powerful, often traumatic, experiences that preceded their births but that were nevertheless transmitted to them so deeply as to seem to constitute memories in their own right" (103). For instance, in "The Funeral Singer," Freda becomes a funeral singer when her father drowns himself in the ocean after being tortured by *macoutes*. She sings at funerals to reclaim her father and to mourn his loss. When she is asked to sing at the national palace, she refuses and has to leave Haiti (cf. *DB* 172). As a consequence, her songs additionally become her means of resisting the people who killed her father.

However, not only the victims' children in *The Dew Breaker* suffer from postmemory. The dew breaker, too, suffers from a so-called perpetrator's trauma of guilt, shame, remorse and horror (cf. Fuchs 143–48; cf. La Capra 79), aspects of which he in turn passes on to his daughter Ka. After her father's confession to her in "The Book of the Dead," Ka is no longer capable of working as an artist (cf. *DB* 31) because her father as victim had been her only subject. Imagining his nightmares, they become her own: "Maybe he dreams of dipping his hands in the sand on a beach in his own country and finding that what he comes up with is a fistful of blood" (*DB* 30). Thus, perpetrators also pass on their burdens of guilt to their progeny. This state, which could be called 'post-guilt,' also carries with it trauma's horrific symptoms.

Another point to remember is that victims' and perpetrators' traumas, though alike in many ways, are distinguishable in other regards. Victims' traumas are mental survival reactions and posttraumatic stress disorders that the historical scientist Ruth Leys describes as emanating from the split of the mind that is:

> unable to register the wound to the psyche because the ordinary mechanisms of awareness and cognition are destroyed. [...] The experience of the trauma, fixed or frozen in time, refuses to be represented *as* past, but is perpetually re-experienced in a painful, dissociated, traumatic present. (2; emphasis original)

Perpetrators, in contrast, rather suffer from guilt and shame. Additionally, as in the dew breaker's case, they fear persecution and punishment, which is why they often do not admit their crimes. Consequently, they prevent themselves from coming to terms with their guilt.

As a former Haitian torturer anonymously living in the US, the dew breaker hides his real name beneath the fake identity 'M. Bienaimé' in order to avoid detention and persecution. His psychological disturbances become obvious in his obsession with *The Egyptian Book of the Dead*, which he uses to indirectly confess his guilt, for instance by constantly quoting from the part "The Negative Confession." After reading to his daughter "I am not a violent man" (*DB* 23), he tells her that she "should have heard something beyond what he was reading. [She] should have removed the negatives" (*DB* 23; cf. Fuchs 144). He needs decades before he is able to tell her the truth. In spite of these fundamental differences between traumas felt both by victim and by perpetrator, both trauma types have something in common: they often result in silence and a continuation of the trauma's power.

To make matters worse, the difficulty of speaking about a trauma is further reinforced by the fact that language is hardly reliable in expressing pain and runs the risk of trivializing and homogenizing experienced violence (Assmann 260; Scarry 4). Thus, language is at one and the same time both deficient for expressing trauma and necessary for the healing of wounds. Faced with this paradox, the traumatized person's subconscious looks for alternative forms of communication to soothe the remnants of pain and suffering. And, again, in another paradox, silence itself is among the alternative forms of communication, for silence has the capacity to relativize the contradictory impact of language and support the process of de-encapsulating trauma. A trauma is often encapsulated, that is, isolated from consciousness. Caruth, therefore, describes trauma as:

> not simply an effect of destruction but also, fundamentally, an enigma of survival. It is only by recognizing traumatic experience as a paradoxical relation between destructiveness and survival that we can also recognize the legacy of incomprehensibility at the heart of the catastrophic experience. (58)

Indeed, by interpreting silences in this way, I argue here that Danticat's use of silence and speech is not conflictive, but complementary. Rather than being absolute opposites, silence and speech are interrelated entities in constant tension, and this tension is reflected in the formal interrelations between the story chapters within the short story cycle.

Since storytelling itself is an act of speaking, it includes and helps to bear silences resulting from traumatizations. For Danticat, writing is an act of survival. In her earlier story cycle *Krik? Krak!* (1996), she has one of her characters utter: "You thought that if you didn't tell stories, the sky would fall on your head. ... This fragile sky has terrified you your whole life. Silences terrify you more than the pounding of a million pieces of steel chopping away at your flesh" (223). In *The Dew Breaker*, Danticat, just like her character Ka, becomes "the keeper of both speech and silence" (*DB* 32). The writer builds words around these terrifying silences to come closer and closer to the core, to the event that caused a trauma. Rather than being mere gaps saying nothing as a consequence of an encapsulated trauma, silences in her texts always communicate something and become tools of communicating if speaking is impossible or too painful. This is particularly important, since a society that immerses itself in speechlessness rather than trying to face its own traumas always runs the risk of being drawn into new maelstroms of violence (Borst 219).

In *The Dew Breaker*, silence has many empowering features. For instance, in "The Book of the Dead," the dew breaker finally manages to break his silence and tells his daughter that "your father was the hunter, he was not the prey" (*DB* 20), thereby facing her rejection and his own shame and guilt. In "The Dew Breaker," the preacher breaks the silence about the regime's violence through radio broadcasts and is ready to be tortured and killed rather than stay silent. His act of breaking an enforced silence is revolutionary and costs him his life. In the same story chapter, Valia, one of the dew breaker's torture victims, keeps silent about her husband's whereabouts, which her tormentor wants her to give away. Her silence protects a critic of the regime and makes the torturer realize that he is not almighty. Dany in "Night Talkers" suffers from his parents' violent death caused by the dew breaker—a death that he has witnessed as a boy. He comes to Haiti to talk about the trauma with his aunt. Although they are unable to do so due to his traumatization, they nevertheless have a conversation in his dream and keep silent in reality (Fuchs 119–39). These different forms of silence are all directly linked to the dew breaker and his torturing. However, in "Water Child," Nadine suffers from a trauma that can only very indirectly be linked to the Haitian dictatorship.

Silence in "Water Child"

Nadine is a Haitian immigrant who came to the US to work as a nurse. Working in an "Ear, Nose and Throat" section of a hospital (*DB* 55), Nadine has to care for patients after laryngectomies and has to acquaint them with the shock that "they would no longer be able to talk" (*DB* 55) after their operations. Rather than merely observing others' voicelessness and concomitant pain, Nadine suffers from her own trauma: an abortion. Her ex-lover Eric is the connection between Nadine and the dew breaker. In the previous story chapter ("Seven)," Eric is introduced as one of the dew breaker's tenants. After seven years of separation from his wife, Eric brings her from

Haiti to the US, which means the end of his relationship with Nadine and their decision to abort their child. Eric is married to another woman and is not willing to found a family with her. Alone, she cannot raise the child, since she works not only to earn her own livelihood, but also to help her poor and sick parents in Haiti, who sacrificed everything for Nadine to help her realize her dream of "seeing the world, of making her own way in it" (*DB* 63). This is why she wants to repay them for what they had done for her with "half her salary every month, and sometimes more" (*DB* 63).

Since the abortion, Nadine has not been able to communicate with others. With her colleague Josette, Nadine "barely spoke at all" (*DB* 55). Her other colleagues dislike Nadine because of her "cold silence" (*DB* 59). She has been incapable of calling her parents in Haiti (cf. *DB* 54). After dialing their number, she cannot speak because she thinks "her voice might betray all that she could not say" (*DB* 57). Direct speech would give away too much and "[c]alling them … always made her wish to be the one guarded, rather than the guardian, to be reassured now and then that some wounds could heal, that some decisions would not haunt her forever" (*DB* 63). In addition, "[t]hey never spoke of difficult things during these phone calls…" (*DB* 64), which is why Nadine does not find the courage to put her pain into words.

Her trauma capsule remains intact. Nadine mourns in silence, traumatized by her own decision to abort her child, an act Eric persuaded her to perform. She feels guilty and isolates herself from all the people around her and from those she loves, and also from Eric, who regularly calls her. Even though Eric speaks on her answering machine in English, French, and Creole, no language reaches her. Instead, she collects the cassettes of her answering machine with his voice on them and puts them on the altar she has erected for their dead child, the Water Child. The Japanese shrine to her aborted child symbolizes the child's absence and Nadine's loss: the altar features a pebble in a jar filled with water. The "dried red roses that Eric had bought her as they'd left the clinic after the procedure" (*DB* 57) stand for their withered love. Nadine's preservation of Eric's words can be interpreted as an act of comforting herself through language (cf. Murphy 13). But the tapes also contain a negative connotation, which turns Danticat's image of the altar into a questionable symbol.

Even though Nadine's act of collecting cassettes with Eric's voice on the altar stands for her unresolved trauma, it also leaves a bad taste (at least in the minds of some readers) that she leaves cassettes with the voice that had talked her into the abortion on their aborted child's shrine. Nadine is still not capable of using language herself, but immerses herself in silence. Additionally, the cassettes show that she still has not cut off relations with Eric. She even tries to contact him. This behavior adds to her trauma's power instead of contributing to healing it. In "Seven," we learn that to Eric, "[t]hose women, most of whom had husbands, boyfriends, fiancés, and lovers in other parts of the world, never meant much [...] anyway" (DB 38). Probably, Nadine in "Water Child is one of these women. Reading "Seven" before "Water Child" hence complicates our sense of the couple's relationship and destabilizes the notion of Nadine as a helpless victim. Seemingly, Nadine was not aware of the provisional nature of Eric's dating practices. Either she was totally naïve, or she is as accountable for the abortion as Eric. Unfortunately, Danticat is silent about Nadine's thoughts with respect to her relationship. Without giving any hints, Danticat presents Nadine as a rather pathetic character, incapable of bearing responsibility and of speaking to others or asking for help.

Nadine's inability to communicate with the people around her also becomes obvious by her substituting real conversations with artificial ones. She surrounds herself with "voices from the large television set that she kept on twenty-four hours a day" (DB 56). The television, magazines, and newspapers crammed into her apartment are "her way of bringing voices into her life that required neither reaction nor response" (DB 56). But even the TV voices are not enough sometimes to help her bear her self-imposed silence (also cf. Shoop 82–83). At such times, Nadine reads her parents' letters, which she always carries with her, and dials their number without actually calling them. Interestingly, the silence between Eric and Nadine is also echoed by the silence between Eric and his wife. Eric betrayed his wife with Nadine, and his wife betrayed him with her neighbor in Haiti. Eric's wife "wanted to tell her husband about that neighbor.... Only then would she feel like their future would be true" (*DB* 48). Instead, she listens to the radio (cf. *DB* 47) and, just like Nadine, distracts herself with external voices instead of voicing her own sorrows and fears.

By presenting Nadine as a pitiable and rather flat character, "Water Child" emerges as one of Danticat's weaker stories in the story cycle. Furthermore, the connection between the story chapters indicates that Nadine in not merely a victim of Eric's ruthlessness and of her dire circumstances as an immigrant in the US. Instead, the connection indicates that both Nadine and Eric must be held responsible for their child's death. Consequently, the altar for the Water Child is not only the image of trauma and pain, but also becomes a more complex symbol of shame, guilt, and remorse.

To sum up, the phrase "Water Child" partly signifies Nadine's shrine to her aborted child. Secondly, it stands for her experienced losses and, thirdly, for her unresolved trauma, accompanied by her feelings of guilt, shame, and remorse. Lastly, if we look at other of Danticat's writings, we can discern in the image an evocation of those lost during the Middle Passage, a historical trauma that still affects Haiti's present as postmemory. The water imagery furthermore evokes the many Haitian boat people who drowned on their way to a supposedly better life in the US. Danticat describes these boat people in "The Children of the Sea" in *Krik? Krak!*. However, in addition to bearing these negative connotations, water also has positive meanings in Caribbean thought. The Barbadian writer Edward Kamau Brathwaite characterizes the Caribbean identity as submarine: "the unity is submarine / breathing air, our problem is how to study the fragments / whole" (1). The sea interconnects the Caribbean islands and constitutes the bridge to the rest of the world, so that water sometimes implies hope for a better future.

A more positive example of Danticat's use of water as an image in *The Dew Breaker* (and a story to contrast "Water Child") can be found in the story chapter "Monkey Tails." Danticat has Michel, Eric's cotenant, tell the story of his youth in Haiti, especially on the day Jean-Claude Duvalier went into exile in 1986. It is a story about

Michel's relationship with his father, who never acknowledged him as his son, and about the Haitian people's revenge on the *Tonton macoutes* after Baby Doc's escape. In spite of the terror and violence that Michel encountered, his is a story of empowerment that he wants to tell. He speaks it onto cassettes for his unborn son (*DB* 151). In contrast to Nadine, who is freshly affected by the trauma of her abortion, Michel encountered violence eighteen years earlier, and he has had time to stay silent and heal. The act of speaking the story on cassettes for posterity might be Michel's attempt to protect his son from haunting postmemory through immediate and direct communication. One day, Nadine might also be able to tell her own story and let people, to whom she will be able to tell everything, get close to her. Michel thus balances Nadine's silence and her sad story of loss, death, and irresponsibility by facing his traumas and passing on his story to his unborn son, who has an optimistic and hopeful future in spite of the violence his father encountered in the past.

Yet, Nadine's story is not entirely pessimistic. While Aitor Ibarrola Armendariz writes that "Nadine seems to see her trauma in more relative terms when she compares her situation to that of other people" (44), the present essay further argues that Nadine's silence is paralleled by the silence of one of her mute patients, Ms. Hinds, who literally lost her voice when her larynx was removed. Nadine and Ms. Hinds are doubles in their silence, but each woman is limited by a different kind of silence. Ms. Hinds is physically limited, and her silence is only temporary. Speech therapy and an artificial voice box will enable her to speak and continue working as a teacher. Nadine's psychologically caused silence depends on the healing of her trauma, which may never be overcome. While Ms. Hinds has her parents with her who take care of her, Nadine is all alone and avoids any human contact out of fear that her trauma capsule might open and that she might have to feel the erupting pain coming to the surface.

Due to their common silence, Nadine is able to understand Ms. Hinds' anger and rage at being mute (cf. *DB* 59). The other nurses want to tie the hysterical Ms. Hinds up and "put restraints on her arms and legs" (*DB* 59). Yet Nadine comprehends how trapped Ms. Hinds feels in her silence. Nadine feels the same kind of entrapment when she keeps "staring at the barred windows on the brown building across the alley..." (*DB* 66) during her solitary lunch hours. She orders her colleagues to release Ms. Hinds, who relaxes because "her need to struggle [is] suddenly gone..." (*DB* 60). When Ms. Hinds tries to speak to Nadine, "all that came out was the hiss of oxygen and mucus filtering through the tube in her neck" (*DB* 60). Due to their common voicelessness, the two women understand each other and start to communicate when Ms. Hinds begins using a pad and pen.

Ms. Hinds writes that she feels like a "basenji," a "dog that doesn't bark" (*DB* 62). Danticat leaves the precise meaning of Ms. Hinds's declaration unclear, though Nadine seems to take it as a declaration of her patient's feeling of powerlessness. However, if we examine the term 'basenji' more closely, it suggests another meaning. A basenji is a dog originally from the Congo and Egypt. The Ancient Egyptian pharaohs used basenjis as palace dogs, a fact that is documented by statues. Additionally, since the late nineteenth century, basenjis have been highly valued as hounds and watchdogs in the headwaters of the Nile and the Congo Rivers because they are almost totally silent (Walker). Indeed, it is because of their ability to be silent that they have been "so highly esteemed ... that they are regarded as having equal rights with their masters" (Walker n.p.). Thus, even though Ms. Hinds feels limited by her enforced silence, the image of the basenji also implies a positive connotation. Silence is sometimes necessary with respect to trauma because trauma takes time before it can be overcome.

Ms. Hinds's literal loss of voice parallels Nadine's loss of her Water Child, the loss of her parents as guardians, the loss of her lover Eric, the loss of Haiti as her homeland, and the loss of herself in the diaspora. Ms. Hinds has to accept that she lost her voice. Nadine begins to realize that she, in contrast, has an option. Ms. Hinds, rather than Nadine's parents (who depend on her like children), makes Nadine realize that "some wounds could heal, that some decisions would not haunt her forever" (*DB* 63). This chance at overcoming her traumatization inspires Nadine to attempt at communicating and transcending her self-imposed, frustrating silence. But rather than calling her parents or people who are friendly toward her (such as Josette), Nadine tries to call Eric, from whom she can expect nothing. When his wife arrived from Haiti, he changed his number. Then Nadine finally calls her parents even though she knows she will not tell them about the abortion, since they never talked about "failure or losses, which could spoil moods for days, weeks, and months, until the next phone call" (*DB* 64). This behavior shows that Nadine is still far from uttering her trauma and coming to terms with it.

Nadine remains as silent as Ms. Hinds who, in the course of her hospital stay, has begun to accept her new situation. While Ms. Hinds was panicking the day before her discharge and would almost "yank out the metal tube inserted in her neck and suffocate" (*DB* 59), the next day, "she reached up and stroked the raised tip of the metal tube in her neck…" (*DB* 65). However, Nadine knows that Ms. Hinds will have to go through the shock of voicelessness again and again (cf. *DB* 66), just like Nadine has to cope with her own traumatic losses anew every day. The voicelessness of both Nadine and Ms. Hinds becomes a silent connection of mutual understanding to bear loss.

This new connection and relation culminates in the scene when Ms. Hinds is discharged and leaves the hospital. After the elevator door closes behind Ms. Hinds and her parents, Nadine faces the "distorted reflection of herself in the wide, shiny metal surface…, the widened, unrecognizable woman staring back at her from the closed elevator door" (*DB* 68). As her double, Ms. Hinds makes Nadine aware of her self-alienation and her traumatization. While staring at her distorted image in the elevator door behind which Ms. Hinds has vanished seconds before, Nadine remembers that her aborted baby "would likely have been born today, or yesterday, or tomorrow, probably sometime this week, but this month for certain" (*DB* 68). Then she thinks of "her parents, of Eric, of the pebble in the water glass in her bedroom at home, all of them belonging to the widened, unrecognizable woman staring back at her from the closed elevator doors" (*DB* 68).

Nadine starts to acknowledge the voicelessness that is a consequence of her losses. At the same time, she realizes that her life continues and that she has options in the future, symbolized by the elevator that may take her out of the hospital—the place where she feels most trapped. If Ms. Hinds is able to leave and start a new life, so is Nadine. She realizes that she has become an unrecognizable woman due to having lost touch with her own self. Now, she has the chance to reclaim herself. Ms. Hinds works as a catalyzer for Nadine. Their shared silence is the time in which they become conscious of their muteness, accept it, and then find new ways of living with it. Thus, Nadine is not a hopeless character, and the story finishes with an open end. It is followed by "The Book of Miracles," which provides the reader with a view on the dew breaker through his wife, Anne. Due to the dew breaker's violent past and her own feelings of guilt for being his co-conspiratorial wife, Anne starts to believe in miracles, hoping that "atonement, reparation, was possible and available for everyone" (*DB* 242). Thereby, Anne continues Nadine's ambiguous position as a voiceless, yet responsible, character, even though Danticat equips Anne with a more complex personality.

Works Cited

Assmann, Aleida. *Erinnerungsräume: Formen und Wandlungen des kulturellen Gedächtnisses.* München, Germany: Beck, 1999.

Borst, Julia. "Geschichten der Zer/Verstörung: Zur Fiktionalisierung der traumatischen Gewalterfahrung der Post-Duvalier-Ära im zeitgenössischen haitianischen Roman am Beispiel von Lyonel Trouillot und Yanick Lahens." Dissertation. *Universität Hamburg,* 2014. Web. 11 Oct. 2015. <http://ediss.sub.uni-hamburg.de/volltexte/2014/7010/pdf/Dissertation.pdf>.

Brathwaite, Edward K. "Caribbean Man in Space and Time." *Savacou* 11–12 (1975): 1–11.

Caruth, Cathy. *Unclaimed Experience: Trauma, Narrative, and History.* Baltimore, MD: Johns Hopkins UP, 1996.

Chancy, Myriam J. A. *From Sugar to Revolution: Women's Visions of Haiti, Cuba, and the Dominican Republic.* Waterloo: Wilfrid Laurier UP, 2012.

Conwell, Joan. "Papa's Masks: Roles of the Father in Danticat's *The Dew Breaker*." *Obsidian* III 6/7.2/1 (2006): n.p. Web. 21 Mar. 2011.

Danticat, Edwidge. *The Dew Breaker*. New York: Knopf, 2004. [Referred to as *DB* in the text].

_____. *Krik? Krak!* New York: Vintage, 1996.

Fuchs, Rebecca. *Caribbeanness as a Global Phenomenon: Junot Díaz, Edwidge Danticat, and Cristina García*. Trier, Germany/Tempe, AZ: WVT & Bilingual Press, 2014.

Hirsch, Marianne. "The Generation of Postmemory." *Poetics Today* 29.1 (2008): 103–28.

Ibarrola Armendariz, Aitor. "The Language of Wounds and Scars in Edwidge Danticat's *The Dew Breaker*, A Case Study in Trauma Symptoms and the Recovery Process." *Journal of English Studies* 8 (2010): 23–56. Web. 17 Apr. 2015.

Ingram, Forrest L. *Representative Short Story Cycles of the Twentieth Century: Studies in a Literary Genre*. The Hague: Mouton, 1971.

Kalisa, Chantal. *Violence in Francophone African and Caribbean Women's Literature*. Lincoln: U of Nebraska P, 2009.

Kaussen, Valerie. *Migrant Revolutions: Haitian Literature, Globalization, and U.S. Imperialism*. Lanham, MD: Rowman & Littlefield, 2007.

Kilomba, Grada. *Plantation Memories: Episodes of Everyday Racism*. Münster, Germany: Unrast, 2008.

LaCapra, Dominick. *Writing History, Writing Trauma*. Baltimore: Johns Hopkins UP, 2001.

Leys, Ruth. *Trauma: A Genealogy*. Chicago: U of Chicago P, 2000.

Mehta, Brinda J. *Notions of Identity, Diaspora and Gender in Caribbean Women's Writing*. New York: Palgrave Macmillan, 2009.

Murphy, Annie. "Fragments, Traces, Echoes: Authorship and Authority in Edwidge Danticat's *The Dew Breaker* and *Brother, I'm Dying*." *Predicate: An English Studies Annual* 1 (2011): 1–27. Web. 17 Apr. 2015.

Parisot, Yolaine. "Mémoire occultée, mémoire littéraire: le roman haïtien en puzzle dans La Brûlerie d'É. Ollivier et dans Le Briseur De Rosée d'E. Danticat." *Le roman haïtien: Intertextualité, parentés, affinités*. Eds. Yves Chemla & Alessandro Costantini. Lecce: Alliance Française de Lecce, 2007. 209–27.

Scarry, Elaine. *The Body in Pain: The Making and Unmaking of the World.* New York: Oxford UP, 1987.

Thomas, Katherine. "Edwidge Danticat's *The Dew Breaker.*" *Journal of Caribbean Studies* 20.1/2 (2006): 93–102.

Walker, Bernice. "Nature's Masterpiece: The Basenji." *Basenji University.* Basenji University, n.d. Web. 15 Apr. 2015.

The Constructed Island: Experimentation and Reference in Ana Menéndez's *Adios, Happy Homeland!*

Alli Carlisle

Ana Menéndez's 2011 short story collection *Adios, Happy Homeland!* fits neatly into a large body of Cuban diasporic fiction that deals with the limitations of national borders in defining national identity and belonging. As Antonia Domínguez Miguela writes, "Cuban American narrative questions the idea that to be a Cuban it is necessary to reside in Cuba" (268). Cuban American narrative, she adds, clearly demonstrates the "deterritorialization of the concepts of nation and culture as a consequence of exile and migration" as well as "the appearance of a new concept of *cubanidad* and therefore of national identity;" Cuban Americans, even those who have never been to Cuba, "identify with an idea of *cultural nation*," rather than a geographically limited political nation (Domínguez Miguela 268). These trends are embodied in the works of first- and second-generation Cuban and Cuban American writers alike, as well as in what Gustavo Pérez Firmat has called the "one-and-a-half" generation, born in Cuba and raised in the United States, "neither *aquí* nor *allá*" (7). Menéndez's writing epitomizes this desire to broaden the discussion of identity in relation to the concrete bounds of the political nation, both in *Adios* and her previous works, particularly the much-lauded story collection *In Cuba I Was a German Shepherd* (2001) and the novel *Loving Che* (2003).

Adios, Happy Homeland! is an experimental collection of short stories that, on its surface, seeks to deconstruct structures of identity, authorship, and belonging. The book is built around a device: it is a fictional anthology of Cuban authors compiled by an Irishman who is driven by a passionate identification with Cuban culture. The stories and poems are held together by a commitment to formal experimentation: one story uses the Oulipan constraint of omitting

165

the letter 'e,' while another is a series of famous Cuban poems filtered through Google Translate. Many of the stories are held together by an internal intertextuality, with authors and characters appearing in each other's stories, and most of the names of the stories' purported authors are references to real Cuban authors. However, underneath these experimental trappings is a continuous thread that ties together the stories with a lyrical, sentimental voice. Throughout *Adios, Happy Homeland!*, Menéndez uses a wide variety of Cuban literary references to construct an appearance of heterogeneity and authoritative access to the Cuban literary canon. Meanwhile, a privileging of affective engagement over academic reading works to support a unified, somewhat homogeneous story. The book's invisible hand, often obscured by the playfulness surrounding the fictional anthologist, links the stories into one continuous thread through creative anachronism and experimental techniques. Ultimately, the idea of text as unifying solution to a fragmented community turns the book into a vague, nostalgic claim to a lost homeland rather than a nuanced portrait of a diverse community.

Literary References and the Debate over Authority

The chapter entitled "Prologue"—not a true prologue—introduces the themes that tie together *Adios*. It is signed "Herberto Quain, La Habana 1936." Readers of Borges, perhaps tipped off by the first of the book's two epigraphs (one from Borges, one from Martí), will recognize Herberto Quain from "Examination of the work of Herbert Quain" ("Examen de la obra de Herbert Quain," 1941). This Borges story is a kind of literary obituary for a figure who we could read as a mediocre version of Borges—just as Menéndez's Quain could be read as her avatar. Quain's writing is experimental and includes a novel called *The God of the Labyrinth*, in which the reader, discovering a hidden solution to the detective story, is allowed to feel "more perspicacious" than the detective protagonist; another of Quain's texts, which the narrator calls a "retrogressive, ramifying" novel and explains with mathematical figures, is dated 1936, as is Menéndez's "Prologue" (Borges 109). Borges's Quain claimed that true readers were extinct, so he wrote stories that allow their readers to believe they have invented them; the narrator claims he himself fashioned "The Circular Ruins" (a real Borges story) from one of Quain's stories.

Menéndez's Quain begins the "Prologue": "The modern reader may well wonder what impels me, an Irishman molded in the nineteenth century, to imagine I have anything to add to the literature of that Caribbean island" (*Adios* 3). An attached footnote, mirroring Borges's story, explains that Cuba is "actually an archipelago" and gives the Greek source-word. The footnote claims to be quoting from Aleksandr Solzhenitsyn's *The Gulag Archipelago*, a book about prison labor camps. This sense of whimsy around this reference, blending real with invented literature, belies its harsh political critique. The opening line of the "Prologue" also establishes the questions of national belonging that run throughout the collection. Can this fictional Irishman be an authority on Cuba? Can a second-generation Cuban raised in the United States, like Menéndez, be an authority on Cuba? This device frames the book's discussion of authority and entitlement, a discussion that clearly argues that belonging is not limited to residence within a nation's political borders. The first words are also an interpellation of the book's intended reader—perhaps a reader set up by Borges's Quain stories to think she is smarter than the text in front of her. The reader we are expected to be at the beginning of this experience might have certain expectations about the proper correspondence of passion to national borders, but those will be broken down.

The questions about experience and entitlement in relation to nationality, collectivity, and cultural authenticity come plainly into view later in the collection, in a pair of letters between the collective authors of the book and Quain. In the first of these, "From: The Poets / To: Herberto Quain / Date: May 23, 1923 / Re: Your book," the authors object to being grouped together and called Cuban. They ask: "Are you actively working to keep us tied to a single identity? [...] much of our lifework was and continues to be dedicated to the idea of escaping the bonds imposed by others. And now you come, an outsider, to impose on us a doomed structure" (Menéndez 99). Their self-proclaimed commonality is their dedication to escaping oppression (perhaps as close as we can get to Menéndez's definition of what it means to be Cuban). Quain's foreignness is as offensive as the fact that he is not "even real" (Menéndez 100). The poets ask, "What gives you the authority? To be done properly, this collection should be put together by a genuine scholar, preferably Cuban himself, and not an Irishman who faked his qualifications to work for our National Library" (Menéndez 100). Lastly, they ask Quain to contact their representative, Jane Smith, whose email address "jsmiththecuban@gmail.com" is a humorous combination of a completely Anglo-sounding name and an epithet clearly explaining, and claiming, her Cubanness.

The response, "From: Herberto Quain / To: The Poets / Date: August 9, 1912 / Re: Re: Your book," makes several counterarguments (and forms an entertaining anti-chronological series). Quain argues that the poets are ignorant of the structure they form: "You need me to give you meaning, but you are too full of individual self-importance (your 'joint' letter notwithstanding) to understand this" (Menéndez 105). He tells the writers they are invented and that people who are not Cubans can understand Cubans—"Or are Cubans the only ones in this world looking for a hidden passage, a way out of our maze?" (Menéndez 105). He ends his brief response with a series of mathematical equations (a direct reference to Borges's Quain). He identifies the paradox of their complaint about identity: "You object to being tethered to a single identity and yet you retreat into it for protection" (Menéndez 106). He thus echoes Frederic Jameson's famous observation about the deterministic role of the nation as allegory in "third world literatures." The writers fall into the unavoidable trap of the collective complaint that can only serve to unify them more.

In other cases, the use of literary references takes a different form. In these cases, references appear as adopted literary voices that are used to tell stories in which certain details correspond with the sources (the stories often feel like scavenger hunts of partially hidden clues), but the narrative voice maintains a lyrical consistency that has little to do with those references. The first story in the collection, after the "Prologue," is "You Are the Heirs of All My Terrors." The name of the fictional author, Celestino D'Alba, is a reference to Reinaldo Arenas's novel *Celestino antes del alba* (1967), and the title of the story is part of a line from his suicide note (which he intended for publication): "You are the heirs of all my terrors, but also of my hope that Cuba will soon be free" (Arenas 317). In the story, a nameless protagonist is chased by two men who "looked like brothers, except one was bearded and the other hairless"—a fairly transparent image of the Castros (Menéndez 15). The story called "Redstone" is attributed to a "C. Casey," a nominal reference to Calvert Casey that seems to contribute nothing substantial to the story itself, which is a granddaughter's reminiscence about her grandfather's participation in missile development in World War II.

Another story is a rewriting of Alejo Carpentier's story "Viaje a la semilla" (written in 1944, published in 1956 in *Guerra del tiempo*), in which the numbered fragments of the story take us, in reverse time, from an old man's deathbed backward through the significant incidents of his life to his infancy. Menéndez's version is called "Journey Back to the Seed (¿Qué Quieres, Vieja?)," and its fictional author is Alex Carpenter. The title is a direct translation, and the parenthetical addition is the first line of the original story, the "viejo" modified to suit a female main character here. Menéndez's rewrite is fairly literal, though with a slightly different focus: the journey of refugees from Cuba to the United States, in this case in reverse.

The opening sentence makes it obvious that we are beginning at the end of the story: "In the end, she is surrounded by strangers" (Menéndez 145). That we begin at the end is not initially apparent in Carpentier's story, but rather comes into focus through the reading. The title of Menéndez's story will make the time-reversal device obvious immediately for a reader who knows the reference; perhaps the clue in the first line is placed there for those who do not. Menéndez's story uses Carpentier's structure, which in its time was strikingly experimental, to talk about dementia, memory, and exile (and, to a lesser extent, gender and the family structure). An overheard conversation provides an interesting comment on memory: "Memory marks and makes us. Not intelligence, it's not that. For a beast, every morning is new; the past is oblivion. Only man looks back, caresses his gathered history as if it were a beloved parent" (Menéndez 148). We see the main character's children grow from adults into babies; we see her "leave America for home," where "soldiers return the bracelet that her mother gave her before she died. They tear up the false bottoms of their suitcases and put in all their old diplomas, the marriage certificate, the photographs, and the newspaper clippings. The soldiers take dollars out of their own pockets and tear up the soles of her shoes so that they can stuff them with money before closing them again with the slash of a knife" (Menéndez 152). These are iconic images from narratives of Cuban refugees. We know her story because it's a general one shared by many. Interestingly, both stories present upper class characters who suffer loss: in Carpentier's story, the regressive decline of the marquis reveals attentively documented nuances of class and race; Menéndez's rewrite does not observe any of these social forces, instead casting those chased out of Cuba during the Revolution as the only victims. This homogenization is consistent in *Adios*, which sometimes attends to gender, but has no consciousness of class, race or sexuality.

Another story also employs allusions, but uses a different methodology—instead of a rewritten story, we have a story that features a historical author as its main character. This story, "The Poet in His Labyrinth," is attributed to Silas Haslam and a translator, Joseph Martin. Again Menéndez uses a reference to Borges to elaborate the thematic backdrop of her book. The figure of labyrinth appears in "Herbert Quain" as well as in many Borges stories; Silas Haslam is a fictional character from Borges's "Tlön, Uqbar, Orbis Tertius," author of *A General History of Labyrinths*. "Tlön" is a story in which real and fictional worlds are difficult to distinguish, and academic research exists on both sides of the blurred line; the character Silas Haslam shares a last name with Borges's English ancestors.

In Menéndez's story, a nameless poet awakens in a place he cannot recognize, remembering verses he has written, but now finding them automatically, irreversibly translated into English. The poet is José Martí, transported in time to the Havana airport that is named after him. Martí tries to remember his history, but it is held just out of reach. He is trapped in translation, unable even to think in Spanish, existing only in his own alienation. The narrator tells us, "He understood then that he had woken on the other side of something, a place that he had no name for" (Menéndez 173). This "something" Martí has slept through could be several things. One is death. Another is the ascendance of the United States empire Martí was so prescient in foreseeing; another is the ascendance of the Cuban regime that fetishizes his image and stridently claims his legacy.

The airport, the site of Martí's reawakening, suggests yet another reading—the airport is a facilitator of cultural exchange, representing transit and globalized connectivity. It is also, to use Marc Augé's term, a non-place: "a space which cannot be defined as relational, or historical, or concerned with identity," but is rather a cultural void of supermodernity (77–78). Menéndez puts an amnesiac Martí into this site representative of the paradox that is globalization: it symbolizes hyperconnectivity along with the loss of context and cultural specificity. The airport also suggests exile, although it is not as obvious a symbol for Cuban exile as are the scenes of boat journeys we see elsewhere in *Adios*. More than exile, perhaps, the airport represents tourism, the necessary evil that has sustained Cuba since the loss of Soviet support. In this way, it symbolizes perhaps the ultimate exile, the nation's commodification and sense of foreignness from itself.

This story integrates real quotations from Martí's writings, a technique that is not present in other stories. The quotations are taken from Martí's letters and poems—many of them refer to flying, some of them to the sea. The quotations are not hidden, but rather italicized (and the truly "modern reader" knows to look to the modern paratext, the copyright information, and so will be aware of the quotations already). Menéndez also inserts her own work (her name appears later among the fictional authors); Martí encounters a copy of her novel *Loving Che* and assumes it was left by a tourist. (Despite his confused awe at the airport, apparently his reading of the airplanes as "cylindrical train cars, each of them winged, waiting like giant birds atop their wheeled legs" allows him to identify that this is a place of tourism [Menéndez 176]). One quote comes from Martí's poem "Odio el mar" ("I hate the sea"): "That I am a dead man, still walking, is clear" (Menéndez 173). The line indicates Martí's acute awareness of his mortality, but in this story, the quotation is used literally, to point to the fact that Martí finds himself alive over a century after his death. In the last lines of the story, strange men lead Martí away, and he recites to them a line that comes from a letter the real Martí wrote the day before he died: "'there are affections of such delicate honesty...'" (Menéndez 177).

José Martí fought and died for Cuban independence from the Spanish; historical distance, intervening changes in the arrangement of political power, and the fact of his long exile from Cuba all make his symbolic capital available to present-day exiles as well as the socialist government. Martí is possibly the most used symbol of *cubanidad*, and a claim to his legacy is the ultimate claim to Cuban authenticity. The Martí of this story is the agent of a nostalgia that has an unidentified loss as its object; the quotations show us that Menéndez has done her research, but don't explain exactly why. Here his words lose their specificity, and his aura of authenticity gives weight to the generalized longing that defines Menéndez's portrayal of Cubanness.

Literature: World of Study or World of Affect?

If we return to the "Prologue," we find that it also introduces a tension between academic and affective reading that underscores the argument for a kind of sentimental community of the nation. Quain's attachment to Cuba is emotional: it consists of an anachronistic, transnational longing that needs academic engagement as its Other. Quain's house, described in a nostalgic register, gives structure to his affective engagement with Cuba. The architecture of the house, he tells us, is unusual for Ireland, but common to Cuban beach houses. It has *vitrales* (Spanish for stained-glass windows). The house is both a transplanted cultural artifact and a labyrinth: "Through the kitchen and around to the side of the house was a small sitting area, and here the house began its first turn inward, toward its origin. [...] And so the house wound deeper and deeper, around rooms and sitting areas, some of them closed off since before I was born" (Menéndez 6). In the center of the house is a library that contains a hidden room with a message in Gaelic over the door, untranslated in the book, signifying "'I am not a scholar, and don't wish to be', as the fox said to the wolf" (MacDonald). According to MacDonald, this line comes from a folk tale in which a fox tricks a wolf into reading an inscription on an ass's hooves by praising him as a scholar. The wolf gets kicked in the head and the fox eats the ass. The quote is a warning about the dangers of scholarship, but a tongue-in-cheek one, since to understand it one has to perform some scholarship to decipher the reference. Quain calls this decontextualized message "an odd thing to assert," as "most would agree;" again we see the appeal to a general population. This declaration, inscribed in the heart of a library, is a political choice of one kind of readership over another, of folk knowledge over academic.

The prologue uses the "secret text" device to establish a relationship of romantic belonging between Quain, a reader out of his time and place, and Cuba, the object of his scholarly-non-scholarly desire. In the library at the center of the labyrinthine house, Quain finds books that hold the "promise of new worlds and adventures" among "cracked leather covers" (Menéndez 9). Quain says he "understood that my own yearning for the future, for escape from the long history of Ireland, was a reaching out for the words now before me. It seemed to me that whoever had written this book had written it especially for me" (Menéndez 8–9). Reading, for Quain, is an experience of personal ownership.

The most important book in the library is *A Brief History of the Cuban Poets*, supposedly written by Victoria O'Campo in 1902. The historical Victoria Ocampo was an Argentinian modernist writer most famous for publishing the literary magazine *Sur* (she was not a Cuban scholar and was twelve years old in 1902). The book turns out to be endless—Quain says he doesn't believe he ever reached the end—"Perhaps I was afraid of the hollow that exists at the conclusion of every story, the disconsolate sense of loss"—

and he also never removes the book from the library (Menéndez 9). The house and the book have parallel structures: they are endless, seductive, secretive, and affective. The *Brief History* is an outsider's book that draws the reader in; similarly, Quain is an outsider who gets pulled into a love for Cuba, eventually to the point that he travels to Cuba and lives there, moving from his childhood library to a post at the Cuban National Library, infiltrating this academic institution with his foreign affective readerliness. Describing his job at the National Library, Quain tells us that he was hired by Domingo Figarola Caneda (Figarola Caneda being the historical first director of Cuba's National Library, beginning in 1901): "In those years, Cuba was beginning to move away from imperial influences. For some reason, old Domingo saw in this Irishman someone who could purge the library of its foreign mannerisms and replace them with something like Creole honesty" (Menéndez 11). This comment is obviously tongue-in-cheek: like much of Menéndez's humor here, it pokes a gentle fun, but does not deconstruct its object. That a "Creole" characteristic is portable to an Irishman is perfectly within the realm of the book's logic.

Herberto Quain finishes off his "Prologue" by affirming his non-academic authority to talk about literature, saying he is "not, in fact, a doctor of letters from Trinity College or anywhere else" (a claim he made to secure his job at the National Library). The reference to a doctorate is also likely a reference to the final verse of Martí's first "Verso sencillo," quoted later in the collection, in which Martí hangs up his doctoral hood. However, Quain says, "I know something of imagination, having sheltered under its enormous shadow-wings. And, though I may not be Cuban, I have learned to speak the language of escape. Untether your expectations; be lifted by these unseen poets struggling to translate that which has no translation" (Menéndez 11). A degree is not necessary to understanding, but is represented as a kind of official dogma against which to rebel. Quain's real credentials are his lived experience with imagination and his fluency in the "language of escape." The idea that a non-scholar might productively direct a section of the National Library parallels the idea that a non-Cuban might help Cuba return to a kind of national, cultural authenticity—and the idea that an exile could be the truest Cuban of all.

Modern Translations: Literature Meets Machine

One of the most technically unusual segments of the book is the eponymous chapter, "Adios Happy Homeland: Selected Translations According to Google." The chapter is dedicated to translations of poems by Cuban authors, including Martí, Gertrudis Gómez de Avellaneda, José María Heredia, Julián del Casal, and another handful of lesser known poets, all presented in English here thanks to one of the contemporary world's most prominent agents of globalization. The results are often charmingly puzzling, for instance in the case of Martí's "Simple Lines (fragments)" ("Versos sencillos"):

> I am an honest man
> From where the palm grows,
> And before I die
> Browse verses from my soul.
>
> I come from everywhere to everywhere
> And: I am art among the arts,
> in the mountains I am.
> [...]
> Callo, and understand,
> and I take the pomp of rhyming:
> hang a withered tree in my hood doctor.   (Menéndez 182–184)

The importance of the "Versos sencillos" (and indeed, the figure of Martí) to Cuban literature and culture would be difficult to summarize. Martí's narrator contemplates mortality, freedom, and the impending danger of empire. In a normal translation, produced by a human, the last stanza of this first poem (of the 46) is as follows:

> Without a word, I've understood
> And put aside the pompous muse;
> From a withered branch, I choose
> To hang my doctoral hood. (Martí, trans. Tellechea)

Tellechea's translation is not word for word, but it follows the meaning of the verse. Google Translate obviously cannot find a translation for "callo" ("I fall quiet"), and doctoral hood becomes "hood doctor"; the syntax is destroyed and prepositions lose their referents, so that rather than hanging the hood on the tree and relinquishing the academic artifact to the natural world, the speaker hangs the tree in the "hood doctor." This last line of Martí's poem underscores, perhaps inspires, the book's anti-academic strain.

Another of the mechanical translations is the source of the title of Menéndez's book. The poem by Gertrudis Gómez de Avellaneda, here called "The Breaking," but originally "Al Partir" ("On Leaving"), reads as follows: "Adios happy homeland, dear Eden! / Where'er the wrath of fate impels me. / Your sweet name flatter my ear!" The verse is about keeping the homeland present even in absence, one of the most prominent themes of *Adios*. Consistently, the automatic translation renders syntactically complex verses into jarring, discrete phrases and nonsensically linked subjects and verbs. From a poem by José Jacinto Milanés y Fuentes, we get:

> My hope is not error,
> and although the tocoloro apronte
> his pen, which adds to the mountain
> will have their song by husky
> as always and everywhere trunk
> the mockingbird sings better. (Menéndez 187)

The automatic translation renders this series of poems both hilarious and largely incoherent. The destruction of structure—syntax, phrasing, rhythms, and most fundamentally a continuous meaning—comments on the fundamental disjuncture of exile and those gaps of translation that are uncrossable. As Herberto Quain tells us at the end of his "Prologue," many of the "poets" collected in his anthology are "struggling to translate that which has no translation" (Menéndez 11). We might also recall the debate between Quain and "The Poets," in which they argue over the role and function of structure. In this instance, translation destroys the internal structure of the poem, perhaps in the same way exile destroys a certain coherence of identity. In a sense, much of *Adios* is asking if there is some structure that can overcome these disjunctures. The arrival of the foreign anthologist Herberto Quain turns these pieces into a book, with his very foreignness creating, by contrast, that category "Cuban," which, although offensive to the writers, gives them a meaningful shape.

The mechanism behind Google Translate has its own particular poetics: as David Bellos tells us, it is a "statistical machine translation system, which means that it doesn't try to unpick or understand anything"; rather than deconstructing and reconstructing the sample, it instead searches for "similar sentences in already translated texts" using "an incredibly clever and speedy statistical reckoning device"; once it finds a similar enough match, "Google Translate coughs it up, raw or, if necessary, lightly cooked." Perhaps even more intriguingly, Bellos explains that most of the data available to Google Translate comes from materials prepared by international organizations: "Thousands of human translators working for the United Nations and the European Union and so forth have spent millions of hours producing precisely those pairings." This image of a parasitic machine feeding off the massive scale labor of a sea of human laborers seems like the perfect representation of the phrase "human resources;" it also fills out the sparse image that comes to mind when we imagine the passionless functioning of the automatic translator. And yet, despite this reminder of the human trace, the body of referents for, in this case, translated poetry, is official, bureaucratic discourse. This makes Google Translate and its sources the equivalent of the airport; it is the non-place of literature.

In the case of this chapter of the book, Google Translate is not the only operation performed on the structure(s) of the poems. Their grouping is a small-scale version of what the poets accuse Quain of doing: reducing their heterogeneity to a single identity, eliding the differences in their temporal, ideological, and artistic contexts. Do we need to know which of these authors is a modernist and which a neoclassicist, which was influenced by Darío and which by Schiller? Not all Cuban poetry is the same, although the broken-robot aesthetic uniformly applied to them here makes them seem as if they were uniform to begin with. One of the poems Quain includes consists, in fact, of a few lines of prose from Alejo Carpentier's novel *Los pasos perdidos*, not only computer-translated, but also transformed by Menéndez into a poem through line breaks. Menéndez has offered in an interview what is perhaps a clue to the unifying aesthetic that fetishizes the poem throughout *Adios*: "in the case of Cuba, I think it's all poetry, even when labeled prose" (interview with Melissa Scholes Young). Here, as elsewhere in *Adios*, the construction of continuity elides nuanced difference.

The Secret Text at the Center of the Library

The endless text mentioned in the "Prologue" appears in *Adios, Happy Homeland!* as a chapter titled "A Brief History of the Cuban Poets." For a reader expecting the marvels and wonders the young Herberto Quain felt upon reading it, this story provides a disappointing contrast. This chapter processes a series of heterogeneous stories through one homogenizing function, not a computerized approximation, but rather a very human reshaping. The chapter begins, in the style of a dark fairy tale, "There once was a country of dark wounds, known for exiling and murdering its poets" (Menéndez 205). The story is a series of short prose accounts of unnamed poets who were exiled or executed by "the oppressors" (or "the next round of oppressors"—this term includes the Spanish, Batista, and Castro governments alike). The list of poets includes Martí, Gertrudis Gómez de Avellaneda, Virgilio Piñera, Lydia Cabrera, Heberto Padilla, Pablo Armando Fernandez, and others.

The conflation of these stories into a series of pithy accounts that all involve exile, imprisonment, and death is a device that obviously forms the backbone of the chapter. It frames all of the writers as poets (continuous with the rest of the book) despite their commitments to various other genres, and it frames them all as victims of an evil that is essentially the same, be it colonial, republican, or socialist. In fact, not all the oppressors are even Cuban—Alba de Céspedes y Bertini makes the list, described as the "granddaughter of a great national hero," (Carlos Manuel de Céspedes, who agitated against Spain). As we learn from this chapter, she "was born in Rome in 1911, but could not escape the curse of the island poets," but we do not learn that she lived her life in Italy, wrote her works in Italian, and was "jailed for agitating against the oppressors" who ruled Italy, not Cuba (Menéndez 207). Another poet, Pablo Armando Fernandez, born in 1930 and "forced to flee the oppressors in 1945," returned to Cuba in 1959 and lived out his life under the socialist government described in other anecdotes as "the oppressors" (Menéndez 207). Is it solely for the purpose of continuity that we do not learn that Virgilio Piñera, the poet born in 1912 who "would be exiled by one oppressor for his politics and isolated by another for his tendencies" was isolated because those tendencies were homosexual? The same goes for Reinaldo Arenas, the last author referred to in this story, whose "various offenses against the empire of reason" include, here, "a proclivity for writing poems on the leaves of innocent trees" and whose 1990 suicide in exile is mentioned, but not his wasting away due to AIDS. In turning Piñera, Arenas, and others into matching characters in matching anecdotes, this chapter creates silence around the range of complicated ideological commitments that comprised the lives and works of the real authors.

That this chapter is the secret text contained in the larger text is indicative. In the "Prologue," Quain tells us that he spent hours reading this book, which contained multitudes such that Quain could never finish it. This chapter illustrates the magical coexistence of what Quain, in a sense the author of the book's wholeness, experiences as the endless worlds of the stories and what we can see as the reductive narratives of the immediate text. This coexistence is an element of the particular fictional universe Menéndez constructs, which seems to feel the "weight of history" very acutely and creates its own magical reality with a blend of literary reference, metafiction, and fantasy. It is also an element of the less apparent homogenizing operation of this fictional universe. The stories combined in this chapter ignore cultural specificities in their effort to present a continuous story, and in creating that coherence the master narrative enacts its own violence on its content. It is worth noticing that this operation has a particular place in the ideological debate that takes place in Cuban American narrative. The story of the lost homeland, however it is deconstructed, displaced, and projected onto a variety of forms and references, is posited as the only loss. This continuity, this centering of a generalized nostalgic story of loss, is justified by a continuous privileging of experiential, affective engagement in a personally felt and owned world of literature rather than an academic reading that might actually account for difference. It is, after all, Herberto Quain's secret childhood library, and not, say, the Cuban National Library he later inhabits, that is the site of real knowledge.

Works Cited

Arenas, Reinaldo. *Before Night Falls*. Trans. Dolores M. Koch. London: Profile Books, 2010.

Augé, Marc. *Non-Places: Introduction to an Anthropology of Supermodernity*. Trans. John Howe. London: Verso, 1995.

Borges, Jorge Luis. *Collected Fictions of Jorge Luis Borges*. Trans. Andrew Hurley. New York: Penguin, 1998.

Domínguez Miguela, Antonia. "Geographies of Identity in Cuban American Narrative." *Evolving Origins, Transplanting Cultures: Literary Legacies of the New Americans*. Ed. Laura P. Alonso Gallo & Antonia Domínguez Miguela. Huelva: Universidad de Huelva, 2002. 267–275.

MacDonald, T. D. *Gaelic Proverbs and Proverbial Sayings*. Great Britain: Eneas Mackay Stirling, 1926. *Internet Archive*. Web. 15 Jul. 2015.

Martí, José. *Versos sencillos*. Trans. Manuel A. Tellechea. Houston: Arte Público Press, 1997. E-book.

Menéndez, Ana. *Adios, Happy Homeland!* New York: Black Cat, 2011.

_____. Interview with Amy Letter. *The Rumpus*. The Rumpus, 2011. Web. 15 Jul. 2015.

Pérez Firmat, Gustavo. *Life on the Hyphen: The Cuban-American Way*. Austin: U of Texas P, 1994.

Artistry, Thematic Criticism, and Two Short Stories by Randa Jarrar————————————

Robert C. Evans

What makes a short story—or any literary text—worth reading? A broad sampling of practically any body of recent commentary on practically any body of literature seems to yield an absolutely clear answer: a literary text is worth reading because of the *ideas* the text expresses. Stories (or poems, dramas, novels, etc.) are, according to this view, not so much stories *per se* as essays in disguise. We read them because we are interested in arguments, points of view, perspectives, issues, or "themes." This critical approach to literature, in fact, is often called "thematic" criticism, and it is one of the most widespread analytical approaches currently practiced. In fact, it is one of the most widespread approaches *ever* practiced. In many ways, it reflects the instinctive responses of "regular readers"—that is, nonacademic, nonprofessional readers, who are not paid to read and interpret texts. After all, one of the most common questions asked, when we tell a friend about having read a new book, is "What's it about?" Partly this question may indicate an interest in plots and characters, but it is also often another way of asking "what's its meaning?"

Much current academic criticism is centrally concerned with this question of meaning or themes. To the extent that the question is a question about *the unifying ideas* of the text—the ideas that help make the text cohere and help hold it together—this question about meaning is partly a question about *form* or *structure*. In other words, when the question is about unity (or the lack thereof), it is really a question about the work as a *work of art*. But that is not usually (at least in recent years) how the question is or has been treated. Partly this change in the meaning of "theme" has occurred because recent critics have often lost much interest in form or structure. Or they think that unity and coherence are either impossible or boring. Or they are interested mainly in the *ideological* impact of literature—the ways it reflects and/or shapes the actual thinking of individuals, groups, and/or cultures. For whatever reasons, then, questions about themes and meanings are, today, less often questions about form, unity, and structure than they are questions about themes and meanings in and of themselves. Literature today is often read (at least by academics) less for *how it is actually written* than for "what it has to say."

This is especially true, perhaps, when academics consider literature written by members of various minority groups, such as immigrant writers. Precisely because immigrant or ethnic writers often write about immigrant or ethnic experiences, it is all-too-tempting to treat their works as sociological, anthropological, or political tracts. Sometimes, indeed, the primary authors themselves seem to offer their works more as reflections on culture than as finely crafted works of art. And often this is how they are read—as mirroring the experiences of groups of people rather than as skillful pieces of writing. Of course, these two ways of reading are not by any means mutually exclusive. But in much commentary on "ethnic literature," the emphasis tends to be more on the adjective (*ethnic*) than on the noun (*literature*).

Dinarzad's Children

Consider, for instance, two stories by the wonderfully talented Arab American writer Randa Jarrar. These stories—"A Frame for the Sky" and "Lost in Freakin' Yonkers"—appear side-by-side in the first edition of *Dinarzad's Children: An Anthology of Contemporary American Arab Fiction* (2004). Edited by Pauline Kaldas and Khaled Mattawa, this volume is an exceptionally valuable (and still unusual) collection of short fiction by American writers with strong connections to the Middle East. Some of the writers represented are immigrants themselves; others are the children of immigrants. The brief biography of Jarrar at the end of the volume says that she "was born in Chicago in 1978 and grew up in Kuwait. She moved back to the United States after the [first] Gulf War" (315).

Simply as literary performances, Jarrar's two stories are among the highlights of *Dinarzad's Children*. While some tales included in that book seem pedestrian in style and structure (as is true of a majority of literary anthologies), Jarrad's stories grab our interest right from the start and hold it throughout. One of the stories ("Lost in Freakin' Yonkers") is primarily comic; the other ("A Frame for the Sky") seems more richly tragicomic. "Lost in Freakin' Yonkers" is laugh-out-loud funny; "A Frame for the Sky" is also often hilarious, but it is sometimes more deeply serious as well. Both works are very much worth reading, but "A Frame for the Sky" seems more likely to last as *literature*—that is, as a piece of writing that is richly written, with real depth and complexity of every sort. It seems unfortunate, then, that "A Frame for the Sky" has been omitted from the book's second edition. The reasons it may have been dropped can easily be imagined: "Lost in Freakin' Yonkers" is so obviously and effectively funny that it provides some real balance in a volume that might otherwise seem predominantly serious. Still, the absence of "A Frame for the Sky" is a real loss to the second edition of *Dinarzad's Children.*

One way to read Jarrar's two stories is to deal with them in terms of their themes. Thus, one recent article on these tales argues that they show how:

> [m]ental and physical borders are disputed, and global hegemonic forces contend for control. Subaltern cultures are compelled to admit the hegemonic in "being-made," but there is also room for "self-making" in the individual's adaptation of culture to suit his or her needs. In "Frame" and "Lost," the forces that occupy Arab-American cultural citizenship are global. . . . In an occupied cultural citizenship, the "ambivalent and contested relationships" are not constrained between the individual and one territorial state. Instead, a multitude of global forces—sometimes aligned, sometimes opposed—act upon the individual. For immigrants, these vectors may include a connection to one's country of birth, political antagonisms outside the region where one resides, and supranational affiliations, which become inscribed on the individual's construction of cultural citizenship. (Simmers 79–80)

Let us concede that everything just quoted about these stories may very well be true. What (one may still ask) does any of this have to do with the stories *as stories*? The quoted comments might just as easily have been written about two *essays* by Jarrar. As in so much contemporary literary criticism (or perhaps we should call it "cultural critique"), the literary aspects of the literature are overlooked. The emphasis is less on Jarrar's (or anyone's) writing than on ideas, issues, topics, and the ways plot summaries support claims about such matters as "global hegemonic forces," "being-made," "self-making," "cultural citizenship," and so on. The literary aspects of the literature under discussion are almost beside the point. The kind of analysis just quoted is the kind most in fashion today—a kind in which the literature gets (to coin a phrase) lost not in Yonkers, but in sociological, cultural, and political jargon.

"Lost in Freakin' Yonkers"

Of the two stories by Jarrar included in the original version of *Dinarzad's Children*, the one that seems most immediately appealing is "Lost in Freakin' Yonkers." Even its title—with its colloquial, slangy tone and its promise of humor and mystery—is instantly appealing. The story itself is often (*quite* often) laugh-out-loud funny. Any writer could have explored or expressed the *ideas* Jarrar treats in this story. Only a writer as skilled as Jarrar could have shown the mastery of tone, atmosphere, detail, rhythm, voice, sound effects, and phrasing in general that Jarrar displays in this tale. Consider, for instance, the story's opening paragraph:

> New York, during the summer of '96, sees its highest temperatures on record, and it is toward the end of this summer that I sit, my enormous pregnant belly to accompany me, on an 80 percent acrylic, 20 percent wool covered futon. I look over the tag again, and under the materials it says, made in ASU. So I'm sitting on the futon, sweating—we have neither an air conditioner nor a fan, and our window is held up by an embarrassingly huge copy of *Dirtiest Jokes Volume III*—and wondering: should I marry my worthless boyfriend? and: was the tag maker dyslexic? (Jarrar, "Lost" 43)

From a strictly *literary* point of view, what this passage "says" cannot be separated from its skillful writing. For instance, the mere use of "'96" rather than "1996" already suggests much about this speaker's informal, unpretentious tone. Already she sounds like a stereotypically no-nonsense, fast-talking New Yorker. The fact that her window is propped up not simply by a dirty joke book, but by the *third* volume in a *dirtiest* joke book series implies much about her literary tastes and/or those of her "worthless boyfriend." The reference to the dirty joke book also foreshadows much of the rest of the narrative's frank, uninhibitedly sexual tone, while the reference to unrelieved, intense heat already suggests part of the story's literally and figuratively oppressive, fiery atmosphere, which will be full of tensions and antagonisms. Because the narrator sits on a simple futon (rather than, say, an elegant sofa), she seems anything but wealthy—an assumption reinforced by the lack of an air conditioner or even a fan. The fact that she doesn't simply *have* "an enormous pregnant belly" but feels "accompany[ied]" by one already suggests her sense of alienation from her own flesh—an alienation stressed throughout the tale. Finally, the skillfully delayed reference to her "worthless boyfriend" (followed immediately by the comic, anticlimactic question about the possibly dyslexic tag maker) already suggests the combination of frustration and humor that will dominate the tone of the whole story. While characterizing her surroundings, the narrator inevitably also characterizes herself.

Even a commentary as detailed as this only begins to scratch the surface of the artistic skill of Jarrar's opening sentences. The fact that the narrator is pregnant but unmarried is itself significant, as is her description of herself as "sweating" rather than "perspiring." Practically every single detail here is rich with implications, and the same is true of almost every sentence in the entire story. Anyone who reads this work simply for its "themes" or "meanings" is missing most of its artistry and, ironically, much of its precise meaning as well. The meanings of this story, after all, are not merely its *paraphraseable* meanings ("this story is about a young unmarried pregnant Arab-American woman frustrated with her life and boyfriend"). Nor are its meanings the larger themes that can abstracted from the text ("this story is about the narrator's resistance to the cultural hegemony of a racialist, patriarchal, phallogencentric late-capitalist American regime"). Rather, the story's meanings inhere in practically every single, apparently small, detail. The fact that the futon, for example, is "covered" in "80 percent acrylic, 20 percent wool" implies a great deal. If it were clad in leather, or even if the percentages of acrylic and wool were reversed, an entirely different socio-economic status for the narrator would be implied. What matters first and foremost, from a literary point of view, is the precision and vividness of Jarrar's individual word choices.

Analyses that go straight for the most-easily paraphraseable "messages" of a literary text are, arguably, not *analyses* in the strictest sense at all. Instead, they are arguably abstractions, simplifications, reductions, distillations. Rather than encouraging us to see literature (and life) as richly complex, they encourage us to think of literature (and perhaps of life as well) in terms of broad, general categories or stereotypes—or, even worse, in terms of simple arguments or slogans. "She-is-a-poor-Arab-American-woman-with-a-worthless-boyfriend" may be the *main* meaning of these opening sentences, but it is hardly the only meaning or even the meaning that matters most if we treat these sentences as *literature*—that is, as words interesting in, of, and for themselves and in, of, and for the skill with which they are arranged.

Of course, any analysis that tried to examine even a very *short* short story (let alone a novel) sentence-by-sentence and word-by-word would be enormous both in length and in complexity. But there is something to be said for pausing, often, to remind readers that the best literature *is* immeasurably complex and skillfully crafted. It is precisely such complexity and craftsmanship that makes it worth reading *as literature*. And being reminded of the complexity of *any*thing, in any *way*, is a valuable experience. It is an experience that can be chastening. Such reminders are cautionary and humbling: they discourage us from rushing (or jumping) to conclusions of any and every sort.

"A Frame for the Sky"

"Lost in Freakin' Yonkers" is an instantly appealing and consistently funny comic story. "A Frame for the Sky," however, is in many ways even more impressive. It begins with an exceptionally long opening sentence—a stylistic *tour de force* (Jarrar, "Frame" 31). This sentence not only immediately begins to suggest the complexity of the late-middle-aged, first-person male narrator, but also establishes many of the story's main themes and much of its persistent imagery. Like much of the rest of the story, this opening sentence is at once serious and amusing. It creates real interest in the narrator's personality, in his life, and in the story he has to tell. The long opening sentence is then followed by a much shorter one, and the two sentences together imply a major concern of the tale as a whole—a concern with time, with the past, present, and future. And, as readers will discover when they reach the end of the narrative, the opening paragraph also foreshadows an important paragraph near the very close of the tale. In short, even after reading the story's first paragraph, we sense that we are in the hands of a real writer. Jarrar can create a narrator not only like herself (as she does when she creates the witty young female narrator of "Lost"); she can also create a narrator (a middle-aged man with a wife and children) with whom she herself seems at first to have little in common.

One of the most effective structural aspects of the story involves the narrator's constant references to various "worst days" of his life, which he obsessively ranks from most worst to least worse and vice versa. This technique symbolizes the story's effective combination of seriousness and humor: the fact that the narrator has had so many "worst days" is inherently serious, but the fact that he obsessively ranks them is funny. (The day of his mother's death was the worst day of his life; the day of his father's death was only the "sixth-worst" [Jarrar, "Frame" 41].) In this respect, the "worst days" motif epitomizes the complex tone of the work as a whole. Sometimes we find ourselves laughing at (and/or with) the narrator, while, at other times, we find him someone with whom we can deeply sympathize and empathize. He is not simply a comic figure, nor simply a tragic figure, but a complex combination of the two.

In the story's second paragraph, we discover that the narrator is a Middle Easterner living temporarily in New York but eager to return to Kuwait in the days after the 1991 American-led invasion, which expelled the Iraqi forces that had recently invaded that country. The narrator refers in passing to his teenaged son, but he also mentions the son's earlier boyhood, thereby reiterating again the themes of change and passing time so important to the rest of the tale. The second and third paragraphs (which conclude the first main segment of the narrative) also establish other key motifs, including the impact of international political events on personal lives, the importance of nationality in determining an individual's fate, and the odd ways in which people can be affected by events beyond their control and through no personal fault of their own. The narrator admits that he shed a tear when discovering that because he was a Palestinian, he was forbidden from returning to Kuwait (Jarrar, "Frame" 32). Yet for the most part, his tone is anything but maudlin. Mainly he seems stoic, and in that sense, he also seems mature. As we will discover, he is a man who longs for love and who is capable of giving it, but he is never paralyzed by self-pity. No sooner does he learn that he is an exile than he is capable of seeing some humor in this new situation (32). He is, indeed, in some ways a comic character, but he is also a character for whom we develop increasing respect as the story continues. He is that rare, difficult thing to achieve in creative writing: a fully believable, richly rounded human being.

As the story progresses, both the narrative and the characters seem increasingly complex and multifaceted. On the one hand, the narrator is a talented architect, but on the other hand, he can't find a job (Jarrar, "Frame" 33). On the one hand, he is a political exile, but on the other, he can afford a beachfront apartment for his exiled wife in Alexandria, Egypt (34). On the one hand, his wife's father served as an officer in the Jordanian military, but after retiring he managed a "silk-manufacturing factory" (34). On the one hand, the narrator longed, as a young man, to return to the Middle East, but he was also a fan of John Travolta in *Saturday Night Fever* (34). When he initially saw *Playboy* magazines, he was "nauseated *at the first viewing*" (emphasis added), but he nevertheless "packed them for friends back home" (34). As all these examples suggest, little about this character or his life is predictable. Practically every paragraph contains surprises about him, his experiences, his reactions, and so on. We continue reading partly because neither the narrator nor the narrative is ever boring. The narrator is not a stereotype, nor is his story stereotypical. Paradoxically, Jarrar makes us feel real affection for her narrator not because he is simply a "representative type," but because he is a credible individual with whom we can easily identify on many different levels and in many different ways. She succeeds in undermining any prejudices that her non-Arab readers may have initially felt about an Arab protagonist. And she does so neither by making the protagonist a representative Arab nor by ignoring his ethnicity altogether, but instead by making him a representative *human being.*

But Jarrar's story is impressive not only in the ways it characterizes the narrator and others, but also in many other ways as well. No sooner, for instance, does the narrator feel politically exiled and professionally rejected than he has a chance encounter with friends who invite him to lunch. Instead of talking to him, however, the friends at first walk with him in silence. Then, just when he and they reach (ironically) a red "DON'T WALK" sign, a chance question leads to a job offer that ironically allows the narrator to move on with his professional career and establish a new, solid personal life in the United States. The story is full of these kinds of twists and turns of fate and fortune, yet none seems contrived or merely convenient. They contribute to one of the tale's larger themes—that real life (like a good narrative) is unpredictable.

Typical of the story's unpredictability are the following sentences, which describe the narrator's wife's reaction when he phones her in Egypt to ask if she would like to come and live in America [slash marks added]: "'Of course I would!' she screamed into the phone when I called her and gave her the good news, and she began packing // what little we had. That afternoon, my son and I walked around the East Village and looked at brownstones, // fantasizing about living in one" (Jarrar, "Frame" 35). I have added the slash marks to these sentences in order to call attention to a major source of the narrative effectiveness of Jarrar's story. We recall, for instance, that the wife is living in a beachfront apartment in Egypt. This location implies that this family enjoys some real wealth. No sooner does the wife begin "packing," however, than we are reminded that the family actually owns very "little." Then, no sooner are we reminded of their relative poverty than the narrator describes how he and his son looked at expensive brownstone apartments, suggesting a real intention to purchase one. But then we discover that their looking is mere "fantasizing." Again and again throughout the story, Jarrar seems to give with one hand and then take away with another. Her narrative method keeps us on our toes; we can never safely predict exactly what she will say next.

One especially effective illustration of this method occurs when the narrator describes the day of his mother's death—"the absolute worst day of my life, full stop" (Jarrar, "Frame" 36)—and then describes her history and personality. This is one of the richest sections of an unusually rich story. Once again, I have added slash marks to indicate the sudden juxtapositions that occur so often in this story, and especially in this section:

> So she'd gone, // like that. I wept in front of my children, // I refused my wife's embrace. // I thought of the way mother cooked eggplant, and how her head, which she never covered, would always part with a single black hair, // dispatching it into the sauce, and that her hair would always find its way into my dish, // into my mouth; // and just when I thought I'd reconciled with the fact // of never tasting it again, // I screamed, unspooling all my sorrow. . . . Nobody really knew Mother; // she spent most of her days away from us, and when she was present // she rarely conversed. Her favorite thing to do // was to spread cold cream on the pale skin of her face, // and tell my father what to do. (Jarrar, "Frame" 36)

The picture that emerges from this passage (and indeed from the whole story) implies an unusually complex relationship between the narrator and his mother. On the one hand, he obviously loved her and still does. He loved her so intensely that he cries in front of his children when he learns she is dead—*but* he refuses to allow his wife to comfort him. He is full of intense emotion, *but* he immediately thinks of something as pedestrian and quotidian as the way she cooked eggplant. *Then*, just when we might expect a loving description of this process, he focuses instead on a detail (the wayward hair) that might seem literally distasteful. *But*, just when we might assume that he would recall with disgust the sensation of the hair in his mouth, we discover that he actually misses that strange kind of contact with his mother. *And*, he misses it so much that the sense of loss literally makes him scream. *But then*, just when we sense his intense attachment to his mother, he admits that neither he nor anyone really knew her. *And*, he notes that even when she was physically present she seemed symbolically distant. The mother who has inspired such strong attachment in the narrator was *also*, apparently, vain, and, *in addition,* she was a comically bossy hen-pecker. No sooner do we get one impression of the narrator's relation to his mother than he switches to something else—usually something a reader could never have predicted from what came just before.

As this description of the mother proceeds, in fact, it becomes even more complicated: we discover that the mother herself, when a girl, was abandoned by her *own* mother. *But* then we discover that her own mother was in fact forced to abandon the girl in order to save her own life. But *then* we discover that the daughter, despite her mother's victimization, never forgave the mother for leaving the daughter to be raised by relatives. And *then* (perhaps most surprisingly of all) the narrator emphasizes his mother's

> utter coldness and… obstinate refusal to forgive. I am not sure if this was the source of her angry composure during my entire childhood, her selfish aloofness, the gulf of distance she placed between us, her children, and herself; I only know that she gave each of us a generous morsel of the attitudes, which we all carry in ourselves—selves which reside in nine different countries—to this day. (Jarrar, "Frame" 37)

The picture that emerges from pages 36–37 is thus exceptionally rich and complex. The speaker is stunned and moved by the death of his mother, *but* he concedes her deep flaws. He loved her and wanted to be loved *by* her, *but* he depicts her as cold, distant, unforgiving, vain, and bossy. But *then*, just when it might seem that he is focusing on his mother's flaws, he makes them seem comprehensible *and* also concedes his own. Accusing her of being unforgiving, he runs the risk of seeming unforgiving himself. All in all, the writing here is not only aesthetically complex, but morally complicated. Indeed, the two kinds of complexity reinforce one another.

No sooner, however, do we make our way through this very rich reminiscence of the narrator's mother than we discover that the narrator has regained not merely his composure but also the sense of humor that helps make the entire story so emotionally diverse. He reports, for instance, that on

> Saturday nights, I used to watch *Saturday Night Live* with my children, and even began a list of Jewish men that my daughters would be allowed to marry, but it still looks like this:
>
> 1. Adam Sandler
> 2.   (Jarrar, "Frame" 37)

Comic passages such as this alternate with darkly meditative passages such as this one (with, once again, slash marks added):

> If I try to remember when it was that I first felt alone, I can only say that it started before language. I could blame our land, the unnamed and desolate, raped, // green // and rocky fact of it. I could blame my mother, // whose demeanor I // inherited, and who // never cared for me as a child—so much so that I cried // at my sister's wedding, thinking my own mother was getting married and leaving me forever. Or can I blame myself? (39–40)

The narrator's complex description of the land ("desolate, raped, green, and rocky") epitomizes the complexity of his vision in general. That one single surprising adjective ("green") suggesting life and growth—right in the middle of other adjectives suggesting lifelessness, violence, and hardness—typifies Jarrar's unpredictable, constantly interesting style. So, too, does the narrator's complicated description (again) of his mother, whom he obviously loves and misses despite the fact that she "never cared for [him] as a child." Yet just when he is tempted to blame her for his sense of loneliness, he also considers blaming himself. The narrator, like the language he uses (indeed, *because* of the language he uses), seems a credibly complex human being. He is not a puppet or a stereotype. He exists not to illustrate some simple political, social, or cultural point, but to evoke our interest, our sympathy, our compassion, and our empathy. Paradoxically, by refusing to treat this narrator as a mere political pawn, used to score some larger geopolitical point, Jarrar wins our genuine interest in him and in people like him. She broadens our sense of humanity not by lecturing us, but by creating a completely believable human being. Her interest seems to be less in instructing us about the means by which "global hegemonic forces contend for control" or the ways in which "[s]ubaltern cultures are compelled to admit the hegemonic in 'being-made.'" Rather, her interest seems to be in creating the kind of memorable characters, embedded in a rich, unpredictable, but coherent work of art, that help make "A Frame for the Sky"—or any literary text—worth reading first and foremost *as* a literary text.

One might easily say more—much more—about the literary success of "A Frame for the Sky." One might note, for instance, the effective use of a comma splice in this sentence: "I wept in front of my children, I refused my wife's embrace." A period, semicolon, or conjunction would have produced a significantly different effect. Or one might note the delicately balanced structure and rhythm of the phrase "cold cream on the pale skin." Ultimately, no analysis can even begin to do full justice to a successful work of art. All it can do is point us back to the work itself, with eyes wide open, ears more alert, and brains fully interested in every seemingly small detail.

Works Cited

Jarrar, Randa. "A Frame for the Sky." *Dinarzad's Children: An Anthology of Contemporary American Arab Fiction*. Eds. Pauline Kaldas & Khaled Mattawa. Fayetteville: U of Arkansas P, 2004. 31–42.

_____. "Lost in Freakin' Yonkers." *Dinarzad's Children: An Anthology of Contemporary American Arab Fiction*. Eds. Pauline Kaldas & Khaled Mattawa. Fayetteville: U of Arkansas P, 2004. 43–55.

Kaldas, Pauline & Khaled Mattawa, eds. *Dinarzad's Children: An Anthology of Contemporary American Arab Fiction*. Fayetteville: U of Arkansas P, 2004.

_____. eds. *Dinarzad's Children: An Anthology of Contemporary American Arab Fiction*. Ed. Pauline Kaldas & Khaled Mattawa. 2nd ed. Fayetteville: U of Arkansas P, 2004.

Simmers, Erich. "The Global War on Culture: The Occupation of Arab-American Cultural Citizenship in Randa Jarrar's Short Fiction." *Anamesa* 17 (Fall 2006): 78–92.

Irony and Epistolary Form in Chitra Banerjee Divakaruni's "Mrs. Dutta Writes a Letter" and Chimamanda Ngozi Adichie's "The Thing Around Your Neck"

Maryse Jayasuriya

What letters communicate and what letter-writers learn shape two important contemporary immigrant short stories: the Indian-American writer Chitra Banerjee Divakaruni's "Mrs. Dutta Writes a Letter" (1998) and the Nigerian writer Chimamanda Ngozi Adichie's "The Thing Around Your Neck" (2009). The epistolary form is most often associated in English literature with the long history of the novel, with such notable works as Samuel Richardson's *Pamela*, Henry Fielding's parodic *Shamela*, and Fanny Burney's *Evelina* serving as early and major examples of the form. The short story has less of an epistolary tradition, so it is striking that both of these writers make letters, actually composed and merely imagined, a central feature of these stories. This use of letters and letter-writing becomes all the more noteworthy at a time when electronic communication is making letter-writing less of a default option for many people. "Mrs. Dutta Writes a Letter" appeared in the midst of the late 1990s' transition to email for personal communications, and "The Thing Around Your Neck" appeared at a time when Skype had already become a verb. The authors' use of physical, paper letters, however, helps to highlight both the cultural adjustments their protagonists are in the process of making as well as the constraints that the middle-aged Mrs. Dutta would face in adapting to more fluid technological media and the material constraints that Adichie's heroine, Akunna, would face in communicating with impoverished loved ones at home. The surprising choice to use epistolary motifs in these two stories parallels the authors' surprising reworking of conventional immigrant success stories.

It is perhaps only natural for people who migrate from one country to another to have great expectations of life in the hostland, a life they hope will be better than the one in their homeland and that will justify the difficulties and even trauma entailed by the relocation. The two short stories mentioned above deal with what happens when immigrants to the United States begin to realize that their expectations of life in their newly adopted country are very different from the reality, and they gradually become disillusioned. This realization is emphasized through the trope of the letter to friends and loved ones back home—a letter that is unfinished or not begun at all because the immigrant does not know what to say about the reality of the immigrant experience, or how to convey hopes that have changed or diminished since the departure from the homeland. Putting words to paper confirms things about which they would rather be silent.

Multiple Generations, Alternate Homes: "Mrs. Dutta Writes a Letter"

The generation gap is a common enough topic but it can add one more layer of complication to life for immigrants in a multigenerational household. In Chitra Banerjee Divakaruni's much-anthologized short story "Mrs. Dutta Writes a Letter" (first published in *The Atlantic* in 1998), the eponymous protagonist is an Indian woman, widowed for three years, who has come to live with her only son Sagar and his family in California. She had been happy enough in her apartment in Calcutta, continuing her long-established diurnal routine even after her husband's death, though friends and family have told her that it is not good for her to live on her own and the cultural norm is for her, a widow, to live with her son. Being confined to bed by a severe attack of pneumonia, however, made her realize that no one needed her anymore and caused depression, propelling her to sell her flat, give away her possessions, and accept her son's invitation to come and live with him in California.

The story focuses on one pivotal day two months after her arrival at her son's house. The sheen and novelty of her presence has worn off, and both Mrs. Dutta and her son's family are experiencing the tensions of living together. She contemplates writing a response to a letter sent by her friend, Mrs. Roma Basu, who is still domiciled in India. Through the mental letter she composes, certain facts about her daily life in the new milieu become evident to readers.

Mrs. Dutta feels homesick—she is full of nostalgia for the life to which she was accustomed back in India, from the brass pots in her kitchen to the vendors constantly passing by in the street. She also has difficulty adjusting to her new environment and constantly experiences culture shock. She has to admit that her expectations of her life with her son, daughter-in-law, and grandchildren were very different from reality. She cannot quite grasp the way in which her son's family has wholeheartedly assimilated to American life.

First, there has been a change in names. Her daughter-in-law is no longer Shyamoli, but "Molli," while her two grandchildren—Mrinalini and Pradeep—now go as "Minnie" and "Pat." While the abbreviation and Anglicization of the Indian names might be considered simply a pragmatic choice, this change seems to suggest, at least to Mrs. Dutta, a desire in her son's family to assimilate completely to the culture of the hostland and a willingness to give up cultural identity for the sake of acceptance and convenience. Unlike Jhumpa Lahiri's protagonist Gogol—a second-generation Indian immigrant attempting to straddle two cultures—in the novel *The Namesake*, Mrs. Dutta's grandchildren display no sense of a divided identity.

Her attempts to regale her grandchildren with stories of her own experiences and educate them about their cultural heritage do not interest them, while her efforts to cook Indian meals for the family are not appreciated by Molli. The gifts that she has brought for her grandchildren—such as the *Ramayana for Young Children*—are not valued or used and the children do not seem to have any time for her: "The children. A heaviness pulls at Mrs. Dutta's entire body when she thinks of them. Like so much in this country, they have turned out to be—yes, she might as well admit it—a disappointment" (Divakaruni 409).

Instead of the joy and fulfillment she expected to find through living with her son's family, Mrs. Dutta experiences guilt and fear—guilt that she cannot, for example, master the instructions for operating the washer and dryer to do the laundry and fear that she is getting in the way. She cannot understand and is embarrassed by public displays of affection between her son and daughter-in-law. She cannot follow the humor in American sitcoms that the family watch on television or comprehend why neighbors do not interact in the same way that they did back in India. If, as Aparajita Sagar has pointed out, "to be at home is to have the sense of a terrain—spatial, epistemological, cultural—which one expects to navigate with smoothness and ease" (237), Mrs. Dutta definitely does not feel at home in her son's house.

The tensions between Mrs. Dutta and her son's family escalate gradually. Her life-long habits of getting up early, taking up time in the bathroom, throwing away what she considered "contaminated" left-over food and beverages instead of putting them in the fridge according to Molli's wishes, and refusing to let her son help with domestic chores, like folding laundry, cause arguments between Sagar and Molli. The latter is exasperated by Mrs. Dutta's inability to comprehend the need for equality in the division of household chores when both partners are gainfully employed outside the home.

The generation gap and cultural difference both come into play here. Mrs. Dutta is appalled at the ways in which Molli, Sagar, and their children have veered away from the Bengali culture that Mrs. Dutta herself has valued and adhered to all her life, such as obeying her mother-in-law's dictates and respecting elders in all matters, even if she didn't agree with them. She is dismayed that Molli does not reprimand her children when they are rude and disrespectful to her, an elder. She cannot understand the concept of privacy—why children are allowed to lock the doors of their rooms and keep parents out. Ngũgĩ wa Thiong'o has famously argued that language carries culture, and this is made evident in the fact that Mrs. Dutta's mother tongue, Bengali, has no word for privacy. By noting the elusiveness of this concept for Mrs. Dutta, Divakaruni calls attention to the fact that Mrs. Dutta is living in translation, trying to understand the culture in which she is living in terms derived from the culture of her birth.

At the point when the story starts, Mrs. Dutta is congratulating herself on her seemingly successful efforts to do things in her own way without her daughter-in-law's knowledge. Since the washer and dryer have defeated her, she washes her clothes in the bathtub (unbeknownst to Molli) and has hung them up to dry on the fence dividing the house from the neighbor's.

The story is propelled forward by the letter that she has received from her old friend, Mrs. Basu—who has asked her whether she is happy in the United States—and the letter she has begun writing and is mentally continuing to craft in reply. Mrs. Basu is her oldest and closest friend, and apparently, one of the few people who still call her by her first name "Prameela" and knows her for herself, not as Mr. Dutta's widow or as Sagar's mother. This epistolary element is significant because Mrs. Dutta's attempts at a response indicate what she does not want to acknowledge to herself—her disappointment in the country to which she has immigrated as well as in her son's family. "And so she has been putting off her reply, while in her heart family loyalty battles with insidious feelings of—but she turns from them quickly and will not name them even to herself" (Divakaruni 407). She has been rationing the nostalgia that she has allowed herself to feel and considers admitting her homesickness to her friend: "*Oh Roma, I miss it all so much. Sometimes I feel that someone has reached in and torn a handful of my chest*" (408). At the same time, she is proud of how she believes she has managed to negotiate her needs in the new environment: "*I'm fitting in so well here, you'd never guess I came only two months back. I've found new ways of doing things, of solving problems creatively. You would be most proud if you saw me*" (412). Her unvoiced critiques of her family are also included in what the third-person limited omniscient narrator refers to as the "mind-letter": the way in which Mrs. Dutta's grandchildren sit mindlessly watching television for hours, and her daughter-in-law's constant complaints and weeping about trivial issues: "*Women need to be strong, not react to every little thing like this. You and I, Roma, we had far worse to cry about, but we shed our tears invisibly. We were good wives and daughters-in-law, good mothers. Dutiful, uncomplaining. Never putting ourselves first*"

(416). She quickly checks herself: "Of course she will never put such blasphemy into a real letter. Still, it makes her feel better to be able to say it, if only to herself" (417).

The letter, in addition to giving Mrs. Dutta the opportunity to express her frustrations and confide her secrets to Mrs. Basu, functions as a sounding board. Mrs. Dutta is not really planning to ask the latter for advice, but is working things out for herself in the act of composing, in her mind, the letter to her friend. The tensions between the letter Mrs. Dutta actually writes, the letter in her mind, and the elements of her current life of which she is unaware constitute concentric circles of irony that Divakaruni uses to illustrate the complexities of the immigrant life that an older immigrant, like Mrs. Dutta, seeks to negotiate.

The letter has another important function in terms of the plot. When Mrs. Dutta goes back into the kitchen to retrieve the half-written letter she has left there, she overhears a weeping Molli talking to Sagar about her—how the neighbor had complained about Mrs. Dutta's hanging the laundry on the fence dividing the two houses. Mrs. Dutta thus learns that her strategies for coping with life in her new milieu have not been successful and are causing difficulties for her son and his family. The moment in which she declared, within the mind-letter, that Mrs. Basu would be "most proud" of her problem-solving skills thus becomes an instance of dramatic irony: we as readers see that the result of Mrs. Dutta's surreptitious laundering is unlikely to be auspicious, but Mrs. Dutta has to learn by hearing the truth from Molli.

The extent to which Molli is upset suggests that she is not as comfortable or confident in the United States as she would have people believe. She seems to be driven by the fear that Americans might think Indian immigrants like her are "savages" (Divakaruni 417), and she makes changes to please them. Ironically, she is not as free as she has believed herself to be—Molli, despite her efforts to free herself from the traditions of her homeland, is constrained by her attempts to fit into what she believes is "American." Mrs. Dutta is thus not the only character in the story who discloses an ironic gap between her perceptions and the reality of her experience.

By letting us hear their voices speak un-self-consciously—Mrs. Dutta's in an imagined letter in the privacy of her mind, and Molli's in the presumptive privacy of a conversation with her husband—Divakaruni helps us enter into the ambivalent feelings of each of their inward experiences of immigrant life.

Mrs. Dutta comes to certain realizations. First, she begins to question whether the dutiful life she has always led—living for other people, being stoic—really is the best idea: *"And what good did it do? The more we bent, the more people pushed us, until one day we'd forgotten that we could stand up straight"* (Divakaruni 417). Perhaps, she thinks, Molli's move away from the cultural norms of her homeland is not something to be condemned, but an action to be emulated. Mrs. Dutta's time in the hostland has held up a mirror to the culture with which she is most familiar and enables her to see the benefits of doing certain things differently. She also interrogates the notion that living with her son and his family in a country that is not familiar to her is the best possible option even though, according to the traditions to which she has always adhered, "everyone knows a wife's place is with her husband, and a widow's is with her son" (412).

Her ability to rethink her choices and beliefs shows that Mrs. Dutta is a woman who has a capacity to grow and develop. Her strength is shown in the way she successfully hides her hurt feelings after eavesdropping inadvertently on Molli's conversation with Sagar and hearing herself being harshly criticized. In addition, Mrs. Dutta bravely acknowledges the truth—that she will be happier back in Calcutta with her old friend than with her own family members. At the end of the short story, when she finally finishes the letter to Mrs. Basu and intimates that she will be returning to India, Mrs. Dutta is acting for herself and becoming empowered. By deciding to return to India, she—for the first time in her life—is making a choice that is not based on duty or cultural values, but her own preference, a choice that seems to have been made possible by her exposure to life and cultural norms in a different society than her own. It is noteworthy that in claiming agency by returning to India, Mrs. Dutta creates an ironic reversal of the standard immigrant narrative;

sometimes, it appears, returning to the homeland can also be a sign of courage, even as, for other immigrants, seeking a new home may demonstrate the strength of one's character.

Diasporic Consciousness and Material Constraints: "The Thing Around Your Neck"

There are instructive similarities between the ambivalent, and at times ironic, approach to the immigrant experience in Divakaruni's story and that taken in a story by one of the present day's most influential West African writers. In the title story of Chimamanda Ngozi Adichie's collection *The Thing Around Your Neck*, the protagonist Akunna also comes to certain realizations about her life as an immigrant in the United States. Unlike Mrs. Dutta, the twenty-two year old Akunna is not from the middle-class in her homeland and lacks the capacity for easy mobility. She has won a green card lottery and leaves her native Nigeria under the impression that she is most fortunate, a view that has been emphasized by envious family and friends who have come to see her off and offer her advice about how to cope in her new environment. Their perceptions of the United States are naïve at best, perhaps influenced by images seen on television or in films: "You thought everybody in America had a car and a gun; your uncles and aunts and cousins thought so, too. [...] they told you: In a month, you will have a big car. Soon, a big house" (Adichie 115). Akunna's actual experience exhibits the ironic frustration of these expectations.

At the beginning, Akunna lives in Maine with the distant relative who originally entered her name in the lottery, along with his wife and children. Once he makes a pass at her, she realizes that she can no longer remain under his roof. Akunna leaves and moves away to Connecticut. She obtains a job in a restaurant by offering to work for a lower wage than the other employees and tries to manage on her own, sending half of her earnings back home to her family despite the fact that she can barely pay her rent. She is unable to pursue her education since going to college is beyond her means.

She finds herself unable to write a letter to enclose in the brown envelope in which she sends money home every month. Unlike Mrs.

Dutta, Akunna cannot actually begin writing a letter to her family because she feels she has nothing worthwhile to say—or nothing that she can disclose to her loved ones without crushing their hopes in the "American dream" and causing anxiety: "You wrapped the money carefully in white paper but you didn't write a letter. There was nothing to write about" (Adichie 118). Another reason for her inability to write home, or her "communicational paralysis" (Braga & Gonçalves 5), is the pressure that she feels to live up to the expectations of her friends and family to gain material success in America and send them gifts: "But you could never afford enough perfumes and clothes and handbags and shoes to go around and still pay your rent on what you earned at the waitressing job, so you wrote nobody" (Adichie 119). Her family's and friends' hypotheses about why she might not write are thus ironically subverted: they might imagine her failure to write as a sign that she has forgotten them amid the pleasures of her new life, when in fact it is the very difficulty of her circumstances that hampers her ability to communicate with them. As Claudio Braga and Glaucia Gonçalves have noted, "the expression 'you wanted to write' […] is repeated seven times throughout the story" (5). The expression becomes a refrain, adding cohesion to the story, even as it emphasizes Akunna's thwarted desire to maintain her connection to her family and friends through letter-writing.

Despite Akunna's inability to put pen to paper, she does want to write about what she has learned about her new country, particularly the aspects of American life that surprise her. She learns from her so-called "Uncle" that "the trick was to understand America, to know that America was give-and-take. You gave up a lot but you gained a lot, too" (Adichie 116). She discovers that as an immigrant, she has to expect insulting or offensive questions based on a "mixture of ignorance and arrogance" (116). She begins to appreciate some of the positive aspects of her hostland—"the surprising openness of people in America, how eagerly they told you […] the kinds of things that one should hide or should reveal only to the family members who wished them well" (118). She is also struck by the reality of the United States: "You wanted to write that rich Americans were thin and poor Americans were fat and that many did not have a big house and car" (119). She is bemused by the deference that parents appear to pay young children and shocked at the way resources are wasted.

Like Mrs. Dutta, Akunna often thinks of home and the good memories she has of her family. She does remember hardships in Nigeria: having to bribe teachers into giving students good grades, deal with universities that are closed for extended periods of time because lecturers are compelled to go on strike just to get paid, and humiliate oneself for the sake of protection from more important and powerful people as her father has had to do, for example. What she really dwells on, however, are the simple pleasures as well as ordinary aspects of life in Lagos that she seems to have taken for granted and only now begins to appreciate:

> [Y]our aunts who hawked dried fish and plantains, cajoling customers to buy and then shouting insults when they didn't; your uncles who drank local gin and crammed their families and lives into single rooms; your friends who had come out to say goodbye before you left, to rejoice because you won the American visa lottery, to confess their envy; your parents who often held hands as they walked to church on Sunday mornings. (Adichie 117–118)

As Daniel Boyarin and Jonathan Boyarin have put it, "We remind ourselves of what we are by reminding ourselves of what we miss" (4).

The entire story is written in the second-person narrative voice. It seems to be an invitation to the reader to identify with the protagonist, for "you" to experience what Akunna experiences as closely as possible. As Elizabeth Jackson has stated, "While pointing out cultural differences from a particular perspective, this narrative at the same time works to reduce distance by insistently using the word 'you,' implying that this could be your perspective" (6). Adichie achieves a profound sort of empathy in her narrative voice through the intimate "you" with which she addresses Akunna, as Jackson suggests, and her readers may well find that the complications of Akunna's immigrant experience come closer to their own uncertainties as a result of this unexpected formal choice.

Akunna is overcome by loneliness, isolation and alienation, the thing "around your neck [...] that very nearly choked you before you fell asleep" (Adichie 119). Jackson has speculated that the title of the story is a reference to Salman Rushdie's short story "The Courter," about South Asian immigrants in Britain and the pull that an immigrant—with metaphorical ropes around his or her neck that function in the manner of a lasso—feels between the homeland and the hostland (3). The reference could also be to Samuel Taylor Coleridge's poem "The Rime of the Ancient Mariner," where the narrator who has recklessly endangered the life of his shipmates by killing an albatross ruefully recounts that "Instead of the cross, the Albatross/ About my neck was hung" (212)—a choice made by an individual that brings on unforeseen negative repercussions.

Akunna's loneliness is eased somewhat by her relationship with an unnamed young white American, a college student with a trust fund and a penchant for travelling around Asia and Africa in an effort to "find himself." At first her interest in him is piqued by his familiarity with her country and culture and by the fact that he appears to see her for herself when she seems to be invisible to those around her. Slowly, she finds herself getting irritated by his obliviousness to the way that others treat them as if they are "abnormal" when they are together as well as by what she understands as his condescension to people who, like her, are from developing countries in Asia and Africa. Akunna views his fraught relationship with his parents as mere self-indulgence. His metaphorical and apparently needless distance from his parents emphasizes her physical distance from her own parents, a distance that she at long last decides to bridge.

When Akunna finally is able to bring herself to write a letter to her parents giving them her address, she immediately receives a response from her mother, informing her of her father's sudden death five months before. Akunna is devastated and realizes the full extent of what she has missed by living in the United States. This gives her the impetus to return to Nigeria. The ending of the story is ambiguous—her future with her boyfriend, or even her return to the United States, is uncertain.

In both short stories, diasporic consciousness—the sense of connection with a distant homeland—results in epiphanic moments for the protagonists. As Edward Said has asserted,

> Most people are principally aware of one culture, one setting, one home; exiles are aware of at least two, and this plurality of vision gives rise to an awareness of simultaneous dimensions, an awareness that—to borrow a phrase from music—is contrapuntal... For an exile, habits of life, expression or activity in the new environment inevitably occur against the memory of these things in another environment. Thus both the new and the old environments are vivid, actual, occurring together contrapuntally. (186)

By using letters as central devices in their stories, Divakaruni and Adichie both allow their characters' Indian and Nigerian identities and experiences to play contrapuntally, to use Said's term, off their experiences in the United States. Although Divakaruni and Adichie, like their characters, are from different generations and continents, both illustrate the complications that arise when immigration is not always a one-way journey and when immigrants can continue to feel the pull of home. This ambivalence is powerfully dramatized through the writers' use of irony and epistolary form, and the artistry of their stories makes the experiences described ring all the more true.

Works Cited

Adichie, Chimamanda Ngozi. "The Thing Around Your Neck." *The Thing Around Your Neck*. New York: Knopf, 2009. 115–127.

Boyarin, Daniel & Jonathan Boyarin. *Powers of Diaspora*. Minneapolis: U of Minnesota P, 2002.

Braga, Claudio & Glaucia R. Gonçalves. "Fictional Representations of Contemporary Diasporas: The Case of the Invisible Diasporic Women of Chimamanda Ngozi Adichie." *The Chimamanda Adichie Website*. May 2014. Web. 20 Aug. 2015.

Burney, Fanny. *Evelina*. New York: Oxford World Classics, 2008.

Coleridge, Samuel Taylor. "The Rime of the Ancient Mariner." 1798. *Lyrical Ballads and Other Poems*. Ware, Hertfordshire: Wordsworth Editions, 2003. 207-27.

Divakaruni, Chitra. "Mrs. Dutta Writes a Letter." *Literature Without Borders*. Ed. George R. Bozzini & Cynthia A. Leenerts. New York: Longman, 2000. 405-420.

Fielding, Henry. *Joseph Andrews and Shamela*. New York: Penguin, 1999.

Jackson, Elizabeth. "Transcending the limitations of diaspora as a category of cultural identity in Chimamanda Ngozi Adichie's *The Thing Around Your Neck*." *The Chimamanda Adichie Website*. June 2012. Web. 22 Aug. 2015.

Lahiri, Jhumpa. *The Namesake*. Boston: Houghton Mifflin, 2003.

Richardson, Samuel. *Pamela, Or Virtue Rewarded*. New York: Oxford World Classics, 2008.

Rushdie, Salman. "The Courter." *East, West*. London: Vintage, 1995. 173-211.

Sagar, Aparajita. "Homes and Postcoloniality." *Diaspora* 6.2 (1997): 237-51.

Said, Edward. *Reflections of Exile*. Cambridge: Harvard UP, 2000.

Wa Thiong'o, Ngugi. *Decolonizing the Mind: The Politics of Language in African Literature*. London: James Currey, 2011.

Immigration, Irony, and Vision in Jhumpa Lahiri's *The Interpreter of Maladies*

Brian Yothers

Characters in Jhumpa Lahiri's short story collection *The Interpreter of Maladies* are defined and redefined by their changing perceptions. As the title of the collection hints, and as Lahiri's own biography as a PhD in Renaissance drama might also lead us to expect, Lahiri's characters are frequently engaged in discerning just what it is that they are seeing, and they attempt to find frameworks into which they can fit these perceptions. Often, the perceptions toward which the characters are struggling are clouded by misperceptions and uncertainties: a white American woman having an affair with an Indian businessman is surprised to learn of the existence of Bengal; a young Indian girl in America discovers Bangladesh's war of independence through a frequent guest at her parents' house; a young immigrant couple disagree on what their relation as Hindus should be to the Christian artifacts left behind in their house; and a family of immigrants to America from India find themselves puzzled by their homeland, and prove puzzling to those at home in India.

One element of these stories that is particularly noteworthy is the way in which they function, not as simple slices of Indian American life, but as intricately crafted pieces of ironic perception, stories in which the unexpected happens more often than what might seem likely, and in which characters are struggling on their way to forming provisional knowledge. In this sense, Lahiri's stories benefit as much from considering how they fit into the artistic traditions of the short story in English, as they do from considering their status as documents that represent the experience of immigration.

Lahiri is a writer who is highly engaged with the traditions of the short story, in English and beyond, and also with the wider literary canon. She earned her PhD in Renaissance literature from Boston University in 1997, completing a dissertation entitled "Accursed Palace: The Italian Palazzo on the Jacobean Stage (1603–1625)." It is worth noting that Lahiri's interest in seventeenth-century English literature was shared by such early masters of the short story form in America as Edgar Allan Poe and Herman Melville, as William E. Engel has discussed in a study of the relationship between Poe, Melville, and seventeenth-century art and literature. In her work that has received the widest circulation, her novel *The Namesake* (since made into a motion picture), she gives her title character the name of Gogol, connecting him directly and explicitly with Nicolai Gogol, the great Russian master of the short story form and author of "The Overcoat." Lahiri's second short story collection, *Unaccustomed Earth*, takes its title from Nathaniel Hawthorne's "Custom-House" introduction to *The Scarlet Letter.* If Lahiri aims to write short stories of the Indian immigrant experience, her emphasis in so doing is at least as much on creating outstanding instances of the short story as a literary genre as on relating the particularity of Indian experiences, and indeed, the two goals depend upon each other.

The four stories I summarize above and discuss below are works that are readily available in literature anthologies (including, for example, Ann Charters's *The Story and Its Writer* and *The American Short Story and Its Writer*, and the nearly ubiquitous *Norton Anthology of American Literature*), and I focus on them precisely because they are works that will likely be used to introduce students both to the art of the short story and to the intercultural aspects of immigrant fiction specifically. I teach each of these stories in my own classes on short fiction, and I find that they are remarkably useful for showing how the interior world of the short story can illuminate the exterior world of events. What makes Lahiri's work so valuable is that her stories embrace both subtle intercultural observation and critique and a devotion to the literary craft of the short story, and indeed, the latter enables much of the subtlety of the former in her work. I discuss the four stories in the order that they appear in *Interpreter of Maladies* in order to demonstrate both the formal qualities of the individual stories and the way in which these stories connect across the collection.

"When Mr. Pirzada Came to Dine": Seeing a Divided Homeland

Lahiri's story of the initiation of a young girl named Lilia into the adult world of politics and political violence via the Bangladeshi war of independence, "When Mr. Pirzada Came to Dine," illustrates how carefully Lahiri crafted her narration of her characters' enlarged consciousness and vision. The opening sentence captures the delicate balance of the physical and intellectual spheres that Lahiri brings off in the story: "In the autumn of 1971 a man used to come to our house, bearing confections in his pocket, and hopes of ascertaining the life or death of his family" ("When Mr. Pirzada" 23). The parallel between the confections in his pocket and the hopes presumably in his heart of good news is both comic and heartbreaking, in a way that resembles the narrator's own expanding vision of the events of her own life and the world of great power politics. The narrator is now an adult, looking back and describing the events of her childhood, but using the constraints on her understanding of geopolitical events as a child to make the events seem contemporaneous rather than simply historical. With admirable economy, the adult Lilia lays the scene for the war between Pakistan and the emerging nation of Bangladesh, identifying the man, Mr. Pirzada, as coming from Dacca (now commonly spelled "Dhaka"), and explaining that Dacca, which is now the capital of independent Bangladesh, was then a war zone, a site of atrocities in which the Pakistani army—fighting to keep Bangladesh, then called East Pakistan, within Pakistan—committed murder and rape.

Not surprisingly, the nine-year-old Lilia mediates these events through a different set of impressions than those that her adult-self narrates so crisply. She reports that Mr. Pirzada was confused by his children's names because they all started with the letter "A," that his seven daughters ate their meals on banana leaves, and that in a black and white photo that he showed her, they all wore braids. As the story goes on, she learns more and more about their precarious circumstances. From her father, she finds out about the violence of the Partition of the Indian subcontinent into India and Pakistan (including, as East Pakistan, Bangladesh). She is puzzled to discover that religious differences led to violence between Muslims and Hindus, who to her eyes seem very similar in the cultural traditions they share, particularly those related to food and hospitality. One of the story's strengths is that just as Lahiri expands the vision of her non-South Asian readers by giving them a view of the ongoing implications of Partition, for immigrants in the United States as well as Indians, Pakistanis, and Bangladeshis at home, the situation of her readers is mirrored in the gradually expanding consciousness of a small, yet precocious child. Another structural strength of the story is the way that Lahiri uses maps as visual objects to show us Lilia's expanding vision: she has been taught only to look at "maps of the thirteen colonies" at the time of the American Revolution in school, but her father introduces her to maps of the subcontinent in the throes of events comparable to those of the American Revolution in their capacity to redraw maps altogether ("When Mr. Pirzada" 28–29).

Food and violence are placed in jarring juxtaposition as Lilia narrates the way in which Mr. Pirzada brings a wider, and often disturbing, knowledge of the world with his candy. Lilia treasures the candy, remembering that "I coveted each evening's treasure as I would a jewel, or a coin from a buried kingdom, and I would place it in a small keepsake box made of carved sandalwood beside my bed, in which, long ago in India, my father's mother used to store the ground areca nuts she ate after her morning bath" ("When Mr. Pirzada" 29–30). The candies thus create a kind of link with her family's past through her grandmother's keepsake box. At the same time that Lilia secretes candies and the family shares the food that unites them culturally to Mr. Pirzada as fellow Bengalis, however, their television set reminds them of how much danger Mr. Pirzada's wife and daughters are in:

> On the screen I saw tanks rolling through dusty streets, and fallen buildings, and forests of unfamiliar trees into which East Pakistani refugees had fled, seeking safety over the Indian border. I saw boats with fan-shaped sails sailing on wide coffee-colored rivers, a barricaded university, newspaper offices burnt to the ground. I turned to look at Mr. Pirzada; the images flashed in miniature across his eyes. (Lahiri, "When Mr. Pirzada" 31)

The crafting of these sentences is subtle enough to miss, but important to note. Lilia's repetition of "I saw" suggests the degree to which this is a revelation for her through the use of the techniques of anaphora (repeated words at the start of sentences) and cataloging (using the cumulative effect of a list for literary effect). When she looks at Mr. Pirzada, she sees the images from the news reflected in his own eyes; in a profound way, she is learning to see by taking on his vision.

The tension and fear associated with the war in Bangladesh builds for Mr. Pirzada throughout the story. Increasingly, as Lilia becomes aware of the degree of danger that Mr. Pirzada's wife and daughters face, what she learns is described in terms of the shared experiences of Lilia (as a second-generation immigrant), her parents (as first-generation immigrants), and Mr. Pirzada (whose status as a visiting scholar is distinct from both). Again, these shared perceptions come together over food, a topic Shweta Garg and Heather Hoyle Peerboom have recently investigated in relation to Lahiri's work. When describing the tension that the family and Mr. Pirzada feel when they are unsure of the fate of his wife and daughters, Lilia relates, "What I remember during those twelve days of the war was that my father no longer asked me to watch the news with them, and that Mr. Pirzada stopped bringing me candy, and that my mother refused to make anything other than boiled eggs with rice for dinner" (Lahiri, "When Mr. Pirzada" 40). The meals had become a kind of religious ritual, binding Lilia's Hindu family and the Muslim Mr. Pirzada in a shared expression of concern: "Most of all, I remember the three of them operating during that time as if they were a single person, sharing a single meal, a single body, a single silence, and a single fear" (41). As before, Lahiri's use of parallelism and repetition underlines the seriousness of the moment, and gives her narration a poetic quality.

Even as Lilia is receiving a firsthand education in international turmoil at home, her time in school is hampering rather than extending her education. Her teacher, Mrs. Kenyon, scolds her for her attempts to learn more about Bangladesh when Bangladesh is not a part of the curriculum (Lahiri, "When Mr. Pirzada" 33). Her father, meanwhile, expresses outrage at the parochialism of an education that leaves out the Indian subcontinent. Elizabeth Jackson has noted that both cosmopolitanism and postcoloniality are important to Lahiri's work (109), and Lilia's father's frustration seems to reflect both a postcolonial concern that the histories of the nations of the decolonizing world be represented in the United States' educational system and a cosmopolitan sense of the interconnectedness of national destines. Lilia's father's reflections on the education she is receiving and Lilia's own experience of having her attention redirected from learning about Bangladesh on her own to following the received curriculum also suggests how closely Lahiri's artistic concern with vision is tied to a concern with representing culture with nuance and integrity.

We might note that by teaching the lessons of Partition (both in its original form in 1947, and again in 1971) Lahiri calls to mind Bapsi Sidwa's novel *Ice-Candy-Man* (1988), which narrates from a Pakistani perspective the agony of the 1947 partition through the consciousness of a young Parsi girl, who because she is Parsi is able to provide a vantage point distinct from either Hindu and Sikh or Muslim versions of Partition. Lahiri balances a range of fictional traditions in her writing from the Renaissance drama that she wrote about as an academic, to the contemporary literature being written by South Asians resident in South Asia. Writing an immigrant story for Lahiri involves an engagement with the stories told in the homeland of the Indian subcontinent and the hostland of the United States alike.

"The Interpreter of Maladies:" Ironic Distance in the Homeland

In the title story, Lahiri brings hostland and homeland perceptions into conflict, and she does so by building a series of ironic frames around her characters' perceptions and misperceptions. The protagonist, Mr. Kapasi, has the task of showing Mr. and Mrs. Das and their three spoiled children around the Sun Temple at Konarak. The mother and father in the Das family are second-generation immigrants whose parents have made good, and they are now experiencing their ancestral homeland as Western tourists, trying at once to preserve a fragile sense of connection to their Indian heritage and to justify the material and economic distance that exists between themselves and an educated Indian domiciled in India, like Mr. Kapasi.

The story uses free indirect discourse to show the family through Mr. Kapasi's eyes. The parents are young and evidently American in culture, as evidenced by Mr. Das's greeting Mr. Kapasi not with two hands pressed together in the manner that Mr. Kapasi uses to greet him, but rather with an excessively firm handshake. Mr. Das's Americanization seems also to make him somewhat juvenile compared to the reserved Mr. Kapasi: he "looked exactly like a magnified version of [his young son] Ronny. He had a sapphire blue visor, and was dressed in shorts, sneakers, and a t-shirt. The camera slung round his neck, with an impressive telephoto lens and numerous buttons and markings, was the only complicated thing he wore" (Lahiri, "Interpreter" 44). Mr. Das's childishness is paralleled by his wife's similarly immature appearance, also captured in a description of her clothing and make-up, from her "close fitting blouse styled like a man's undershirt… decorated at chest level with a calico applique shaped like a strawberry," to her "small hands like paws, her frosty pink fingernails painted to match her lips" (46). The children argue with each other, and the parents argue with them in a way that seems to diminish the distance between the generations still more. The contrast between the entire family and the dignified, scholarly Mr. Kapasi could not be more pronounced, as we come to realize that this shallow family is being driven about by a polyglot whose knowledge of a wide range of Asian and European languages is mirrored by his poetic appreciation of the site to which he is taking the Das family. Mr. Kapasi is discontented with his job and his marriage, but he behaves as an adult in a way that the couple seems incapable of imitating. The job that he holds during the week, that of serving as a translator for a physician, while not his preferred profession, means that his humanistic knowledge of languages is enlisted in the service of matters of life and death, even as his material circumstances are sufficiently straitened that the philistine Das family can employ him as a guide.

The narrator's irony at the expense of the Das family, both parents and children, calls to mind Flannery O'Connor's short story "A Good Man is Hard to Find," where O'Connor lets the children's rudeness and bad behavior accumulate over the course of the story until it speaks for itself. Something similar is at work when Lahiri lets us see the children's and parents' immaturity and gives us the darkly comic scene of the monkeys' attack on one of the Das's spoiled children. Admittedly, this is not a misfortune on par with the murder of an entire family by the Misfit in O'Connor's story, but the confrontations that conclude the story, first between Mr. Kapasi and Mrs. Das in the car, and then between the family and the monkeys outside the temple, pass a similar judgment on what the Das family has lost. In the car, Mrs. Das confesses to the fact that the younger son, Bobby, is not her husband's child, but the result of an affair. Awash in self-pity, she responds contemptuously when Mr. Kapasi suggests that she may not fully comprehend her own feelings about her adulterous affair and its consequences: "He decided to begin with the most obvious question, to get to the heart of the matter, and so he asked, 'Is it really pain you feel, Mrs. Das, or guilt?' She turned to him and glared, mustard oil thick on her frosty pink lips" (Lahiri, "Interpreter" 66). Mr. Kapasi, who had been fantasizing about maintaining a relationship with Mrs. Das, has diagnosed her condition accurately. In so doing, he has severed the line of communication between them because acknowledging Mr. Kapasi's diagnosis would require more self-knowledge than Mrs. Das can manage.

Ultimately, two major gaps in understanding appear in this story: on the one hand, the self-aware Mr. Kapasi recognizes that there is a great deal that he does not understand regarding the Das family, whereas the Das family never fully comprehends their own occluded vision when it comes to their ancestral homeland of India and their even more deficient insight into themselves. Even more than the story's conclusion, in which Mr. Kapasi has to rescue the Das's son Bobby from the monkeys outside the Sun Temple (monkeys that the Das family have failed to take seriously), the end of Mr. Kapasi's conversation with Mrs. Das, when he diagnoses her feelings about

Bobby's conception as guilt rather than pain, demonstrates what Mr. and Mrs. Das, and now their children, have lost in terms of self-knowledge and self-mastery. At the same time, Mr. Kapasi, who is both dissatisfied with his own marriage and attracted to Mrs. Das, demonstrates both self-knowledge and self-mastery when he speaks the truth as he understands it to Mrs. Das regarding her affair. In an ironic reversal of how stories of North Americans, whether South Asian immigrants or otherwise, traveling to India, typically develop, the Das family does not learn anything, apparently, from their visit to their ancestral homeland, nor do they have anything explicit to teach; rather, it is Mr. Kapasi who learns to see clearly both his own motivations and those of the family from abroad and who offers them the opportunity for self-knowledge.

The aspect of vision that plays itself out so frequently in Lahiri's work and is at the heart of "When Mr. Pirzada Came to Dine" is transformed here. The knowledge gained is not the second-generation immigrant's knowledge of her ancestral homeland, but rather a recognition of the vacuity of the Das family's sense of morality. Unlike Lilia, the Das family never seems to learn much, so the illumination that occurs in this story is not theirs, but Mr. Kapasi's. Mr. Kapasi is an "interpreter of maladies," and in this story, the maladies that he examines, and that Lahiri examines, are those of the soul. The Das family may be unable to learn from their experience, but in a well-crafted instance of dramatic irony, seeing them through Mr. Kapasi's eyes offers Lahiri's readers the moment of insight the members of this second- and third- generation immigrant family are denied.

"Sexy:" Awakening to Difference

Lahiri makes the relationship between maps and her characters' attempts at knowledge that appears in "When Mr. Pirzada Came to Dine" most explicit in "Sexy," a story about a young, white, American woman from Michigan in an affair with a Bengali American businessman named Dev. The story moves between two complementary registers: on the one hand, the Mapparium in the Christian Science Reading room provides a window into the wider world for the protagonist, and on the other, the narrative's probing of the meaning of the word "sexy" makes the protagonist look inward, evaluating her own understanding of the meaning of relationships.

Miranda, a recent college graduate from Michigan who is the protagonist in "Sexy," may be older than Lilia in "When Mr. Pirzada Came to Dine," but she is scarcely less innocent in her comprehension of the world. Miranda's only consciousness of South Asian immigrants comes from a family that she knew as a child and from one of her coworkers. Lahiri makes a sort of gesture toward a more conventional sort of immigration story than the one she is writing when she narrates Miranda's childhood experience with Indians. An Indian family named the Dixits had moved into Miranda's community, and Miranda remembers school children taunting them with the words "The Dixits dig shit." She also recalls being invited into the Dixit's house and encountering their Hindu religion by viewing a picture of a goddess with a "necklace composed of bleeding heads." Mrs. Dixit informs her, "It is the goddess Kali… Come please, time for cake" (Lahiri, "Sexy" 96).

All the exotic elements that we might expect to find in an immigrant story are here: food, religion, a general sense of the exotic and mysterious, tied to the casual cruelty that children often employ toward those they see as being different. And yet, this is just a side note in the story Lahiri tells. Miranda's childhood experience of an Indian family remains in the background, with her adult relationship and its implications firmly in the foreground, and we are allowed to see how immigrants and non-immigrants interact as coworkers and as lovers. The question of immigrant status is not the decisive one for the story, even as it consistently helps to shape the direction of the plot. Indeed, between Miranda and her Bengali lover Dev, Miranda's status as a Midwesterner in Boston makes her seem less at home than he is. Dev is not only the person who teaches her about the world beyond the borders of the United States, he is the person who teaches her about the city in which she now lives.

Lahiri's craft becomes particularly evident in the way she narrows down the meaning of the story to one word, "sexy," and then pulls back to take in the entire globe. The word sexy appears in the story when Miranda's lover, Dev, whispers it to her in the midst of the Mapparium, a part of the Christian Science Reading Room in Boston that "was shaped like the inside of a globe but looked like the outside of one" (Lahiri, "Sexy" 90). Dev first gives Miranda a tour of the world, demonstrating both his cosmopolitanism and her parochialism, and then he shows her that the acoustics of the Mappariam are such that he can whisper to her across the room. The words that he whispers are "You're sexy," and they stand in her for all the possibilities that Miranda is experiencing as she learns about the wider world through her affair with Dev (91). The word "sexy" reappears when Rohin, a child whose father has deserted his mother for a younger woman, explains its meaning for him to Miranda: "It means loving someone you don't know" (107). Rohin's definition serves to make the consequences of Miranda's affair clear to her: she realizes that her awakening is coming at the expense of another woman and that this is a price she is unwilling to exact for her own fulfillment.

The story ends with Miranda at the Mappariam after she has ended her affair with Dev, and by the time it does, the young woman from Michigan has experienced as thorough an education as the young immigrant child Lilia in "When Mr. Pirzada Came to Dine." She has ended her relationship with Dev, realizing the anguish that it could cause for his family and the morally compromised position in which it places her. She has also arrived at an understanding of the wider world and her place in it that she could scarcely have imagined at the beginning of the story, and the imagery of the open sky outside the Mappariam at the Christian Science center suggests the openness of Miranda's future as she sits "on one of the benches in the plaza outside the church, gazing at its giant pillars and massive dome, and at the clear blue sky spread over the city" (Lahiri, "Sexy" 110). As with the first two stories, Lahiri's conclusion in "Sexy" is characterized by its open-endedness. We do not where Miranda is headed next, but we can tell that her trajectory has changed.

It is hard not to see at least a little of Lahiri's background as a Renaissance scholar at work in a figure like Miranda, who seems to bear some resemblance to her namesake from Shakespeare's

The Tempest. Like Shakespeare's Miranda, Lahiri's lacks a broad knowledge of the world and has an awakening to the world that works hand in hand with a sexual awakening. In *The Tempest*, Miranda finds her comprehension of the world expanded by her encounter with a handsome stranger from abroad, an awakening that proves to be positive in the context of Shakespeare's play, but more equivocal in the context of Lahiri's story.

"This Blessed House:" Uncertain Conversations

One of the more puzzling stories in the collection for many readers is "This Blessed House," which narrates the story of a Hindu couple who are attempting to come to terms with both their very new marriage and the objects they are continually finding in their new house. Like the previous three stories discussed here, the story uses marriage and family life as a way into its discussion of immigration and culture. To his immense frustration, the husband, Sanjeev, discovers that his wife Twinkle not only regularly finds Christian paraphernalia (often quite kitschy) in the closet and attic of their new house, but also seems compelled to display these items in the most visible areas possible.

"This Blessed House" raises the question of what identity means and what art has to do with it. The story also suggests the archaeological layering of immigrant narratives: the images that have been left in the house are clearly not merely Christian, but specifically Roman Catholic, and thus reflect the fact that Lahiri's Indian immigrant couple are not the first religious minorities to attempt to make a home in this dwelling. This is a connection of which Sanjeev and Twinkle are unaware, but which surely would be evident to Lahiri, a scholar of seventeenth-century English literature. If Sanjeev finds the presence of the Catholic images offensive because they seem to obscure the couple's cultural links to India and to Hinduism, Twinkle seems to find their presence desirable because they connect her, on a human level, with the previous inhabitants of the house. There is no evidence in the story that Twinkle actually wants to convert to Christianity, as Sanjeev at times speculates; rather, she seems to want to discover a history for herself in the house where she now lives, and she finds this in the images that have been left behind by the previous family. The effect of this story is hauntingly equivocal: are we meant to empathize more with Sanjeev's disappointment in Twinkle and her seemingly indiscriminate assimilation to her host country's culture, or are we meant to admire Twinkle's protean ability to appropriate aspects of another culture? Anxieties about identity and how it relates to self-knowledge haunt this story, and Sanjeev's and Twinkle's dilemma is suggestive of recent discussions of mimicry and hybridity by the postcolonial theorist Homi K. Bhabha, but Lahiri provides us with no definitive resolution.

The aesthetic qualities of the items that the couple find in their house are also of interest here. The narrator seems almost bemused in describing the objects, and certainly Sanjeev is, finding them to be tacky and embarrassing. Yet the objects exercise a kind of power through their very tackiness, their lack of evident aesthetic merit. If the Christian images left behind had been beautiful, or culturally significant in any way, Sanjeev could have justified having them displayed in the house. Because they are evidently tacky, expressions of faith by people without a great deal of discrimination, they are able to function as a true test case for how Twinkle and Sanjeev encounter difference.

The matter of seeing, which has been so central to the three stories discussed above, thus becomes central here as well. Twinkle and Sanjeev seem incapable of finding a common vision of their new house, and this inability to harmonize their view of what is in front of them seems to suggest that their life is pulling them in different directions. Lahiri does not offer a simple resolution either by having the couple split from each other or come to agreement, but instead leaves the relationship hovering in the balance.

As with the other stories discussed, "This Blessed House" finds analogues in the longer tradition of the short story. Ernest Hemingway, a writer who may seem at a far remove from Lahiri indeed in terms of subject matter and his treatment of gender, expertly used the ways in which dialogue can fail within a relationship and between the sexes in his stories "Hills Like White Elephants" and "The Snows of Kilimanjaro," and the dialogue in "This Blessed House" provides us with a similar failure of comprehension. Lahiri's stories work themselves out on the uncertain boundary between increasing knowledge and inescapable ignorance, and the drama that is most compelling in them is the internal struggle in characters who strain for insight, but often fail to attain it because of their own lack of self-knowledge.

The combination of dramatic and situational irony in Lahiri's stories has the effect of drawing our attention both to what her characters learn and to what they have been prevented from learning. The path toward some sort of provisional enlightenment in Lahiri's stories resembles the overwhelming "effect" that Poe said in his review of Nathaniel Hawthorne that he hoped to obtain in fictional prose pieces that could capture something of the "supernal beauty," as he described it in the *Poetic Principle* (698–704), of lyric poetry and the indications of "grace" that Flannery O'Connor suggested in *Mystery and Manners* (118) mattered more in her stories than the body counts. One thing that these similarities suggest is that the short story may be a genre particularly well adapted to an era of global exchange and immigration. For many people, comprehension of the varieties of immigrant experiences is clouded by the posturing of politicians, by differences in language, culture, and religion, and by the obscurity that seems to attend upon faraway events. The ability of the short story in the hands of an expert teller like Lahiri to cast a concentrated, illuminating ray on these matters and still do justice to their complexity is a signal instance of how the aesthetic form and cultural content of the stories we tell can transform, and expand, our own range of vision. If we can comprehend how short stories of the immigrant experience can engage both accurate social representation and analysis and visionary artistic insight, we will be better readers, students, teachers, and critics of the very finest immigrant short fiction, of which Lahiri's work is a rich and suggestive exemplar.

Works Cited

Baym, Nina, et al. *The Norton Anthology of American Literature.* 8th ed. Vol. E. New York: W.W. Norton, 2011.

Bhabha, Homi. *The Location of Culture*. New York: Routledge, 1994.

Charters, Ann. *The American Short Story and Its Writer*. Boston: Bedford St. Martin's, 2000.

_____. *The Short Story and Its Writer: An Introduction to Short Fiction*. 8th ed. Boston: Bedford St. Martin's, 2014.

Engel, William E. *Early Modern Poetics in Melville and Poe: Memory, Melancholy, and the Emblematic Tradition*. Aldershot, UK: Ashgate, 2012.

Garg, Shweta. "Interpreting a Culinary Montage: Food in Jhumpa Lahiri's *Interpreter of Maladies*." *Asiatic* 6.1 (2012): 73–83.

Hawthorne, Nathaniel. *The Scarlet Letter*. 1850. A Norton Critical Edition. Ed. Leland S. Person. New York: W. W. Norton, 2005.

Hemingway, Ernest. "Hills Like White Elephants." *The Complete Short Stories of Ernest Hemingway*. New York: Simon & Schuster, 1987. 211–214.

_____. "The Snows of Kilimanjaro." *The Complete Short Stories of Ernest Hemingway*. New York: Simon & Schuster, 1987. 39–56.

Jackson, Elizabeth. "Transcending the Politics of 'Where You're From:' Postcolonial Nationality and Cosmopolitanism in Jhumpa Lahiri's *The Interpreter of Maladies*." *ARIEL: A Review of International English Literature* 43.1 (2012): 109–125, 142.

Lahiri, Jhumpa. "The Interpreter of Maladies." *The Interpreter of Maladies: Stories of Bengal, Boston, and Beyond*. New Delhi: HarperCollins India, 1999.

_____. *The Namesake: A Novel*. New York: Houghton Mifflin, 2004.

_____. "Sexy." *The Interpreter of Maladies: Stories of Bengal, Boston, and Beyond*. New Delhi: HarperCollins India, 1999.

_____. "This Blessed House." *The Interpreter of Maladies: Stories of Bengal, Boston, and Beyond*. New Delhi: HarperCollins India, 1999.

_____. *Unaccustomed Earth*. New York: Vintage, 2009.

_____. "When Mr. Pirzada Came to Dine." *The Interpreter of Maladies: Stories of Bengal, Boston, and Beyond*. New Delhi: HarperCollins India, 1999.

O'Connor, Flannery. "A Good Man is Hard to Find." *The Complete Stories*. New York: Farrar, Straus & Giroux, 1971.

_____. "On Her Own Work." *Mystery and Manners: Occasional Prose.* Ed. Sally Fitzgerald & Robert Fitzgerald. New York: Farrar, Straus & Giroux, 1969. 107–18.

Peerboom, Heather Hoyle. "As American and Mom and Chicken Curry: Home as Metaphor in Jhumpa Lahiri's *Interpreter of Maladies.*" *JASAT* 42 (2011): 49–55.

Poe, Edgar Allan. "Nathaniel Hawthorne." 1842. *The Selected Writings of Edgar Allan Poe: A Norton Critical Edition.* Ed. G. R. Thompson. New York: W.W. Norton, 2004.

_____. *The Poetic Principle. The Selected Writings of Edgar Allan Poe: A Norton Critical Edition.* Ed. G. R. Thompson. New York: W.W. Norton, 2004. 698–704.

Shakespeare, William. *The Tempest.* New York: Simon & Schuster, 2004.

Sidwa, Bhapsi. *The Ice-Candy-Man.* New Delhi: Penguin India, 1988.

RESOURCES

Works of Contemporary Immigrant Short Fiction

The following is a chronological listing of recent stories and short story collections by and/or about:

Arab Americans

Geha, Joseph. *Through and Through: Toledo Stories.* 1990.

Noble, Frances Khirallah. *The Situe Stories.* 2000.

Serageldin, Samia. *Love Is Like Water and Other Stories.* 2009.

Orfalea, Gregory. *The Man Who Guarded the Bomb: Stories.* 2010.

Armenian Americans

Antreassian, Antranig & Ardavast (Jack) Antreassian. *The Cup of Bitterness and Other Stories.* 1979.

Bedrosian, Margaret & Leo Hamalian, eds. *Crossroads: Short Fiction by Armenian American Writers.* 1992.

Chinese Americans

Chin, Frank. *The Chinaman Pacific and Frisco R.R. Co.: Short Stories.* 1988.

Ping, Wang. *American Visa: Short Stories.* 1994.

Chang, Lan Samantha. *Hunger: A Novella and Stories.* 1998.

Jen, Gish. *Who's Irish?: Stories.* 1999.

Li, Yiyun. *A Thousand Years of Good Prayers: Stories.* 2005.

Ping, Wang. *The Last Communist Virgin: Stories.* 2007.

Cuban Americans

Milanés, Cecilia Rodríguez. *Oye, What I'm Gonna Tell You: Stories.* 2015.

Czech Americans

Slouka, Mark. *Lost Lake: Stories.* 2012.

Dominican Americans

Díaz, Junot. *Drown.* 1997.

Filipino Americans

Santos, Bienvenido N. *Scent of Apples: A Collection of Stories.* 1979.

Galang, M. Evelina. *Her Wild American Self: Short Stories.* 1996.

Villanueva, Marianne. *Mayor of the Roses: Stories.* 2005.

Tenorio, Lysley. *Monstress: Stories.* 2012.

Greek Americans

Petrakis, Henry Mark. *The Collected Stories of Harry Mark Petrakis.* 1987.

Papanikolas, Helen. *Small Bird, Tell Me: Stories of Greek Immigrants in Utah.* 1993.

_____. *The Apple Falls from the Apple Tree: Stories.* 1996.

Hispanic, Chicano, & Latino Americans

Cisneros, Sandra. *Woman Hollering Creek and Other Stories.* 1992.

González, Ray, ed. *Mirrors Beneath the Earth: Short Fiction by Chicano Writers.* 1992.

Augenbraum, Harold & Ilan Stavans, eds. *Growing Up Latino: Memoirs and Stories.* 1993.

Martin, Patricia Preciado. *El Milagro and Other Stories.* 1996.

Canales, Viola. *Orange Candy Slices and Other Secret Tales.* 2001.

Garcia, Lionel G. *The Day They Took My Uncle, and Other Stories.* 2001.

Quintana, Leroy V. *La Promesa and Other Stories.* 2002.

Hernández, Lisa. *Migrations and Other Stories.* 2007.

Shapard, Robert, James Thomas, & Ray González, eds. *Sudden Fiction Latino: Short-Short Stories from the United States and Latin America.* 2010.

Indian Americans

Lahiri, Jhumpa. *Interpreter of Maladies: Stories.* 1999.

Divakaruni, Chitra Banerjee. *The Unknown Errors of Our Lives*. 2001.

Vaswani, Neela. *Where the Long Grass Bends: Stories*. 2004.

Mukherjee, Bharati. *The Middleman and Other Stories*. 2007.

Deckha, Nitin. *Shopping for Sabzi: Stories*. 2008.

Reddi, Rishi. *Karma and Other Stories*. 2009.

Divakarun, Chitra Banerjee. *Arranged Marriage: Stories*. 2011.

Mehta, Rahul. *Quarantine: Stories*. 2011.

Sidhu, Ranbir Singh. *Good Indian Girls: Stories*. 2012.

Iranian Americans

Rachlin, Nahid. *Veils: Short Stories*. 1992.

Siletz, Ari B. *The Mullah with No Legs and Other Stories*. 1992.

Irish Americans

Goran, Lester. *Tales from the Irish Club: A Collection of Short Stories*. 1996.

_____. *Outlaws of the Purple Cow and Other Stories*. 1999.

Winch, Terence. *That Special Place: New World Irish Stories*. 2004.

Lordan, Beth. *But Come Ye Back: A Novel in Stories*. 2005.

Gordon, Mary. *The Stories of Mary Gordon*. 2006.

Italian Americans

Papaleo, Joseph. *Italian Stories*. 2002.

Japanese Americans

Yamamoto, Hisaye. *Seventeen Syllables and Other Stories*. 1988.

Saiki, Jessica Kawasuna. *From the Lanai: And Other Hawaii Stories*. 1991.

Sasaki, R. A. *The Loom and Other Stories*. 1991.

Jewish Americans

Howe, Irving, ed. *Jewish-American Stories*. 1977.

Helprin, Mark. *Ellis Island, and Other Stories*. 1981.

Malamud, Bernard. *The Stories of Bernard Malamud*. 1983.

Korean Americans

Pak, Ty. *Moonbay: Short Stories*. 1999.

Mexican Americans

Rice, David. *Give the Pig a Chance and Other Stories*. 1996.

Soto, Gary. *Baseball in April and Other Stories*. 2000.

Rice, David. *Crazy Loco: Stories*. 2001.

Casares, Oscar. *Brownsville: Stories*. 2003.

Saldaña, Jr., René. *Finding Our Way: Stories*. 2003.

Soto, Gary. *Help Wanted: Stories*. 2005.

_____. *Facts of Life: Stories*. 2008.

Rice, David. *Heart-Shaped Cookies and Other Stories*. 2011.

Pakistani Americans

Rahman, Imad. *I Dream of Microwaves: Stories*. 2004.

Puerto Rican Americans

Agüeros, Jack. *Dominoes and Other Stories from the Puerto Rican*. 1993.

Cofer, Judith Ortiz. *An Island Like You: Stories of the Barrio*. 1995.

_____. *The Year of Our Revolution: New and Selected Stories and Poems*. 1998.

Thomas, Piri. *Stories from El Barrio*. 2005.

Polish Americans

Bukoski, Anthony. *Children of Strangers: Stories*. 1993.

Petesch, Natalie L. M. *The Immigrant Train and Other Stories*. 1996.

Bukoski, Anthony. *Polonaise: Stories*. 1999.

_____. *Time Between Trains: Stories*. 2003.

_____. *North of the Port: Stories*. 2008.

Collections of Recent American Immigrant Short Fiction

Brown, Wesley & Amy Ling, eds. *Imagining America: Stories from the Promised Land*. 1991. Rev. ed. New York: Persea Books, 2003.

Casey, Daniel J. & Robert E. Rhodes, eds. *Modern Irish-American Fiction: A Reader*. Syracuse, NY: Syracuse UP, 1989.

Chernoff, Dorothy A., ed. *Call Us Americans*. Garden City, NY: Doubleday, 1968.

Gallo, Donald R., ed. *From First Crossing*. Carmel, CA: Hampton-Brown, 2004.

Gillan, Maria Mazziotti & Jennifer Gillan, eds. *Growing Up Ethnic in America: Contemporary Fiction About Learning To Be American*. New York: Penguin, 1999.

Goodman, Henry, ed. & trans. *The New Country: Stories from the Yiddish About Life in America*. Syracuse, NY: Syracuse UP, 2001.

Grossman, Sari & Joan Brodsky Schur, eds. *In a New Land: An Anthology of Immigrant Literature*. Lincolnwood, IL: National Textbook Co., 1994.

Kaldas, Pauline & Khaled Mattawa, eds. *Dinarzad's Children: An Anthology of Contemporary Arab American Fiction*. 2004. Rev. ed. Fayetteville: U of Arkansas P, 2009.

Kanellos, Nicolás, ed. *Short Fiction by Hispanic Writers of the United States*. Houston, TX: Arte Público Press, 1993.

Mendoza, Louis & Subramanian Shankar, eds. *Crossing into America: The New Literature of Immigration*. New York: New Press, 2003.

Miller, Ingrid Watson, ed. *Afro-Hispanic Literature: An Anthology of Hispanic Writers of African Ancestry*. Miami, FL: Ediciones Universal, 1991.

Newman, Katharine D., ed. *Ethnic American Short Stories*. New York: Washington Square Press, 1975.

Novakovich, Josip & Robert Shapard, eds. *Stories in the Stepmother Tongue*. Buffalo, NY: White Pine Press, 2000.

Obejas, Achy & Megan Bayles, eds. *Immigrant Voices: 21st Century Stories*. Chicago: The Great Books Foundation, 2014.

Spencer, Sharon & Dennis Toner, eds. *Ellis Island, Then and Now*. Franklin Lakes, NJ: Lincoln Springs Press, 1988.

Rosenfeld, Max. *New Yorkish and Other American Yiddish Stories*. Philadelphia: Sholom Aleichem Club Press, 1995.

Trueblood, Kathryn & Linda Stovall, eds. *Homeground*. Berkeley, CA: Before Columbus Foundation; Hillsboro, OR: Blue Heron, 1996.

Vatanabadi, Shouleh & Mohammad Mehdi Khorrami, eds. *Another Sea, Another Shore: Stories of Iranian Migration*. Northampton, MA: Interlink Books, 2004.

Key Secondary Works

Adams, Bella. *Asian American Literature*. Edinburgh, UK: Edinburgh UP, 2008. Edinburgh Critical Guides to Literature Ser.

Aldama, Frederick Luis. *Latino/a Literature in the Classroom: 21st Century Approaches to Teaching*. New York: Routledge, 2015.

Augenbraum, Harold & Margarite Fernández Olmos, eds. *U.S. Latino Literature: A Critical Guide for Students and Teachers*. Westport, CT: Greenwood Press, 2000.

Baker, Houston A. Jr., ed. *Three American Literatures: Essays on Chicano, Native Americans and Asian American Literature for Teachers of American Literature*. New York: MLA, 1982.

Balogun, F. Odun. *Tradition and Modernity in the African Short Story: An Introduction to a Literature in Search of Critics*. New York: Greenwood, 1991.

Bendixen, Alfred & James Nagel, eds. *A Companion to the American Short Story*. Malden, MA: Wiley-Blackwell, 2010.

Boddy, Kasia. *The American Short Story since 1950*. Edinburgh: Edinburgh UP, 2010.

Brians, Paul. *Modern South Asian Literature in English*. Westport, CT: Greenwood Press, 2003.

Brown, Julie, ed. *Ethnicity and the American Short Story*. New York: Garland, 1997.

Cheung, King-Kok, ed. *An Interethnic Companion to Asian American Literature*. New York: Cambridge UP, 1997.

Cowart, David. *Trailing Clouds: Immigrant Fiction in Contemporary America*. Ithaca, NY: Cornell UP, 2006.

Dale, Corrine H. & J. H. E. Paine, eds. *Women on the Edge: Ethnicity and Gender in Short Stories by American Women*. New York: Garland, 1999.

Davis, Rocío G. *Transcultural Reinventions: Asian American and Asian Canadian Short-Story Cycles*. Toronto: TSAR, 2001.

Emenyonu, Ernest, ed. *Writing Africa in the Short Story*. Rochester, NY: Boydell & Brewer, 2013.

Fallon, Erin, et al., eds. *A Reader's Companion to the Short Story in English*. Westport, CT: Greenwood, 2001.

Ghymn, Esther Mikyung. *The Shapes and Styles of Asian American Prose Fiction*. New York: P. Lang, 1992. American University Studies Ser.

Hassan, Salah & Marcy Jane Knopf-Newman, eds. *MELUS: The Journal of the Society for the Study of Multi-Ethnic Literature of the United States*. Special Issue: Arab American Literature 31.4 (Winter 2006).

Huang, Guiyou, ed. *Asian American Short Story Writers: An A-to-Z Guide*. Westport, CT: Greenwood Press, 2003.

_____. *The Columbia Guide to Asian American Literature since 1945*. New York: Columbia UP, 2006.

_____. *The Greenwood Encyclopedia of Asian American Literature*. 3 vols. Westport, CT: Greenwood Press, 2009.

Jin, Ha. *The Writer as Migrant*. Chicago: U of Chicago P, 2008.

Kanellos, Nicolás. *Biographical Dictionary of Hispanic Literature in the United States: The Literature of Puerto Ricans, Cuban Americans, and Other Hispanic Writers*. New York: Greenwood Press, 1989.

_____. *Hispanic Literature of the United States: A Comprehensive Reference*. Westport, CT: Greenwood Press, 2003.

Kevane, Bridget A. *Latino Literature in America*. Westport, CT: Greenwood Press, 2003.

Knippling, Alpana Sharma, ed. *New Immigrant Literatures in the United States: A Sourcebook to Our Multicultural Literary Heritage*. Westport, CT: Greenwood Press, 1996.

Kuortti, Joel & Mittapalli Rajeshwar, eds. *Indian Women's Short Fiction*. New Delhi: Atlantic, 2007.

May, Charles E., ed. *Critical Survey of Short Fiction*. 4th ed. 10 vols. Ipswich, MA: Salem Press, 2012.

Meanor, Patrick. *American Short-Story Writers Since World War II.* Detroit: Gale Research, 1993.

_____ & Gwen Crane. *American Short-Story Writers Since World War II.* Second Series. Detroit: Gale, 2000.

_____ & Richard E. Lee. *American Short-Story Writers Since World War II.* Third Series. Detroit: Gale Group, 2001.

_____ & Joseph McNicholas. *American Short-Story Writers Since World War II.* Fourth Series. Detroit: Gale, 2001.

_____ & Richard E. Lee. *American Short-Story Writers Since World War II.* Fifth Series. Detroit: Thomson Gale, 2007.

Muller, Gilbert. *New Strangers in Paradise: The Immigrant Experience and Contemporary American Fiction.* Lexington: U of Kentucky P, 2008.

Nelson, Emmanuel S., ed. *Asian American Novelists: A Bio-Bibliographical Critical Sourcebook.* Westport, CT: Greenwood Press, 2000.

_____. *Ethnic American Literature: An Encyclopedia for Students.* Westport, CT: Greenwood Press, 2015.

_____. *The Greenwood Encyclopedia of Multiethnic American Literature.* 5 vols. Westport, CT: Greenwood Press, 2005.

_____, ed. *Reworlding: The Literature of the Indian Diaspora.* Westport, CT: Greenwood Press, 1992.

Oh, Seiwoong, ed. *Encyclopedia of Asian-American Literature.* New York: Facts On File, 2007. Encyclopedia of American Ethnic Literature Ser.

Orfalea, Gregory. *U.S.-Arab Relations: The Literary Dimension.* Washington, DC: National Council on U.S.-Arab Relations, 1984.

Parekh, Pushpa Naidu & Siga Fatima Jagne, eds. *Postcolonial African Writers: A Bio-Bibliographical Critical Sourcebook.* Westport, CT: Greenwood Press, 1998.

Payant, Katherine B. & Toby Rose, eds. *The Immigrant Experience in North American Literature: Carving out a Niche.* Westport, CT: Greenwood Press, 1999.

Peck, David R. *American Ethnic Literatures: Native American, African American, Chicano/Latino, and Asian American Writers and Their Backgrounds—An Annotated Bibliography.* Pasadena, CA: Salem Press, 1991.

_____, ed. *American Ethnic Writers*. 2000. Pasadena, CA: Salem Press, 2008.

_____ & Eric Howard, eds. *Identities and Issues in Literature*. 3 vols. Pasadena, CA: Salem Press, 1997.

Poey, Delia. *Latino American Literature in the Classroom: The Politics of Transformation*. Gainesville: UP of Florida, 2002.

Ramanan, Mohan & Pingali Sailaja, eds. *English and the Indian Short Story: Essays in Criticism*. New Delhi: Orient Longman, 2000.

Salaita, Steven. *Modern Arab American Fiction: A Reader's Guide*. Syracuse, NY: Syracuse UP, 2011.

Sandín, Lyn Di Iorio & Richard Perez, eds. *Contemporary U.S. Latino: A Literary Criticism*. New York: Palgrave Macmillan, 2007.

Sanga, Jaina C. *South Asian Novelists in English: An A-to-Z Guide*. Westport, CT: Greenwood Press, 2003.

Shell, Marc & Werner Sollors, eds. *The Multilingual Anthology of American Literature: A Reader of Original Texts with English Translations*. New York: New York UP, 2000.

Simone, Roberta. *The Immigrant Experience in American Fiction: An Annotated Bibliography*. Metuchen, NJ: Scarecrow, 1994.

Sollors, Werner, ed. *Multilingual America: Transnationalism, Ethnicity and the Languages of American Literature*. New York: New York UP, 1998.

Werlock, Abby H.P. & James P. Werlock, eds. *The Facts On File Companion to the American Short Story*. 2nd ed. New York: Facts On File, 2009.

About the Editor_____

Robert C. Evans is I. B. Young Professor of English at Auburn University at Montgomery, where he has taught since 1982. In 1984, he received his PhD from Princeton University, where he held Weaver and Whiting fellowships as well as a university fellowship. In later years, his research was supported by fellowships from the Newberry Library, the American Council of Learned Societies, the Folger Shakespeare Library, the Mellon Foundation, the Huntington Library, the National Endowment for the Humanities, the American Philosophical Society, and the UCLA Center for Medieval and Renaissance Studies.

In 1982, he was awarded the G. E. Bentley Prize and in 1989 was selected Professor of the Year for Alabama by the Council for the Advancement and Support of Education. At AUM, he has received the Faculty Excellence Award and has been named Distinguished Research Professor, Distinguished Teaching Professor, and University Alumni Professor. Most recently he was named Professor of the Year by the South Atlantic Association of Departments of English.

He is one of three editors of the *Ben Jonson Journal* and is a contributing editor to the John Donne *Variorum Edition*, the author or editor of over thirty books (on such topics as Ben Jonson, Martha Moulsworth, Kate Chopin, John Donne, Frank O'Connor, Brian Friel, Ambrose Bierce, Amy Tan, early modern women writers, pluralist literary theory, literary criticism, twentieth-century American writers, American novelists, Shakespeare, Renaissance poetry, and seventeenth-century English literature), as well as the author of roughly three hundred published or forthcoming essays or notes (in print and online) on a variety of topics, especially dealing with Renaissance literature, critical theory, women writers, short fiction, and literature of the nineteenth and twentieth centuries.

Contributors_____

Anupama Arora is associate professor of English and women's and gender studies at the University of Massachusetts, Dartmouth. Her area of specialization is postcolonial literatures, especially from South Asia and its diaspora. Her work has appeared in *Ariel: A Review of International English Literature*, *South Asian Popular Culture*, *The Journal of Commonwealth Literature*, and *Women's Studies*, among other journals. She is currently working on a book on early Indo-American encounters.

Alli Carlisle (MA, University of Chicago) is a doctoral student at the University of California, Los Angeles, whose work focuses on identity formation through narrative and the intersections of literary and political discourses in twentieth-century Cuba and Latin America. She has studied Cuban literature and political thought at the University of Havana. Her criticism and reviews have been published in *Full Stop* and *Newcity*.

King-Kok Cheung is professor of English and Asian American studies at the University of California, Los Angeles; director of the University of California Education Abroad Program Study Center in China (2008–2010, 2015–2017); and the 2012–2013 recipient of the Hoshide Teaching Award in Asian American studies. She is the author of *Articulate Silences* (Cornell, 1993) and *Chinese American Literature without Borders* (Palgrave Macmillan, forthcoming); editor of *Words Matter* (U of Hawaii P, 2000), *An Interethnic Companion to Asian American Literature* (Cambridge, 1996), *"Seventeen Syllables"* (Rutgers, 1994), *Asian American Literature: An Annotated Bibliography* (MLA, 1988); and coeditor of *The Heath Anthology of American Literature*. Her articles have appeared in *Amerasia Journal*, *American Literary History*, *Biography, Bucknell Review*, *Cambridge Journal of China Studies, MELUS, Milton Studies, PMLA, Positions, Shakespeare Quarterly*, and *Transnational Literature*.

David A. Colón is associate professor of English and director of the Latina/o Studies Program at Texas Christian University. His essays have appeared in *Jacket2, Transmodernity, Cultural Critique*, the *Journal of Latino/Latin American Studies, The Princeton Encyclopedia of Poetry and*

Poetics, and many other publications. His edited anthology, *Between Day and Night: New and Selected Poems, 1946–2010* by Miguel González-Gerth (2013) was named an "outstanding title" by the Association of American University Presses. His novel, *The Lost Men* (2012), was nominated for the Arthur C. Clarke Award. A recipient of grants and fellowships from Stanford University, the University of California at Berkeley, the Social Science Research Council, and the Woodrow Wilson National Fellowship Foundation, he is currently working on a book titled *Juan Diego's Burden: Masculinities of Matriarchy in Chicano Fiction*.

Natalie Friedman is currently dean of studies at Barnard College. Prior to working at Barnard, she was assistant dean of students at New York University. She spent eight years teaching English and running the Learning and Teaching Center/Writing Center at Vassar College, and she has also taught at Marymount College and at Boston University. She received her PhD in English from New York University in 2001 and her BA in French and English from Vassar College in 1995. She has published scholarly articles and literary nonfiction in journals such as *Critique, Legacy, MELUS: Multiethnic Literature of the United States, The Connecticut Review, The Equals Record*, and the *Blue Lyra Review*. A native New Yorker, she is the daughter of immigrants, the first person to receive an American college degree in her family, and the first in her family to receive a PhD.

Rebecca Fuchs studied American studies, book history, and cultural anthropology at the Johannes Gutenberg University in Mainz, Germany. She wrote her dissertation as part of the interdisciplinary graduate program "Formations of the Global" School of the Humanities at the University of Mannheim, Germany, and spent one semester as a visiting scholar at Duke University in Durham, North Carolina. Her thesis, *Caribbeanness as a Global Phenomenon: Junot Díaz, Edwidge Danticat, and Cristina Garcia* (WVT & Bilingual Review Press, 2014), focuses on the fictional works *The Brief Wondrous Life of Oscar Wao* (2007) by Junot Díaz, *The Dew Breaker* (2004) by Edwidge Danticat, and *The Agüero Sisters* (1997) by Cristina García, which are read in dialog with Caribbean and decolonial theories. In her current research, she examines transcultural temporal concepts in Native American, African American, Euro-American literature.

Maryse Jayasuriya is associate professor in the Department of English at the University of Texas at El Paso. She received her PhD from Purdue University. She is the author of *Terror and Reconciliation: Sri Lankan Anglophone Literature, 1983–2009* (Lexington, 2012), which explores the English-language literature that has emerged from Sri Lanka's quarter-century-long ethnic conflict. She has published articles on South Asian and Asian American literature in such venues as *South Asian Review*, *Journeys*, *Margins*, and *The Journal of Postcolonial Cultures and Societies*. She coedited a special issue of *South Asian Review* (33.3) entitled *Sri Lankan Anglophone Literature*.

Bridget Kevane is professor of Latin American and Latino studies at Montana State University. She has published widely on Latino literature and culture. Her publications include *Latina Self-Portraits: Interviews with Contemporary Women Writers*, *Latino Literature in America*, *Profane & Sacred: Latino/a American Writers Reveal the Interplay of the Secular and Religious*, and *The Dynamics of Jewish Latino Relationships: Hope and Caution*. She has also published essays in the *Los Angeles Review of Books*, *Tablet*, the *Forward*, *Moment*, and the *New York Times Book Review*.

John Paul Russo is professor of English and classics and chair of the Department of Classics at the University of Miami. He has published books and essays on the theory of criticism, ethnicity, and history of culture. *I. A. Richards: His Life and Works* appeared in 1989. Recipient of three Fulbright fellowships to Italy, he has taught at the universities of Palermo, Rome, Genoa, and Salerno. He is book review editor of *Italian Americana* (1990–present) and coeditor of *RSA* (*Rivista di Studi Nord Americani*) (2009–12). His *The Future Without a Past: The Humanities in a Technological Society* was awarded the 2006 Bonner Prize. His study of representations of Italy, Italians, and Italian Americans, cowritten by Robert Casillo and entitled *The Italian in Modernity*, was published by the University of Toronto Press in 2011.

Te-hsing Shan is distinguished research fellow of the Institute of European and American Studies, Academia Sinica, Taiwan, and distinguished adjunct professor of humanities, Lingnan University, Hong

Kong. His publications include *Inscriptions and Representations: Chinese American Literary and Cultural Criticism*; *Translations and Contexts, Transgressions and Innovations*; and *Edward W. Said in Taiwan*. He has also published three collections of interviews: *Dialogues and Interchanges: Interviews with Contemporary Writers and Critics*; *In the Company of the Wise: Conversations with Asian American Writers and Critics*; and *Then and Now: Conversations with Contemporary Writers and Critics*. Moreover, he has translated nearly twenty books from English into Chinese, including *Writers at Work*; *The Challenge of the American Dream*; *Representations of the Intellectual*; *Gulliver's Travels*; and *Power, Politics, and Culture: Interviews with Edward W. Said*. His research areas include comparative literature, Asian American literature, translation studies, and cultural studies.

Brian Yothers is professor and associate chair of English at the University of Texas at El Paso. He is associate editor of *Leviathan: A Journal of Melville Studies*, coeditor of the interdisciplinary journal *Journeys*, editor of the Camden House Press book series Literary Criticism in Perspective, and a member of the editorial boards for the digital humanities projects *Melville's Marginalia Online* and the *Melville Electronic Library*. His books include *Sacred Uncertainty: Religious Difference and the Shape of Melville's Career* (Northwestern, 2015); *Melville's Mirrors: Literary Criticism and America's Most Elusive Author* (Camden House, 2011); and *The Romance of the Holy Land in American Travel Writing, 1790–1876* (Ashgate, 2007). He has published on South Asian literature and culture in the *South Asian Review*, *Journeys*, and *Margins*.

Solveig Zempel is professor emerita of Norwegian at St. Olaf College, Northfield, MN, where she taught Norwegian language and literature as well as American immigrant literature. Zempel received her MA and PhD from the University of Minnesota. Her scholarly publications include articles and reviews of Norwegian and Norwegian American literature, translation of Norwegian immigrant letters (*In Their Own Words: Letters from Norwegian Immigrants*, U of Minnesota P, 1991), and translations of three works by O. E. Rølvaag: *The Third Life of Per Smevik* (Dillon P, 1971, rpt. Harper Perennial Classics, 1987), *When the Wind Is in the South and Other Stories by O.E. Rølvaag* (Center for Western Studies,

1984), and *Concerning Our Heritage* (NAHA, 1998). From 2002 to 2008, she served as associate dean for interdisciplinary and general studies, and from 2009 to 2012, she held the O. C. and Patricia Boldt Distinguished Teaching Chair in the Humanities at St. Olaf College.

Index